HJ
2381
.G73   The Great American
        tax revolt

The
Great
American
Tax
Revolt

The Great American Tax Revolt

Edited by Lester A. Sobel

Contributing Editors: Mary Elizabeth Clifford,
Joe Fickes, Stephen Orlofsky

Indexer: Grace M. Ferrara

Facts On File
119 West 57th Street, New York, N.Y. 10019

The Great American Tax Revolt

Library of Congress Cataloging in Publication Data

The Great American tax revolt.

Includes index.
1. Taxing—United States.   2. Local taxing—United States.
3. Taxing—Law & legislation—United States.
I. Sobel, Lester A.   II. Fickes, Joseph.
III. Hill, Ray 1946.   IV. Facts On File Inc., New York.
HJ2381.G73   336.2-00973   79-19421
ISBN 0-87196-2918

Contents

Introduction

ACCORDING TO AT LEAST one observer*, "1978 . . . will go down as the year of the Great American Tax Rebellion." For many people with similar views, an outstanding victory of the tax revolt was the approval by California voters June 6, 1978 of state Proposition 13, the Jarvis-Gann proposal to limit real estate taxes in California to a maximum of one per cent "of the full cash value of such property [real estate]."

As with most good revolutions, the tax revolt of 1978 had a number of ardent leaders. The most prominent was Howard Arnold Jarvis, the 75-year-old unpaid chairman of the American Tax Reduction Movement and author of Proposition 13. Jarvis, a conservative Republican businessman, had headed West from Utah in 1934 and had been prospering in California for 44 years as an outspoken rugged individualist. A mark of his leadership and of the strength of the tax rebellion is the fact that a record 1,300,000 Californians—800,000 more than necessary—signed the petition that put Proposition 13 on the ballot.

For Jarvis was leading a highly popular movement in a tradition that goes back, in North America at least, to before the American revolution and seems to have counterparts on all continents and in most countries. Benjamin Franklin's wry observation that "in this world nothing is certain but death and taxes" appears to have fallen only slightly short of the mark: where there are taxes, there is also bound to be opposition to taxes—

---

* Arthur Zich in the June 12, 1978 issue of *New Times*.

1

and certainly opposition to levies that are considered oppressive
or unfair.

The struggle against such taxation is often conducted with a

Howard Arnold Jarvis

fervor that is almost religious. Yet the zeal may also be understandable in light of Chief Justice John Marshall's 1819 warning that "the power to tax involves the power to destroy." Inspiration to battle against onerous taxes may also be traced to Grover Cleveland's assertion that "when more of the people's sustenance is exacted through the form of taxation than is necessary to meet the just obligations of government and expenses of its economical administration, such exaction becomes ruthless extortion and a violation of the fundamental principles of a free government." Tax rebels may assent to the dictum of Justice Oliver Wendell Holmes, Jr. that "taxes are what we pay for civilized society." But they are not prone to quote Plato's assertion that "when there is an income tax, the just man will pay more and the unjust less on the same amount of income."

A common view of the fairness of the tax system can be inferred from this bit of doggerel read into the *Congressional Record* by Rep. Tennyson Guyer (R, Ohio) April 11, 1978 as a comment on the situation of the American farmer:

> His horse went dead, and his mule went lame,
> He lost six cows in a hurricane.
> Then a cyclone came on a summer day
> And blew the house where he lived away.
> Then an earthquake came—when that was gone,
> It swallowed up the land that his house stood on.
> Then the tax collector, he came round
> And charged him for the hole in the ground.

The complaints of the tax rebels of the 1970s are varied. A recurring theme, of course, is that taxes are too high. It is also felt that tax laws are often unfair, that they favor special groups—for example, business, the rich, the church, the poor, the lazy—at the expense of others. Many homeowners hold that it is especially inequitable to make taxes on real estate the principal support of the schools. It is said that a racial issue exists, under the surface at least, in the assertion that excessively high costs of welfare and social services are a major reason for excessively high taxes. It is pointed out that taxes have been rising in response to many other factors as well, among them inflation, the large increases in oil prices and the costs of the arms race and war in Vietnam.

Sen. Joseph R. Biden, Jr. (D, Dela.) discussed some of the complaints Aug. 14, 1978 in a statement that accompanied his submission of legislation to encourage state and local governments to provide property tax relief. Biden said in his statement:

"Local governments, faced by soaring costs as a result of inflation, but in many cases, with property tax bases still eroded from the recession, have been forced to increase their property taxes in an ever upward spiral.

"Tax revolts are an integral part of American history. There is a new tax revolt with us today, in modern form. It is the increasing dissatisfaction with the property tax. People feel not only that it is too high but also that it is inequitable. In a recent survey taken in Delaware, when people were asked whether—if necessary to continue essential state services—they favored an increase in income taxes, a sales tax or a statewide property tax, only 16% opted for the property tax. Yet on the local level particularly, the property tax is the only major revenue source for providing essential local services. One usually thinks of the homeowner as bearing the burden of property taxation. The fact is that many of the people who can least afford it pay property taxes through their rent, as the owner passes along tax increases in the rent he charges. Thus no one is immune from the burden which this tax imposes and which together with inflation eats away at the money needed for subsistence.

"Last year, property tax relief was enacted in one form or another in 23 states. But such relief is essentially hit or miss and that does not begin to take care of the problem. . . . In the decade from 1966 to 1976, state and local property taxes have climbed at an amazing rate of 131%. Total revenues from property taxes in 1976 were $57 billion, a staggering sum that is about half of all federal collections from the individual income tax. The per capita real property tax burden grew from $135 per capita to $266 in the decade.

"The two groups often hit the hardest are the elderly who live on fixed incomes in these inflationary times and families of modest incomes seeking to raise and educate a family. In particular, the elderly find that the property tax can threaten a secure future in their own home, no matter how carefully that future was planned. For modest income families it is a barrier to a reasonable standard of living and to our national goal of a decent home for every family. This reliance on the property tax places a strain on local governments which are the backbone of our federal structure of our government. In some ways, the federal government, by virtually monopolizing the income tax, has forced this reliance on property taxes. The federal government has an obligation to help ease the burden on those unable to bear it. . . ."

Rep. Benjamin A. Gilman (R, N.Y.), who also had introduced legislation on the real-property tax issue, amplified the tax rebels' views Jan. 24, 1979 in a statement in the *Congressional Record:* "Our nation's taxpayers have reached the limits of their ability to absorb astronomical real estate taxes, runaway welfare expenditures, the costs of escalating social service programs, soaring utility bills, growing federal and state income taxes and substantial state and municipal sales taxes," Gilman declared. "They are being crushed by the high costs of living in an economy already strained by the high rate of inflation and unemployment. The Proposition 13 fever which swept our nation last year sent this message to public officials at all levels of government. . . ."

Sen. George S. McGovern (D, S.D.) had told the Senate as far back as March 21, 1972 that "the American people are angry with a tax system which has become increasingly unjust and which places an enormous burden on property owners. It is no exaggeration to say that we face a full-fledged tax revolt. While the President and the Congress would have to decide on the use of revenues resulting from tax reform, I believe that we must place a high priority on their allocation for the purpose of reducing the property tax."

Six years later, speaking in Washington June 17, 1978 at the annual convention of Americans for Democratic Action, McGovern recalled his remarks of 1972: "I urged military economies and tax reform to finance property tax relief. . . . Today the fault for the heavy burden of unfair taxes rests not on liberal programs but on needless war, a reckless arms race and an unjust tax system designed and continued by selfish special interests. . . . [V]oters are offered a degrading hedonism that tells them to ask what they can take from the needy. . . ." He added that "[w]hile the tax revolt expresses profound and legitimate anger, it also has undertones of racism. . . . A news weekly quoted one California voter: 'It's those social services that annoy . . . me—social services for the colored, the Mexican, and so forth.' Sixty percent of the [public] employees who may be laid off in Los Angeles [as a result of government spending cuts attributable to Proposition 13] are members of minority groups."

An attack on "unfair" tax laws was made by Rep. James C. Corman (D, Calif.) Jan. 15, 1979 as he reintroduced tax equity proposals that were first offered in 1971. "The prime objective of all tax reformers,'' Corman said in a statement accompanying his bill, ''is to make the code more equitable, that is to insure everyone is taxed according to ability to pay. We began to establish preferences within the code in order to better define a taxpayer's real ability to pay. To look only at income would be unfair. Certain other factors have to be considered such as expenses incurred in producing income, family size and even unusual medical costs. Unfortunately, over the years, these basic considerations have been joined by other preferences that severely strain the limit of credibility. The problem with many of them is that they are available only to a select group of taxpayers usually in the higher income brackets.

''The liberalization of the treatment of capital gains that took place last year is a perfect example of law that chiefly benefits the wealthy. Of the $2.5 billion revenue loss incurred by these changes, 78% will benefit taxpayers with incomes of $50,000 and over. . . . Preferences such as these provide tax cuts that are unevenly distributed among taxpayers. The revenue lost could provide significant savings for all Americans if applied across the board in the form of general tax cuts.

''Some of the preferences found in the tax code were put there to accomplish certain social goals. Many of them have actually backfired by directing capital into investments that are not economically sound, but which provide tax shelters for wealthy investors. The Tax Reform Act of 1976 accomplished a great deal in closing up tax shelters in the areas where the most abuse has occurred. The Revenue Act of 1978 went further by limiting opportunities for sheltering in all other areas except for one notable exception—real estate. Investors in real estate enjoy a multitude of tax breaks that were established in the hope of providing employment in the construction industry. However, most have served chiefly to make speculators wealthy. In addition, these tax preferences have contributed to the shocking rise in real estate prices which have far outstripped even the soaring rates of inflation we have seen in the past few years. . . .

''Taxes, like every other family expenditure, hit hardest at those in the lowest income brackets. A 1977 Brookings Institute study showed that all American families earning $50,000 and less paid out almost the same percentages—about 30%—of their incomes in taxes, including federal, state and local income taxes, payroll taxes, property taxes, and sales and excise taxes. This leaves little discretionary income for someone who earns less than $10,000 a year but is not nearly so painful for those in the $50,000 bracket. Of course, the regressivity of such taxes as the sales and payroll taxes make this picture as bleak as it is. . . .''

Corman pointed out that "the $1,000 personal exemption . . . now reduces the taxes of someone in the highest bracket by $700 and the lowest bracket by only $140. . . .''

Calling for an "immediate" tax cut, Rep. Virginia Smith (R, Neb.) pointed out in an April 5, 1978 statement that, according to the Internal Revenue Service, Americans in 1977 "paid $16.7 billion more in taxes than they spent on the three basic necessities of food, clothing and housing. . . . [E]ach of us—every man, woman and child—paid some $2,200 in taxes while spending a total of $2,100 on food, clothing and shelter. . . .'' She added that "the tax burden imposed on all Americans . . . has risen by 144% over the last ten years.'' Mrs. Smith recalled, however, that "in the early 1920s, the government reduced taxes and the economy boomed. In the early 1960s, a similar reduction in taxes produced real investment growth at the highest rate in modern history with the lowest growth rate for inflation.''

Tax cut proposals often "fail to come to grips with the realities of the distortions that inflation introduces into the tax system,'' Sen. Harry F. Byrd Jr. (D, Va.) told the Senate April 24, 1978. "The reason that inflation is a problem is that the tax system treats every increase in income as if it were real income. The tax system does not take into account the fact that a worker's real income has increased less than nominal income because the entire nominal income gain is taxed. Thus, with the sustained high inflation in recent years, workers have had wage increases reduced not only by inflation but also by the higher taxes that must be paid as inflation pushes incomes into higher tax brackets.'' Furthermore, Byrd held, "the rule has been *ad hoc* tax cuts, usually in elections years, in response to continuing inflation. Normally these reductions have been just enough to offset the effects of inflation, but only past inflation not future inflation. . . .''

As one way of showing how the tax burden weighs on Americans, the Tax Foundation, Inc. calculated that the average American had to work 126 eight-hour days in 1979 to pay his federal, state and local taxes. In 1978 the period was 124 days. Or "calculated in another way, the typical American worker labors two hours and 45 minutes per eight-hour day [in 1979] to pay his tax obligations,'' the Tax Foundation said. The foundation reported that the average worker's taxes would take 34.3% of his earnings in 1979, compared with 33.5% in 1969, 18.6% in 1959, 22.7% in 1949, 17.4% in 1939 and 10.8% in 1929. One additional Tax Foundation calculation: In 1979 the typical worker would have to work four months and six days to pay his taxes and thus would have less than eight months' pay left for himself.

Paul Craig Roberts, former economic counsel to Sen. Orrin G. Hatch (R, Utah), called attention to the fact that high taxes apear to act as a "brake" on economic activity. He asserted in an article in the *Wall Street Journal* Jan. 11, 1979 that "the two most important prices governing production" are (1) "the price of leisure in terms of foregone current income" and (2) "the price of current consumption in terms of foregone future income." Roberts said that "the lower these prices are, the lower production will be." When taxes on additional earnings are high, the after-tax income from additional work and investment is low while leisure and current consumption are cheap "in terms of foregone income." Thus, Roberts wrote, "high tax rates encourage leisure and consumption and discourage work and saving."

Much of the effort to cut taxes comes in the form of efforts to limit government spending. Conservative economist Milton Friedman explained the reasoning behind this in an article in *Policy Review*: "As long as high government spending remains, we shall have the hidden tax of inflation. The only true tax cutting proposal would be a proposal to cut government spending. . . ." Efforts to impose balanced budgets may result not in tax cuts, Friedman suggested, but probably in a combination of increases in levies (as legislators vote for tax raises as a means of eliminating deficits) and in "the hidden tax of inflation." "I would far rather have total federal spending at $200 billion with a deficit of $100 billion than a balanced budget at $500 billion," Friedman declared. He indicated that "what government spends" (rather than merely budget deficits) is "the measure of the amount [of taxes] we turn over to the bureaucrats. . . ."

THIS VOLUME IS DESIGNED to serve as a record of "the Great American Tax Revolt" of the 1970s. It chronicles the various charges, proposals, statistics and similar data involved in the issue. The material that follows consists principally of the developments recorded by FACTS ON FILE in its ongoing examination of world affairs. A conscientious effort was made to keep this book free of bias and to make it a balanced and trustworthy reference tool.

LESTER A. SOBEL

New York, N.Y.
July, 1979

Mounting Protest: 1969-72

'Revolt' Foreseen, Tax Reform Limited

Taxpayer grumblings during Richard M. Nixon's first term as President resulted in some tax-reform legislation, but critics characterized Congress' action as limited and insufficient.

'Revolt' Predicted. The Johnson Administration's outgoing Treasury secretary, Joseph W. Barr, warned Jan. 17, 1969, in testimony before the Joint Economic Committee of Congress, of "the possibility of a taxpayer revolt if we do not soon make major reforms in our income taxes." The revolt would come, he said, not from the poor but from "middle-class" taxpayers with $7,000-$20,000 incomes because of their concern and anger "about the high-income recipients who pay little or no federal income tax." He estimated that more than $50 billion in revenue would be lost to the federal government in 1969 because of "loopholes" [special provisions] in the tax laws.

(A Nixon Administration pledge to seek "equity" in the tax laws was made in a statement released Feb. 7 by incoming Treasury Secretary David M. Kennedy.)

Surplus & Tax Reform Urged. Members of the Congressional Joint Economic Committee stressed in their annual report April 1, 1969 a need to lessen inflationary pressures and to reform taxation.

Republican and Democratic members of the committee agreed on the necessity of achieving a "significant" federal budget surplus as an anti-inflation move. They also agreed on the need to extend the 10% income tax surcharge. But the Republicans, in their minority report, suggested giving the President authority to reduce the rate unless Congress objected within a specific time period. The Democratic majority said the surtax was necessary unless the same effect on the economy could be achieved by reducing federal expenditures "at least $12 billion" or by enacting "quick and drastic" tax reform.

There was bipartisan agreement that tax reform was "long overdue" and should be a "major objective." There was disagreement over the 7% investment tax credit for business. Democrats, identifying the tax credit as "one of the most important sources of the recent inflation," advocated repeal. Republicans called repeal unwise.

11

Tax Reform Enacted. The Tax Reform Act of 1969 was passed by Congress Dec. 22 and signed by President Nixon Dec. 30. It was passed by overwhelming votes in both houses—381-2 in the House and 71-6 in the Senate.

The total individual income tax reductions provided by the bill, once all of its provisions were in effect in 1973, were estimated at $9.1 billion annually; in the same period, tax collections would be increased by $6.6 billion annually.

The bill's major provisions were a 15% rise in Social Security benefits, an increase in the personal exemption and standard deduction, a reduction in the oil depletion allowance to 22%, extension of the income tax surcharge at a 5% rate through June 1970, postponement of scheduled reductions in telephone and automobile excise taxes and repeal of the 7% business investment tax credit.

The bill also contained a "minimum tax" designed to cover large incomes heretofore escaping federal tax (except for interest on bonds of state and local governments, which remained tax exempt), plus stiffer provisions for foundations, those with capital-gain income and real estate operators.

The final version of the bill, as worked out by the House-Senate conferences— the 14 senior members of the House Ways and Means and Senate Finance Committees—was close to Administration recommendations in its net revenue effects, excluding those of the Social Security increase. The Administration version had called for a net revenue increase of $7.1 billion in 1970, $615 million in 1971 and a net revenue decrease of $2.3 billion in 1972; the final version provided for a net increase of $6.5 billion in 1970, $288 million in 1971 and a $1.8 billion loss in 1972. After 1972, the final version would cost the government from $500 million to $1 billion a year more than the Administration proposals. The figures excluded the effects of the 15% rise in Social Security benefits provided by the bill, which would cost about $1.5 billion more a year than the 10% increase requested by President Nixon.

The conferees revised the Senate version, which would have reduced tax collections from individuals by $1.2 billion a year, to conform largely to the net effects of the House version, which would have raised collections from individuals by $1.4 billion.

The bill was passed under a threat of a Presidential veto, but Senate Republican leader Hugh Scott (Pa.) said after a meeting with President Nixon Dec. 20 that the inflationary effect of the Senate bill, against which Mr. Nixon had directed his threat, had been "considerably reduced" by the conferees' version.

The conferees revised the personal exemption from its current $600 to $650 on July 1, 1970, to $700 in 1972 and to $750 in 1973. On the Social Security provision, the 15% increase in benefits was retained but the Senate's increase in the minimum monthly benefit payment to $100 was deleted.

Among other final provisions:

(a) A minimum standard deduction was set at $1,100 for 1970, $1,050 for 1971 and $1,000 for 1972; (b) the standard deduction was increased from 10% of income or $1,000 (whichever was lower) to 13% or $1,500 for 1971, 14% or $2,000 for 1972 and 15% or $2,000 for 1973; (c) a special new tax rate for single persons would begin in 1971 to keep them from paying more than 20% more tax than married couples with the same taxable income; (d) a maximum tax on earned income was set at 60% for 1971 and 50% thereafter; a "minimum tax" provision would apply to heretofore tax-sheltered income in excess of $30,000—from this the taxpayer would subtract the tax paid on his regularly taxable income and be taxed 10% on the remainder; (e) the depletion allowance for minerals currently at more than 22% rate, such as sulphur and uranium, was reduced, like the allowance for the oil and gas industry, to 22%; molybdenum, currently at 15%, was raised to 22%, most now at 15% were cut to 14% except for gold, silver, copper, oil shale and iron ore; depletion allowance for foreign operations of oil firms was retained at its current level; (f) the capital gains holding period was retained at six months, the amount of capital gains that could be taxed on the alternative tax rate of 25%, was set at $50,000, above that the rate would rise as high as 35%; (g) the first income tax on private foundations was set at 4% of investment income, and foundations would be required to distribute an amount equal to at least 6% of their income; restrictions were set on a foundation's financing of voter registration drives, on controlling interests in business corporations and on lobbying activities; (h) on real estate, the double depreciation, currently available for all new construction, would be limited to new housing; other new building could be depreciated at a 150% rate, all used construction would be permitted only straight-line depreciation except residences with a useful life of more than 20 years, which were permitted a 125% rate; a new provision was written for "recapture" of excess depreciation, permitting a 1%-

a-month phaseout of the recapturable amount after an 8¼-year period; (i) individuals with an extraordinary income in a single year (exceeding 120% of the five-year average) would be allowed to pay lower rates on the excess by treating it as if it were earned over five years; (j) certain deductions were permitted for direct costs of moving not reimbursed by an employer.

The conferees eliminated from the final bill: (1) a Senate amendment for a $325 tax credit for college student expenses; (2) a proposal for unlimited medical deductions for the elderly; (3) Senate-approved exemptions from the repeal of the 7% investment credit—on the first $20,000 of such investment and on investment in depressed areas or for watershed development.

In signing the bill, Nixon called it "unbalanced" with "both good and bad" in it. He considered the tax reforms, on the whole, good but its effect on the budget and cost of living bad. It "unduly favors spending at the expense of saving," he said, "at a time when demands on our savings are heavy." And it would make the anti-inflation effort "more difficult." He chided Congress about its "reluctance . . . to face up to the adverse impact of its tax and spending decisions." Tax reduction must be accompanied by corresponding expenditure reduction, he cautioned, pointing out that in this session Congress had not done this but had cut revenues by $3 billion while increasing spending $3 billion over his recommendations.

School Tax Problems

Southern school tax exemptions backed. Federal attorneys representing the Internal Revenue Service (IRS) contended in a brief filed May 15, 1970 that the tax-exempt status granted to newly chartered segregated academies in the South was legal, even if the private schools were established to avoid integrated public schooling.

The IRS attorneys held that the tax exemptions did not constitute a form of government subsidy and was therefore legal.

The government's opinions were contained in the brief filed in the U.S. District Court for the District of Columbia, in a case brought by black parents in Holmes County, Miss., where several private all-white academies had recently been opened. The parents of the county's black pupils contended that the ability of donors to the all-white academies to deduct their contributions on their tax returns constituted government support of segregated education. The Holmes suit was the same case that led the court to order that the IRS suspend all tax-exemption privileges to donors while the case was being tried.

(The court had ruled Jan. 13 that the segregated private schools that already had been granted tax-exempt status could retain them until the suit was decided.)

The government's contention, presented by Assistant Attorney General Johnnie M. Walters, relied heavily on the language of the Supreme Court's 7-1 decision May 4 sustaining the right of local governments to exempt the property of churches from local taxation.

Walters said the IRS, rather than lending aid or support to racial discrimination, was maintaining the same sort of "benevolent neutrality" toward nonprofit educational institutions that the Supreme Court sustained in its decision permitting states to refrain from taxing religious property.

It was the first time the government had used this argument during the months of legal struggles over the tax-exemption issue. Previously the government had taken the position that the parents who had filed the suit had no legal standing on which to base their case. The May 15 brief contended that the black parents had failed to establish any connection between the tax exemptions and the establishment of the academies and that the parents had failed to demonstrate any injury to themselves or their children resulting from the tax exemptions.

The IRS June 26 agreed to an order by the court suspending the tax exemptions pending the conclusion of the suit.

U.S. to tax segregated schools. The Internal Revenue Service announced in a new policy directive July 10, 1970 that private schools practicing racial discrimination in their admissions policies would have their tax-exempt status revoked. The new guidelines brought to an end a year-long debate among government agencies and the White House staff over the tax status of private academies.

According to Commissioner of Internal Revenue Randolph W. Thrower, who announced the new policy, the guidelines would be applied nationwide. The greatest impact, however, was expected to be felt by the racially segregated private academies that had been chartered in the Deep South to afford white students an alternative to integrated schooling.

Such schools had been heavily dependent on contributions regarded as tax exempt. The IRS's new policy would apply to any income or property of the schools, but the major effect would be in the loss of deductibility for contributions made to the schools by their supporters.

White House Press Secretary Ronald L. Ziegler said that President Nixon had seen and cleared the IRS announcement.

The announcement said that schools practicing racial discrimination would be given "a reasonable opportunity" to alter their admissions practices before having their exempt status revoked.

Thrower added that the new policy would not affect parochial schools that limited their students to members of one religion.

Tax System Outdated. The New York Times reported Jan. 11, 1971 that a study group, funded by a $1.9 million U.S. Office of Education grant, had collected data indicating that the traditional method of financing public schools primarily through local property taxes had become outdated. Dr. Roe L. Johns, head of the three-year National Educational Finance Project based in Gainesville, Fla., said: "It's unrealistic to expect an old tax system to finance modern educational needs."

According to the Times, the project staff believed that heavy reliance on property taxes for education was unreasonable in an age when only 9% of the national income came from property and 71% from wages.

The Times reported Johns' belief that by 1980, 10% of school financing should be from local sources, 60% from state and 30% federal. Currently, 52.7% of school revenues came from local government, primarily through property taxes, 39.9% from state and 7.4% federal. The study group estimated that educational costs would double to about $80 billion a year during the 1970s.

The report cited the existence of more than 2,300 well-organized tax protest groups with two million members. Such groups had organized tax revolts that succeeded in repeatedly defeating levy proposals in suburban St. Louis school districts in 1970.

California System Invalid. The California Supreme Court ruled, 6–1, Aug. 30, 1971 that the state's school financing system based on property taxes favored affluent districts and discriminated against children in poorer neighborhoods. The ruling, written by Justice Ralph L. Sullivan, examined a series of U.S. Supreme Court decisions and held that the property-tax system "must fall before the equal protection clause" of the 14th Amendment, which guaranteed every citizen "the equal protection of the laws."

The ruling sent the case back to lower courts where it had been previously dismissed due to a finding that the plaintiffs had no standing to bring suit. The lower courts were instructed to hold hearings to discover a more equitable school financing system.

The California system, followed in virtually every state, raised 56% of the school revenues from local property taxes, 35% from the state and about 9% from federal grants. The California court held that affluent districts could spend more per pupil and, at the same time, have lower property taxes. The ruling objected that the system "makes the quality of a child's education a function of the wealth of his parents and neighborhoods."

Similar suits had been filed in Illinois, Michigan, Texas and Virginia but had met with little success.

The California court modified its ruling Oct. 21, explaining that it had instructed a lower court to make the specific constitutional decision. In any case, the court said, the property tax system of financing would remain valid until an alternative could be devised.

Minnesota system also invalid—U.S. District Court Judge Miles M. Lord ruled in October that Minnesota's school financing system based on local property taxes was unconstitutional, and asked the state legislature to revise it.

In a preliminary ruling, reported Oct. 16, on a state motion to dismiss a private suit, Judge Lord said "spending for a child's education may not be a function of wealth other than the wealth of the state as a whole."

Nixon orders school tax study—President Nixon Oct. 3 ordered a study of the role of local property taxes in financing the nation's public schools.

The President gave the order after meeting with representatives of nine elementary and secondary school organizations. It was the first such meeting since he took office.

Health, Education and Welfare Secretary Elliot L. Richardson, announcing the new study, said education financing should move from "a narrowly based, regressive local tax to a more broadly based national tax."

Nationalization of big-city schools asked—Dr. Mark R. Shedd, superintendent of the Philadelphia school system, told the Senate Select Committee on Equal Educational Opportunity Sept. 21 that the "urban schools of this country are dying . . . from financial strangulation." Shedd proposed that the government nationalize the funding and operation of the 25 largest urban public school systems.

Shedd said the "job of rescuing the nation's urban schools from disaster simply has become too big for the limited resources of state and local governments to accomplish." He said property taxes were an insufficient basis to finance urban schools and that most of the revenues of big cities went to fund other services whereas the major share of suburban tax money could go to education.

California changes school tax. The California legislature completed final action Dec. 1, 1972 on a tax reform measure designed to move the state toward compliance with the ruling invalidating the previous school finance system.

The bill, backed by Gov. Ronald Reagan, would cut property taxes and allow tax credits to renters totaling $488 million a year. The state sales tax would go from 5% to 6%, bank and corporate taxes would go up 1.4% while local business inventory taxes would decline 20%. The provisions would result in a net increase of $332 million a year in education money.

Local School Tax Criticized. The U.S. Office of Education Nov. 2, 1971 released a four-year study of the nation's school financing system that called for the federal and state governments to assume almost all public school costs.

The report contended that the property tax, then supplying nearly all 52% of school costs raised locally, was unfair and already near the point of exhaustion. It asked the federal government to raise its contribution from about 7% to 22% of costs, which were expected to rise from $36 billion to as much as $73 billion by 1980, if early and remedial education programs were adopted.

Federal funds would be distributed in broad-purpose block grants rather than for specific programs, according to the study. States would take into account the needs of cities with a high proportion of disadvantaged pupils in determining per-pupil aid.

The study, called the National Educational Finance Project, was conducted largely at the University of Florida.

Deficits close local schools. Public schools were closed in Independence, Mo. Nov. 1–2, 1971 and in Dayton, Ohio Nov. 5–9 because of budget crises.

The 54,000 Dayton students and 17,000 in Independence were caught in a squeeze of rising costs and voter resistance to property tax referenda that had caused smaller systems to shut down in Ohio, Wisconsin, California and Washington. Teachers in Gary, Ind. voted Dec. 10 to teach the last school week in December even if payrolls were suspended.

The Independence school board decided Nov. 9 to resume classes on the basis of anticipated state aid, despite the failure that day of a tax rise vote. Dayton voters Nov. 12 approved a special property tax increase, enabling the board to borrow on 1972 revenues, and reopen schools that had been closed by the Ohio auditor when he determined that current funds were inadequate for expenses.

Texas school tax overturned. A special three-judge federal panel in San Antonio ruled Dec. 23, 1971 that Texas' public school finance system was unconstitutional and ordered the legislature to adopt an alternate system within two years.

The court ruled that the system, based 40% on local property taxes, discriminated against students in poor districts by violating their right to equal protection under the 14th Amendment.

N.J. Tax Voided. A New Jersey superior court judge Jan. 19, 1972 overturned the system of public school financing through local property taxes as violating the educational and equal protection clauses of the state constitution.

Judge Theodore I. Botter gave the state legislature one year to devise an alternate system that would not discriminate against "pupils in districts with low real property wealth," or "against taxpayers by imposing unequal burdens for a common state purpose."

Gov. William T. Cahill (R) had appointed a commission to study the state's tax structure, and had indicated support for a graduated personal income tax and a statewide property tax.

Plaintiffs in the suit included the mayors of Jersey City, Paterson, East Orange and Plainfield. Since the ruling, unlike similar rulings in California, Texas and Minnesota, was based on the state constitution, it would not be appealed in federal courts.

The state Supreme Court April 3, 1973 upheld the superior court decision. The legislature had rejected in 1972 a plan proposed by Gov. William T. Cahill for a uniform statewide property tax and a graduated statewide income tax.

N.Y. panel favors state property tax. A New York state special education commission, after a two-year study, proposed Jan. 28, 1972 that the state assume the entire cost of school financing, replacing local property taxes with a statewide property tax. The funds would be distributed by the state, and "weighted" in favor of schools with disadvantaged pupils.

Commission asks states to assume full costs. The President's Commission on School Finance submitted a 147-page report to President Nixon March 6, 1972 proposing that the states assume nearly all the costs of public elementary and secondary education, to relieve localities of the growing property tax burden and to guarantee equal educational opportunities within each state.

The report, the product of two years of study by the 18-member commission, did not specify how the states should raise the 52% of education costs now borne locally, but suggested as possibilities statewide property taxes, sales and income taxes. The states would distribute the funds with a view to the greater needs of disadvantaged and handicapped children and the varying costs of education in different parts of each state.

No district would have its budget reduced, but all districts would be prohibited from adding more than 10% over the state contribution, to conform with recent court decisions on equal school expenditures.

As an incentive to the states, the commission proposed that the federal government supply them with about $1 billion a year over five years. The states would need about $6 billion a year in new revenues to equalize spending between poor and wealthy districts, in addition to replacing local revenues, now totaling about $26.6 billion a year.

The commission emphasized that education should remain a state and local responsibility, asking that any major new federal aid be channeled through the states. The commission did not consider proposals for a national value added tax to finance education, according to Chairman Neil McElroy, because the subject had arisen too recently.

Although the report recommended increased aid to private and parochial schools, McElroy dissented along with seven other members. He said legal advisers "could not find any proposal for substantive form of assistance to non-public schools which appeared both practical and a probable winner of judicial challenge."

Nevertheless, the report asked the government to "promptly and seriously consider" the use of tax credits for private schools, tax deductions for parents, and tuition reimbursements, and favored support from all levels of government for less controversial purposes such as lunches, textbooks, transportation and health care.

McGovern for Tuition Credits. The unsuccessful 1972 Democratic Presidential candidate, Sen. George McGovern (S.D.), Sept. 19 endorsed the principle of federal tax aid for private and parochial school tuition. He did so in a speech at a Chicago Roman Catholic high school.

Although he did not support a specific plan, McGovern cited a bill supported by Rep. Wilbur D. Mills (D, Ark.) that would allow a $200 annual credit for each child in a bona fide non-public school.

McGovern said legislation could be drawn to exclude segregated private academies from eligibility.

Public opinion polls had shown the Democratic candidate to be weak among traditionally Democratic Roman Catholic blue collar workers, for whom the crisis in parochial education was a major issue.

Casper W. Weinberger, director of the office of Management and Budget, had told the House Ways and Means Committee Aug. 14 that the credit would cost the federal government $790 million–$970 million a year in lost tax revenues.

Labor spokesmen had opposed the bill in Sept. 8 hearings of the committee, including Andrew J. Biemiller, chief lobbyist for the AFL-CIO, and John J. Murray, head of the American Federation of Teachers non-public school department.

The National Education Association (NEA) also attacked the tax credit plan, in a Sept. 19 telegram to McGovern, saying the NEA "vigorously protests" his stand.

New York Archbishop Terence Cardinal Cooke spoke in favor of the bill Sept. 7 before the Ways and Means Committee, as had Lutheran, Jewish and other religious education spokesmen during August hearings.

Colorado & Ohio Back Property Tax. Among results of the elections Nov. 7, 1972, Colorado voters rejected a plan that would have outlawed the property tax as the source of funding for schools, stipulating that such funds come from income, sales and severance taxes.

Oregon voters, by 3–2, defeated a proposal to prohibit the use of property taxes for school operating costs.

In Michigan, voters rejected a proposal to replace the property tax with a general state tax (such as on sales or income) to finance most education.

Property Tax Cut Rejected. A U.S. advisory panel Dec. 14, 1972 rejected the Administration's plan to provide financial aid to states so that local government units could reduce property taxes.

The Advisory Commission on Intergovernmental Relations, a 26-member panel composed of members of the Cabinet, governors, mayors, county officials and members of Congress and the state legislatures, had been asked by President Nixon to study ways to reduce property taxes while still providing financing for education.

Nixon had pledged a reduction of local property taxes during his Presidential re-election campaign, and aides had drawn up a plan aimed at equalizing spending and tax burdens among state school districts, according to the Wall Street Journal Dec. 15.

The Commission report warned, "States should retain primary responsibility for shaping policies dealing with general property tax relief and intrastate equalization of school finances."

A proposal favored by the Administration and supported by the advisory commission's staff calling for federal grants to states to encourage property tax relief for low income groups was turned down by the commission.

Also rejected was another Administration proposal—the national value added tax.

Michigan System Invalid. The Michigan Supreme Court ruled Dec. 29, 1972 that the state's system of financing education for the 1970-1971 year, through property taxes and state aid, had been unconstitutional. While the court did not invalidate the current, similar system, it said it would accept a court challenge to any 1973-1974 system the legislature would devise, and said the new system would have to cease benefitting rich districts at the expense of poor ones.

Ohio tax credits voided. A three-judge federal panel ruled in Columbus, O. Dec. 29, 1972 that an Ohio law for state sales and local tax credits to parents of nonpublic school children was an unconstitutional violation of the separation of church and state. The law would have gone into effect for parents of about 300,000 children on returns for their 1972 taxes.

School financing by property tax upheld. The Supreme Court ruled March 21, 1973 that states could constitutionally finance schools through use of local property taxes, even when disparities between districts due to differences in affluence resulted.

The court, by a 5-4 vote, overturned a federal district court ruling that held the Texas school financing law unconstitutional because it created unequal educational opportunities. The Texas law had provided "at least a minimum foundation education" for every child through $1 billion in funds from the state's general revenues, a portion of which was distributed according to county property valuations. The districts were further allowed to supplement their funding through local property taxes.

The suit challenging the Texas law was filed by parents from the San Antonio area, where the poorest district had realized $26 per pupil through property taxes and the richest district $333.

Voting with the majority were Chief Justice Warren E. Burger and Justices Lewis F. Powell, Harry A. Blackmun, William H. Rehnquist and Potter Stewart. In the minority were Justices Thurgood Marshall, William J. Brennan, William O. Douglas, and Byron R. White.

Writing for the majority, Powell said, "Education . . . is not among the rights afforded explicit protection under our federal Constitution. Nor do we find any basis for saying it is implicitly so protected."

Powell denied the contention of the San Antonio parents that the system of funding violated the equal protection clause of the 14th Amendment. "At least where wealth is involved the equal protection clause does not require absolute equality of precisely equal advantages. Nor, indeed, in view of the infinite variables affecting the educational process, can any system assure equal quality of education except in the most relative sense."

Powell also argued that the parents had failed to prove they constituted a definable, discriminated-against class as required in past rulings with regard to the equal protection clause. Powell wrote that the appellees had failed to prove the Texas system operated to the "peculiar disadvantage of any suspect class." Moreover, he wrote, they had failed to establish that the poor were even concentrated in the poorest districts.

Powell denied what he referred to as the appellee's "nexus theory," that held the system failed to provide each child with an "opportunity to acquire minimum basic skills necessary for the full enjoyment of the rights of free speech and full participation in the political process." The Texas law, on the contrary, was a commitment on the part of the state to extend and improve the quality of education, he said.

Writing in dissent, Marshall (with Douglas concurring) said, "The court decides . . . that a state may constitutionally vary the quality of education it offers its children in accordance with the amount of taxable wealth. . . . the majority's holding can only be seen as a retreat from our historic commitment to equality of educational opportunity and as unsupportable acquiescense in a system which deprives children in their earliest years of the chance to reach their full potential as citizens."

White, in a separate dissent (joined by Douglas and Brennan), said that if one of the purposes of the Texas law was to encourage local initiative, the state failed "in districts with property tax bases so low that there is little if any opportunity for interested parents, rich or poor, to augment school district revenues."

All states except Hawaii raised funds for their schools primarily through local property taxes levied on a district-by-district basis. The system often led to less spending on educational facilities and materials in poor districts than in wealthy ones.

The syllabus summarizing the Supreme Court decision said:

The financing of public elementary and secondary schools in Texas is a product of state and local participation. Almost half of the revenues are derived from a largely state-funded program designed to provide a basic minimum educational offering in every school. Each district supplements state aid through an ad valorem tax on property within its jurisdiction. Appellees brought this class action on behalf of school children said to be members of poor families who reside in school districts having a low property tax base, making the claim that the Texas system's reliance on local property taxation favors the more affluent and violates equal protection requirements because of substantial interdistrict disparities in per-pupil ex-

penditures resulting primarily from differences in the value of assessable property among the districts. The District Court, finding that wealth is a "suspect" classification and that education is a "fundamental" right, concluded that the system could be upheld only upon a showing, which appellants failed to make, that there was a compelling state interest for the system. The court also concluded that appellants failed even to demonstrate a reasonable or rational basis for the State's system.

Held:

1. This is not a proper case in which to examine a State's laws under standards of strict judicial scrutiny, since that test is reserved for cases involving laws that operate to the disadvantage of suspect classes or interfere with the exercise of fundamental rights and liberties explicitly or implicitly protected by the Constitution.

(a) The Texas system does not disadvantage any suspect class. It has not been shown to discriminate against any definable class of "poor" people or to occasion discriminations depending on the relative wealth of the families in any district. And, insofar as the financing system disadvantages those who, disregarding their individual income characteristics, reside in comparatively poor school districts, the resulting class cannot be said to be suspect.

(b) Nor does the Texas school-financing system impermissibly interfere with the exercise of a "fundamental" right or liberty. Though education is one of the most important services performed by the State, it is not within the limited category of rights recognized by this Court as guaranteed by the Constitution. Even if some identifiable quantum of education is arguably entitled to constitutional protection to make meaningful the exercise of other constitutional rights, here there is no showing that the Texas system fails to provide the basic minimal skills necessary for that purpose.

(c) Moreover, this is an inappropriate case in which to invoke strict scrutiny since it involves the most delicate and difficult questions of local taxation, fiscal planning, educational policy, and federalism, considerations counseling a more restrained form of review.

2. The Texas system does not violate the Equal Protection Clause of the Fourteenth Amendment. Though concededly imperfect, the system bears a rational relationship to a legitimate state purpose. While assuring basic education for every child in the State, it permits and encourages participation in and significant control of each district's schools at the local level.

Oregon Rejects Change. Oregon voters May 1, 1973 reaffirmed their 1972 vote by deciding, by a 3–2 margin, to keep the local property tax as the major source of public school funds.

The vote rejected a proposal, backed by Gov. Tom McCall (R), education leaders and organized labor, to reduce local property taxes and have the state take over 95% of school operating costs. Construction and transportation costs would have remained a local responsibility.

To finance the plan, personal and corporate income taxes would have been increased, and the state would have imposed new taxes on business, real estate and profits. Opponents, including Republican legislators and business leaders, derided McCall's contention that 80%–85% of the state's taxpayers would have a net tax saving and said the business climate would be damaged.

Under the proposal, Oregon's spending range of about $600–$2,500 per pupil would have been narrowed over two years to $900–$1,200, and state funding would have increased from 21% to 95%.

H. Reed Saunders, director of school finance in the U.S. Office of Education, expressed disappointment in the vote May 2 and said if the plan had passed, "it might have started a bandwagon in other states, especially in view of the New Jersey ruling . . . throwing out their school financing system."

Florida aid curb upset. In a 6–1 decision April 5, 1973, the Florida Supreme Court struck down a state law used to withhold $32 million from schools in counties with property assessments lower than market value. State courts had held that property had to be assessed at full market value, but county tax officials had often under-assessed property.

The court said that allowing the state to determine the amount of under-assessment was an unconstitutional attack on the power of county tax assessors.

Nonpublic-School Tax Aid Urged. The presidential Panel on Nonpublic Education, composed of four members of the President's School Finance Commission, proposed April 20, 1972 the enactment of a $500 million annual program of tuition

tax credits to middle-income parents of nonpublic schoolchildren, and grants to poor families with such children.

State Taxes

Increases & New Levies. A variety of state tax developments took place in 1971:

■ New Hampshire Gov. Walter R. Peterson Jr. (R) reversed his campaign position against broadbased state taxes Feb. 11 and asked for a 3% state income tax. In the 1970 election campaign, Peterson had promised to prevent state sales or income taxes. Peterson told the legislature that increasing present levies on alcohol, cigarettes and gambling could no longer support demands on state services.

Peterson's proposal was defeated by 219–157 vote of the state House of Representatives May 27. New Hampshire remained the nation's only state with no personal income or general sales tax.

■ Gov. William G. Milliken (R) proposed a 38% increase in state income taxes to finance a $1.974 billion budget for Michigan, according to a New York Times report Feb. 14.

■ Connecticut Gov. Thomas J. Meskill (R) asked for a 2% state sales tax boost Feb. 16 that would raise state sales taxes to 7%, the highest in the U.S.

■ Rhode Island levied its first income tax Feb. 26 in a bill signed by Gov. Frank Licht (D) minutes after it was approved by the state senate. The tax, to be collected at a rate of 20% of the federal income tax, was enacted for the first six months of the year to offset a projected $24.5 million deficit for the current fiscal year.

■ Pennsylvania Gov. Milton J. Shapp (D) signed into law March 4 a 3.5% income tax as part of a $1.5 billion revenue package for the state. The state's first personal income tax had been approved by the legislature March 3 after Democratic state senators had pushed through an amendment reducing the levy from the 5% requested by Shapp Feb. 2 to 3.5%.

■ Gov. John G. Gilligan of Ohio March 15 proposed corporate and personal state income taxes and a reduction of state property taxes.

■ Maine voters agreed by a 3–1 margin in a Nov. 2 referendum to continue the state's 2-year-old personal and corporate income taxes.

Church exemption upheld. The Supreme Court ruled 7–1 May 4, 1970 to uphold the constitutionality of a New York State tax exemption for church property used solely for religious purposes. Similar laws exempted houses of worship from real estate taxes in all 50 states and the District of Columbia. The court rejected the appeal of Frederick Walz, a New York property owner, who argued that the exemption raised his real estate taxes, forcing him to contribute to religious groups against his will. Walz's appeal was backed by the American Civil Liberties Union.

Justice William O. Douglas, the lone dissenter, said a "strict constructionist" view should be taken in the matter of separation of church and state. He argued the exemption was not neutral because it did not apply to atheistic or agnostic groups.

The majority, in an opinion written by Chief Justice Warren E. Burger, did not deny that the law provided an "indirect economic benefit" to religious institutions but described the exemption as a form of "benevolent neutrality" that did not interfere with religious freedom. He said church property fell "within a broad class of property owned by nonprofit, quasi-public corporations which include hospitals, libraries, playgrounds, scientific, professional, historical and patriotic groups" which were spared "the burden of property taxation levied on private profit institutions." In a concurring opinion, Justice John M. Harlan said that in his view, the New York law was broad enough to permit agnostic and other non-religious groups to profit by similar tax benefits.

Estimates put the total value of church-owned property in the U.S. at $79.5 billion, with the Roman Catholic church holding $44.5 billion, the Protestant denominations with $28 billion and the Jews $7 billion. The government also granted tax deductions for donations to churches; such donations, according to a 1962 study, totaled $5.5 billion that year.

Federal Tax Reform

Congress took preliminary action during 1971 on additional tax reform proposals, but efforts at final action were dropped in 1972 because of the complications of the Presidential election.

House Votes Modified Program. The House passed by voice vote Oct. 6, 1971 a modified version of President Nixon's tax proposals for his new economic policy. The House debated the bill one hour 39 minutes Oct. 5 under a rule barring floor amendments. The version approved was the one reported Sept. 29 by the House Ways and Means Committee, which had modified the Administration's proposals.

President Nixon praised the House action Oct. 6 as reflecting "an overwhelming national will for prompt legislative measures to stimulate the economy, create jobs and halt inflation."

Organized labor, however, called it "a giant raid on the federal treasury that would transfer billions of dollars in public funds into the private treasuries of big business." This view, and an appeal to reject the bill, were contained in AFL-CIO letters to all members of Congress Oct. 5.

The committee revised the Administration program to a total tax revenue reduction of $25.6 billion over a three-year period, calendar 1971 73, compared with the Administration's $27.3 billion total for the same period. During the three years, individual taxes would be reduced by $5.7 billion compared with the Nixon program's $2.2 billion, and business taxes (not including the automobile excise tax repeal) would be cut by $14.1 billion compared with the Administration's $20.1 billion figure.

The committee approved shifting tax relief for individuals from the Administration's program for 67% of the total relief to those with incomes of $10,000 or more, to a program where 62% of the relief would go to those with incomes of $10,000 or less.

One of key labor objections was the continuing tax relief for business, which the AFL-CIO estimated would amount to $80 billion over the next 10 years.

Among the House bill's major provisions:

■ The tax credit for business investment would be reinstated at a 7% rate, retroactive to April 1. It would not apply to equipment manufactured overseas unless the President granted an exemption for specific reasons if there were a monopoly of American production of the item, if there was no other source except the foreign one, of if the import was for the purpose of initiating production of the item in the U.S.

■ The 7% excise tax on new automobiles would be repealed, as would be the 10% tax on trucks weighing up to 10,000 pounds.

■ The liberalized depreciation rates put into effect previously by the Treasury would be incorporated into the bill but without authority to advance the effective date for claiming depreciation.

■ Tax liability for businesses receiving a large part of their receipts from export sales would be deferred according to the amount exports were increased over previous years.

■ The $650 personal exemption for individual taxpayers would rise to $675 in 1971 and to $750 in 1972.

■ The standard deduction would rise in 1972 to 15% of income or $2,000, whichever was lower (currently 13% or $1,500).

■ The minimum standard deduction would rise to $1,300 in 1972 (currently $1,050) and a phaseout, reducing the amount as income increased, would be eliminated.

Tax break shift sought—Chairman Wilbur D. Mills (D, Ark.) of the House Ways & Means Committee and Rep. John W. Byrnes (Wis.), ranking committee Republican, had indicated Sept. 14 in interviews in the New York Times that they were in agreement about repealing part of a depreciation tax break for business, effected earlier in 1971, and applying the recouped funds—$1 billion-$2 billion—to tax relief for poor persons. Both favored reinstatement of the investment tax credit for business but not at the rate

proposed by the President—10% the first year and 5% thereafter. A single rate was suggested, 7% by Byrnes, Mills reserving opinion on a firm figure.

Sen. Russell Long (D, La.), chairman of the Senate Finance Committee, commented Oct. 6 after the House passed its tax bill that "in its present form, the bill appears to be too much of a trickle-down operation, with too little of it ever getting down."

When the committee hearings opened Oct. 7, Treasury Secretary John B. Connally Jr. advocated cutting corporate taxes by $800 million more than the Administration had originally sought—$500 million more in relief through the investment tax credit and $300 million more in tax relief for export firms. Connally accepted as "reasonable" the House bill's new tax relief for low-income families and the provisions for increased personal exemptions and standard deductions.

Senate panel readies bill—The Senate Finance Committee Nov. 8 approved its version of the tax bill to be sent to the Senate floor for consideration. The committee version, which would provide total tax reductions of $26.2 billion over a three-year period for individuals and business, was similar to the tax bill passed by the House in October.

The Senate bill's major provisions would:

■ Increase personal income tax exemptions to $675 on 1971 income and to $750 on 1972 income.

■ Provide a new standard minimum deduction of $1,300 on 1972 income for individuals near the poverty level.

■ Permit standard deductions of up to 15%, with a $2,000 ceiling, effective in 1972, for persons with higher incomes filing non-itemized reports.

■ Repeal the 7% excise tax on automobiles and the 10% excise tax on small trucks, retroactive to Aug. 15 (the retroactive date in the House bill for trucks was Sept. 26).

■ Give U.S. firms a 7% tax deduction for investment in American-made equipment and new depreciation rules (the latter incorporating the system put into effect earlier in 1971 by the Administration).

■ Allow exporting firms to defer taxes of $300 million a year to spur export price cuts.

'Unfairness' Change Opposed. A top Treasury official told the House Ways & Means Committee May 1, 1972 that the

Administration opposed any major revision of federal income tax laws to meet criticism that the system was sometimes unfair to single persons and married couples.

Edwin S. Cohen, assistant Treasury secretary, told the committee, however, that Congress might consider changing the maximum standard deduction for single and married persons. Under the present laws, the deduction was the same for either singles or married persons—15% to a maximum of $2,000.

The Ways and Means Committee had been holding hearings to consider complaints about the effect of tax law changes made in 1969.

Some of those changes reduced the gap between the amount of federal tax paid by a married couple and that paid by a single person with the same income. But under the present system, a maximum difference of 20% remained in some cases.

In addition, the changes since 1969 in at least some instances required husbands and wives who each earned a substantial portion of their joint income to pay more than two single persons would with the same income.

In testimony before the Joint Economic Committee July 21, Cohen was critical of attempts to reform the tax structure in an election year. He declined to reveal specific items in the Administration's tax reform proposals which would not be submitted to Congress before 1973.

But Cohen suggested that Congress rewrite and strengthen a 1969 tax law which attempted to force wealthy persons to pay a minimum tax on their income. Despite his support for a stronger tax law, Cohen said, less than 1% of the rich pay no federal income tax and that most pay huge amounts.

Cohen suggested that the favored tax treatment for capital gains be eliminated and that the top tax rate be reduced from 70% to 35%. The new tax rates would range from 12% on the first $3,000 of taxable income to 35% on taxable income of $48,000 and up. Under Cohen's proposal, personal exemptions would be increased.

Tax reform put off. John D. Ehrlichman, President Nixon's principal domestic affairs aide, informed newsmen May 12, 1972 that Nixon had agreed with Chairman Wilbur D. Mills (D, Ark.) of the House Ways and Means Committee that tax reform legislation would not be considered during the 1972 election year. If re-elected, Nixon would seek major tax reform in 1973, Ehrlichman said.

Ehrlichman attacked Democratic presidential candidates for a "platitudinous approach to tax reform" during the current campaign.

Treasury Secretary John B. Connally also had attacked the Democratic presidential campaigners on the tax reform issue. Appearing before the American Society of Newspaper Editors in Washington April 19, Connally stated his opposition to proposals for heavier taxation of capital gains—"I don't want to see the Dow-Jones hit 500," a reference to the DJ stock average, which on that day closed at 964.78. Connally said he did not regard as "loopholes" the capital gains tax provision or provision for tax exempt interest on state and local government bonds.

An aide, Assistant Treasury Secretary Edwin S. Cohen, in a Boston speech April 29, warned against tax reforms that could impair the economic situation for the oil industry, housing or business investment.

The New York Times then reported May 7 that the Treasury Department would propose that corporations and individuals be required to reinvest the savings which resulted from the oil and gas depletion allowances in the exploration and development of new energy producing properties.

The Times said the proposal, which would primarily affect wealthy individual investors and which had met with no corporate opposition, would be proposed to Congress only as a countermeasure if tax reformers attempted to lower or eliminated the tax depletion allowance.

Rep. Mills May 31 introduced legislation that would force Congress to review 54 tax-code provisions, many considered loopholes, giving special benefits to particular sources of income.

The bill called for the expiration of the 54 provisions, in three annual groupings of 18, the first group to lapse Jan. 1, 1974. Before the provisions lapsed, Congress could re-enact each provision, revise it or let it expire. The other two groups of tax preferences would expire Jan. 1, 1975 and Jan. 1, 1976.

Mills' plan was introduced in the Senate May 31 by Majority Leader Mike Mansfield (D, Mont.).

Mills, in a statement issued by the Ways and Means Committee, said his bill, called the Tax Policy Review Act of 1972, "in no way represents an evaluation or judgment on my part concerning any of these provisions."

He added, "It is expected that many of these terminations will not, in fact, be allowed to occur." Mills said he was seeking to "review each of these various items in an orderly way."

Tax Action, Studies & Protests

Depreciation Tax Liberalized. President Nixon Jan. 11, 1971 ordered liberalized requirements for depreciation writeoffs on business equipment. The new rules would create a $2.6 billion tax reduction for business in 1971. In a statement issued from the Western White House in San Clemente, Calif., the President said the new rules would spur employment, promote economic growth, increase competitiveness of U.S. goods abroad and clarify an important section of the Internal Revenue Code.

The rules, designed to act as a long-range stimulus to capital spending by business, would: (1) set up an "asset depreciation range system" to permit a 20% margin period (shortened or extended) over which business could write off the cost of equipment; (2) introduce various technical changes in permissible methods of figuring depreciation, retroactive to Jan. 1; and (3) drop the "reserve ratio test" standard limiting by means of a time schedule the amount of depreciation write-offs. The new regulations would not apply to equipment purchased by electric, gas and telephone companies.

The Treasury Department estimated that the business tax cut would result in an $800 million loss in federal revenue for fiscal year 1971 (ending June 30), rising to $4.1 billion in fiscal 1976 and declining to $2.8 billion in fiscal 1980.

Two lawyers from the Public Interest Research Group, a Washington law firm founded by consumer advocate Ralph Nader, filed suit in Washington's U.S. district court Jan. 11 to prohibit the Treasury from implementing the new rules. The lawyers sought the injunction on grounds that the changes were illegal because the public had not been notified in advance and public hearings had not been held. The Treasury said the new rules fell under a legal standard for "reasonable deductions" that did not require Congressional action.

The Treasury Department June 22 issued rules for the liberalized write-offs, and a diverse group of plaintiffs filed suit in U.S. District Court in Washington July 7 to block the guidelines. They said that the department had illegally issued the regulations by administratively enacting the changes without asking Congress to amend the tax laws.

The plaintiffs were Nader, Common Cause, the United Auto Workers, the National Rural Electric Cooperative Association, Rep. Henry S. Reuss (D, Wis.) and real estate developer Ramon L. Posel. The diversity was intended to improve the plaintiffs' legal standing to bring the suit. According to the doctrine of legal standing, the plaintiff must show that he was significantly affected by the action he was challenging in court.

In an apparently unprecedented action Reuss alleged that the Treasury action undermined his vote in Congress on the issue and nullified his past opposition as a congressman to subsidies for business taxpayers.

Both Nader and Common Cause contended they would be injured because the tax cut of more than $3 billion annually would reduce federal revenues to finance consumer programs. The UAW argued that the new rules would unlawfully subsidize a "particular class of business taxpayers" and discriminate against UAW members. The rural electric co-ops, mostly exempt from federal taxation, said the tax cut would give their competitors, the private power companies, an advantage that would alter the competitive balance between co-ops and private companies. The Jenkintown, Pa. real estate developer said he would be injured competitively by businesses benefitting under the new rules, since real estate and construction were not covered.

276 avoid '71 income tax. A preliminary Treasury Department study of 1971 tax returns indicated that 276 persons with incomes exceeding $100,000 paid no federal income tax during that year. (72 persons in that group had incomes greater than $200,000.)

Sen. Walter F. Mondale (D, Minn.) of the Senate Finance Committee which was studying tax reform issues, released the data April 1, 1973. "The 276 who paid no taxes at all are the barest tip of the iceberg. Thousands more pay only a pittance in taxes on their huge incomes," Mondale said.

Treasury Department officials, representing the Administration which was on record opposing most tax reform proposals, defended the group, saying that large deductions for interest payments on loans made for business purposes had offset taxable income.

The number of individuals who had avoided 1971 payments was down from 394 in 1970, including 112 in the over $200,000 category.

Big Firms Pay Little or No Tax. Rep. Charles A. Vanik (D, Ohio) reported to the House Aug. 1, 1973 on an updated study of large, profitable American corporations that were paying little or no federal income tax. His statement said:

Despite the fact that the following 11 companies were earning substantial profits in 1972, and paying out dividends, they paid no Federal income tax. What is even more shocking is that some of these companies not only paid no Federal tax but received a credit back from the Treasury.

Those industrial corporations with substantial before tax income reported to shareholders who paid no Federal corporate tax in 1972:

	Income reported to shareholders
McDonnell Douglas	$111,675,000
Republic Steel	43,061,000
Occidental Petroleum	10,419,000

Those transportation and utility corporations with substantial before tax income reported to shareholders who paid no Federal corporate tax in 1972:

Income Reported to Shareholders

Railroad Corporations:
Burlington Northern Inc., $48,711,000.
Airline Corporations:
Eastern Airlines, $59,178,000.
Trans World Airlines (received a credit of $857,000) $43,497,000.
United Airlines (received a credit of $140,000) $32,445,000.
Northwest Airlines (received a credit of $6,174,000) $17,253,000.
Consolidated Edison of N.Y. (received a credit of $1,091,000) $144,781,000.
American Electric Power (received a credit of $6,708,000) $168,103,000.
Penzoil Company (received a credit of $836,000) $62,276,000.

In tax year 1972, there were 11 profitable corporations out of 90 for which data was available that paid no Federal income tax—but this would have little significance even if this were the complete picture. The statutory rate that corporations should theoretically pay is 48 percent, yet in addition to the 3 industrials who paid no tax, 14 out of the remaining 58 industrials for which data was available paid only a 1- to 10-percent Federal effective tax rate.

INDUSTRIAL CORPORATIONS INCLUDED IN THE STUDY WHICH MADE PROFITS AND PAID AN EFFECTIVE FEDERAL TAX RATE OF 1 PERCENT TO 10 PERCENT

Year	Number of corporations	Amount of taxable income on which 1 percent to 10 percent corporate tax was paid
1969	10 out of 78	$3,377,000,000
1970	13 out of 86	3,171,000,000
1971	6 out of 45	2,327,000,000
1972	14 out of 58	3,666,710,000

The average effective Federal corporate tax rate was 29.6 percent in 1971 and 29.0 percent in 1972 for the industrials in the sample. This is nearly 20 tax percentage points below the statutory rate.

Some corporations have decreased their tax burden dramatically in recent years. ITT in 1972 paid an effective rate of 1 percent while its pre-tax income was $376,383,000.

EFFECTIVE FEDERAL TAX RATE OF ITT

	Net income before Federal tax	Effective rate (percent)
1969	$357,345,000	14.4
1970	429,615,000	4.2
1971	413,858,000	4.9
1972	376,383,000	1.0

Let me stress here, Mr. Speaker, that these corporations have done nothing illegal in lowering their tax rates— they have simply taken advantage— quite effectively—of the multitude of tax subsidies which have been enacted into the tax laws over the years.

· · · Our tax policy, whether we like it or not, does much more than just raise revenues. Our tax policy over the years has placed incentives and disincentives into the law hoping to correct specific problems. As the years roll on and the problems come and go, the provisions of the tax code remain, with a constituency and effect that many times has little to do with the original intent of the legislation.

It appears quite obvious that this study confirms my fears described in last year's report—that there is a startling reduction of corporate tax payments. The present laws are designed to insure that large American corporations will pay less and less in the future in support of our Government.

Need for Tax Rise Seen. A Brookings Institution report May 24, 1972 found the federal government "overcommitted" in current budget programs and facing a $17 billion shortfall by fiscal 1975 even assuming a prosperous economy. The study concluded that "lasting new federal initiatives can be financed only with a tax increase."

The $17 billion deficit could be expected, according to the study, in the context of a $300 billion federal budget for fiscal 1975 even if Congress enacted only programs proposed by President Nixon and no other additions. Legisla-

tion now before Congress for increased Social Security benefits could by itself "use up" regular revenue growth of the budget through fiscal 1977, according to the study.

These conclusions were reached even with possible lower defense spending, the study using a minimum defense budget of less spending than projected by the Administration. According to the Washington Post May 25, the suggested defense cutbacks ranged up to $13 billion a year.

In fact, "the total sums involved [in possible expenditure reductions] are small compared to the cost of new programs" already proposed, the study said. The study pointed out that the prospect of budget reduction was further clouded by Congress' past reluctance to cut back traditional subsidy programs.

Two major pessimistic findings of the study: federal spending on civilian programs had been rising since 1966 faster than revenues, and budget programs for major domestic problems too often led to "dead ends" because of uncertainty about the proper solution and insufficient funding or both.

Neither the Administration plan nor the House Ways and Means Committee plan for revenue sharing, the study found, would confront the main problem of the revenue "crisis" of the central cities, which would receive relatively little help under either plan with funding spread among state and local jurisdictions.

The Brookings study also pointed out that alternatives to the burdensome local property tax, currently financing elementary and secondary schools, were facing an insurmountable problem of finding a fair distribution formula.

Tax structure, wealth, income examined—A 1972 study conducted by the Cambridge Institute examining the pattern of wealth and income distribution in the U.S. called for a major overhaul in the federal tax structure.

"The effective rates of the progressive federal income tax are declining, particularly on property income. The regressive Social Security payroll tax and state and local taxes are increasing. Transfer payments are not increasing enough to improve the relative income share of low-income families," the report said.

The researchers concluded that "there is a startling and continuing inequality in the distribution of income in the U.S., and the overall pattern has remained virtually unchanged since World War II. . . . Government programs have had only a marginal impact on the overall distribution of income."

Radicals disrupt war-tax protests. Taxpayers' rallies against the war in Vietnam were staged April 15, 1970 in cities across the nation. The protests coincided with the deadline for filing federal tax returns as the sponsors of the various demonstrations—including the Vietnam Moratorium Committee, the New Mobilization Committee Against the War in Vietnam and the Student Mobilization Committee—hoped to emphasize the economic consequences of the war. Most of the protests were small and peaceful; however incidents of violence occurred when radicals confronted police in Boston, Berkeley, Calif., Cleveland and New York.

Maine timber taxes studied. A task force of law students, sponsored by Ralph Nader's Center for Study of Responsive Law, said June 1, 1971 that Maine woodlands owned by pulp and paper companies had been "grossly underassessed," resulting in an annual loss of a million dollars in state tax revenues. The study group's initial report, released in Portland, said that partly as a result of its investigation, timberland assessments had been adjusted upward in 1970, but that revenues were still more than a half a million dollars below what they should be.

The report said the 10 largest paper companies in Maine owned about one-third of the land in the state and purchased most of the timber grown in the remaining 10 million acres of woodland. The students said that for almost 40 years, the state had contracted out the tax assessment of timberland to a company whose other business, for the most part, came from paper companies and large landowners.

Watergate & Inflation Eclipse Tax Issue: 1973-74

Tax Revolt Smolders, Nixon Avoids Major Changes

Richard M. Nixon had served little more than a year and a half of his second term as President before the Watergate scandal forced him out of office Aug. 9, 1974. Observers held that Watergate had distracted Nixon, his Administration and Congress during these months from effective action on tax reform and many other issues. Such tax action as was considered was often relegated to a subsidiary role by the pressure of inflation, which had risen from a rate of 3% in 1972 to 8.8% in 1973 and then had reached the "double-digit" figure of 10.7% for the 12-month period that ended in May 1974. The question during this period was often: in what way can tax policy be used as a weapon against inflation? Yet embers of tax revolt continued to smolder and were often visible through the flames of the other controversies.

'74 Budget Avoids Tax Change. President Nixon submitted to Congress Jan. 29, 1973 a $268.7 billion fiscal 1974 budget designed to avoid higher taxes and inflation and drastically revamp the structure of federal programs.

Some 112 programs, among them major antipoverty efforts and landmark education-aid legislation, were to be eliminated or reduced. Another 70 programs were to be replaced and encompassed under four special revenue sharing plans, with a total funding of $6.9 billion, covering education, law enforcement, manpower training and urban community development.

In addition to avoiding major new spending initiatives in the new budget, the President abandoned pursuit of some past initiatives for welfare reform and revision of the local property tax structure to relieve, especially, the tax burden for the elderly.

And, despite the negotiated cease-fire in the Vietnam conflict, the budget did not reflect any war-end dividend. Defense spending was budgeted at $81.1 billion for fiscal 1974, almost a third of the total budget and $4.7 billion of the $18.9 billion total budget increase from fiscal 1973 to 1974.

Curb on spending stressed—The President stressed in his budget message the need to hold down government spending at all levels and to avoid a tax increase. Only two tax proposals were made in the budget, involving a $600 million revenue loss to the Treasury in fiscal 1974—an income tax credit for tuition paid to parochial and other nonpublic schools, and a liberalized tax deduction for retirement funds set aside by individuals.

The goal, Nixon said, was high employment prosperity without inflation and without war. His budget proposed, he said, "a leaner federal bureaucracy, increased reliance on state and local governments to carry out what are primarily state and local responsibilities, and greater freedom for the American people to make for themselves fundamental choices about what is best for them."

If Congress abided by his budget recommendations, Nixon said, and if a "disciplined approach to federal spending" were taken, it would be possible to avoid a tax increase "for the foreseeable future."

If Congress exceeded the budgeted outlays, he warned, it would face "the alternative of higher taxes, higher interest rates, renewed inflation, or all three."

Nixon radio appeal. President Nixon had unveiled his budget proposals in a nationwide radio address Jan. 28 when he called on the public to support those legislators "who have the courage to vote against higher spending."

Nixon forecast a new "era of prolonged and growing prosperity" beginning with 1973 but he declared, "The greatest threat to our new prosperity is excessive government spending."

To justify his sweeping cutbacks in federal programs "that have outlived their time, or that have failed," Nixon cited the "sky-rocketing" budgetary costs in recent years. Since 1952, the budget had doubled every 10 years, he said. He predicted that by the 1990s, it could reach "over a trillion dollars."

Nixon offered three reasons for resisting this expansionary fiscal trend: to prevent a tax increase, to offset inflation and to reduce the size of government.

"It is time to get big government off your back and out of your pocket," the President said.

Nixon concluded that what was at stake in his budgetary proposal to Congress was "your job, your taxes, the prices you pay, and whether the money you earn by your own work is spent by you for what you want, or by government for what someone else wants."

Albert attacks Nixon budget. House Speaker Carl Albert (Okla.) characterized President Nixon's new budget Feb. 11 as one that had "its hands in its pockets and its eyes on the ground." It lacked a "sense of affirmation," he said, and was a budget "of limited horizon" and "devoid of any great vision of America." Albert made the remarks in a 10-minute radio address carried by all four major networks as a Democratic rebuttal to Nixon's budget speech.

"Congress will not tolerate the callous attitude of an administration that seems to have no compassion for the down-and-out citizens of this country," he said. It was apparent, Albert said, "that big business will not suffer from the Nixon budget cuts" and neither would "the rich" but the average taxpayer would "continue to pay a disproportionately large share" of his income in federal taxes "while getting fewer federal services in return."

Mandate 'gravely misconstrued'—The Coalition for a Democratic Majority said Feb. 14 that President Nixon had "gravely misconstrued" the mandate he won in the 1972 presidential election. The coalition said that had been given "no ideological proxy to turn back the clock on progress in America."

"The central issue before the nation and before Congress," it said, was "not the fixing of a ceiling on the federal budget but rather the promotion of sound, feasible and beneficial programs and a fair allocation of the burden of paying the tax bill."

Nixon's economic message. President Nixon's state of the union message dealing with economic matters, submitted to Congress Feb. 22, contained no changes in previously stated Administration economic plans.

The report concentrated heavily on a defense of fiscal restraint, proposed White House cutbacks in social assistance programs and general promises of tax relief.

The President promised to "submit a tax program that builds further on those we achieved in 1969 and 1971." No further details were offered. Other tax recommendations the White House said would be submitted to Congress included plans for "alleviating the crushing burdens which property taxes now create for older Americans" and tax credits for parents with children in parochial and private schools.

Herbert Stein, chairman of the President's Council of Economic Advisers, told newsmen attending a Washington economic briefing April 24 that the White House had flatly ruled out a re-imposition of "rigid and comprehensive wage and price controls." He conceded, however, that the Administration was studying the "possibility" of a tax increase to "prevent the rise in demand from becoming excessive." A lowering of the 7% tax credit for investment in business equipment was under specific consideration, he said.

Nixon tax proposals. President Nixon submitted tax reform legislation to the House Ways and Means Committee April 30 but proposed few major changes in the nation's tax code. According to Treasury Secretary George P. Shultz, who presented the plan to Congress, the Administration goal was not a sweeping restructuring of a "basically sound [tax] system," but an attempt to spur economic growth and to provide taxpayers with more equitable and efficient tax laws.

The proposed changes, estimated to cost the government $900 million in lost revenues during the first year of operation, "were essentially neutral in their budgetary effects," Shultz said.

Shultz cited the "dangerously demoralizing effect" of tax avoidance schemes by wealthy individuals as justification for two new provisions designed to replace the four-year-old "minimum income tax." The current law, which was aimed at limiting the ability of individuals to legally avoid payment of most or all of their federal income, had proven inadequate.

In its place, the Administration proposed a complex "minimum taxable income" plan and a "limitation on artificial accounting losses." (The substitute measure would not apply to corporations which would continue paying the single "minimum income tax.")

The Administration offered no proposals for reform of estate and gift taxes, Shultz said, because "Congress is the best place" to formulate changes in those areas.

The White House offered a tax simplification proposal to deal with the "burgeoning complexity" of the tax system. A new form—1040S—a shorter, streamlined version of the basic form 1040, would permit an estimated 20 million taxpayers to make easier calculations of itemized non-wage income; however, some of the current deductions would be eliminated or restricted under the new plan. A "miscellaneous deduction allowance" of $500 would be included in Form 1040S in addition to regular deductions.

Other proposed changes provided property tax relief (up to $500 credit) for the elderly; tax credits of up to $200 for parents of children attending nonpublic schools; direct cash subsidies to state and local governments that issued bonds paying interest which was subject to federal tax (governments would still have the option to issue tax exempt bonds and receive no subsidy); tax checkoffs directly on the tax form for political contributions; and civil penalties and court injunctions against fraudulent or incompetent tax return preparers.

The Administration plan also contained two previously discussed tax proposals: credits for exploratory oil and natural gas drilling and limits on income earned abroad.

No changes in capital gains, depreciation or oil depletion allowance taxes were included in the White House proposal.

House Ways and Means Committee Chairman Wilbur D. Mills (D, Ark.), as well as Democratic proponents of a sweeping overhaul in the tax code, criticized the Administration tax package as inadequate.

Later in 1973, at a Sept. 5 press conference, Nixon amplified Administration views on the situation.

Asked if the tax structure could be "altered in any way to help strengthen the economy," Nixon said a number of his advisers, including Federal Reserve Board Chairman Arthur F. Burns, had "strongly recommended that the answer to this whole problem of inflation is the tax structure . . . that there's this gimmick and that one." As an example, he cited the suggestion to give the President power to move the investment credit from 3% to 15%, which he considered "an excellent idea" but added that "there isn't a chance the Congress is ever going to give the President that power."

A number of suggestions had been made on the tax front which might be helpful in controlling inflation, he said, "but there isn't a chance that a responsible tax bill would be passed by this Congress in time to deal with that problem."

Tax increase considered. President Nixon was considering the advisability of requesting a tax increase from Congress. This reversal of policy from Nixon's often-stated opposition to a tax rise in 1973 was announced by Melvin R. Laird, counselor to the President, at a news conference Sept. 13.

The immediate reaction from Congressional leaders was unfavorable, and Treasury Secretary George P. Shultz, who was attending a conference in Tokyo, said Sept. 14 that Laird should "keep his cotton-picking hands off economic policy."

Laird said two plans were being discussed for possible application to the current inflationary economy:

■ An across-the-board income tax increase on individuals and corporations to be collected during an inflationary period and refunded later, possibly two or three years later, when inflation lessened. Laird said the figure under discussion was in the area of a 10% surcharge on income taxes.

■ Revision of the 7% investment tax credit for business into a variable credit ranging from 4% to 15%, with the rate set low in boom times to discourage business spending for equipment and high in slack times to encourage such spending.

Laird put his announcement in the context of the Administration's "move toward greater openness." "We are having more conversations," he said, "and we are having more confrontation over ideas, and that is important." He said he did not expect enactment of either tax plan in 1973 because of Congress' full schedule of other work, but he offered the possibility that the tax increase might be requested as a means to offset increased spending by Congress.

The switch in Nixon's position was disclosed Sept. 12 by Arthur F. Burns, chairman of the Federal Reserve Board, who told the House Banking Committee that Nixon had indicated to him "very considerable sympathy" for a tax increase to take some of the anti-inflation burden from the board's policy of money and credit restraint. Burns himself advocated a lower investment tax credit rate and a tax on individuals, or possibly only corporations, that would be "impounded" during inflation and refunded during non-inflation times.

Burns, who had conferred with Nixon Sept. 11, was asked by reporters after the House hearing if he expected Nixon to propose a tax increase. "I would not put it in terms of expectations, but I would not be surprised," he replied.

Rep. Al Ullman (D, Ore.), acting chairman of the House Ways and Means Committee, said Sept. 13 he thought Laird's announcement was "a trial balloon—and a weak one."

Sen. Russell B. Long (D, La.), chairman of the Senate Finance Committee, said he would not support a refundable income tax surcharge because he "would not have any confidence that it would be returned."

Laird confirmed Sept. 23 that the Administration would not send any proposals for a tax increase to Congress during 1973. In a televised news broadcast, Laird defended his Sept. 13 remark that the White House was considering a 10% income tax surcharge, saying "now is the time to have open conversation and discussion" about the form future tax legislation might take.

Study calls for tax reform. The Brookings Institution said July 18, 1973 that instead of raising taxes as it had proposed in 1972, Nixon had made cuts in domestic spending while increasing military expenditures. The study concluded that tax reform, rather than an across-the-board tax increase, was a better method of increasing tax revenue.

The study noted that, due to tax loopholes and rising Social Security taxes, federal tax rates were not as progressive as they were thought to be. The report stated that the flat Social Security tax was regressive and that the total federal taxes of a family of four are "actually a smaller percentage if the family earns $25,000 than if it earns $10,000. While the affluent family pays a higher percentage in income tax, this is more than offset by the lower percentage of its income that it pays in payroll tax."

The report emphasized that "without changes in tax structure or defense spending," there would be "little room for initiative in the domestic budget until (fiscal) 1977. Even then, the leeway is modest."

Tax on political parties planned. The Internal Revenue Service (IRS) said Aug. 1, 1973 that it planned to tax political parties and fund raising committees for income derived from stocks given as political contributions.

Donors giving the properties would not pay capital gains taxes but fund raising groups would be required to pay taxes ranging from 7%–35% on stocks which had increased in value between the time the contributor acquired the property and the time it was donated to the political group. Taxes also would be levied on income derived from interest or dividends on investments and on "any ancillary commercial activities" unrelated to a candidate's campaign.

IRS Commissioner Donald C. Alexander said that unless Congress or the courts objected to the proposal, the new ruling would apply to any property given to political groups after Oct. 3, 1972, the day when the IRS had first indicated its "concern" about tax loopholes enjoyed by political groups.

The selection of the retroactive starting date was regarded by observers as a compromise gesture by the IRS permitting the bulk of the stock transfers made during the presidential campaign to escape taxation. Alexander said both political parties already had declared their opposition to the proposal. Political parties had not been required to file income tax returns in the past.

'Windfall' profits tax proposed. President Nixon made a brief appearance before reporters Dec. 19, 1973 to say that the White House would propose legislation to levy an "emergency windfall profits tax" on the oil industry. The measure was actually a misnomer because profits—revenues minus costs—would not be taxed. Instead, an excise-type levy would be placed on crude oil prices that rose above a certain base.

The proposal was designed to offset excess profits accruing to producers as a result of the scarcity of crude oil and the recent enormous increases in the price of petroleum products without diminishing the industry's incentive to spend money on exploration for new oil reserves.

The proposal also had a "fadeaway" provision in which the tax would decrease gradually and then die, probably within five years—a reflection of the Administration's belief that rising oil prices would have reached equilibrium by that time and profits would no longer be considered excessive.

In a parallel announcement Dec. 19, the Cost of Living Council (CLC) authorized an immediate $1 a barrel increase in the price of crude, a 23% boost over the current price of $4.25 a barrel.

The full effect of the increase would not be felt until February 1974. Under current CLC rules, producers could institute one-third on the increase Jan. 1, 1974 and the remainder Feb. 1.

Treasury Secretary George P. Shultz conducted the White House news briefing after President Nixon left without answering any questions. According to Shultz, the windfall profits tax would take effect when oil prices topped $4.75 a barrel. The tax would rise progressively, reaching a maximum 85%.

Schultz estimated that producers eventually would have to charge $7 a barrel to balance supply and demand, but he warned that while new supplies of petroleum were being sought in the interim, prices could reach $9 a barrel before conditions stabilized.

The CLC action would apply only to "old" oil—equal to the volume the producer pumped in 1972. (Old oil represented about 75% of current production.) The price of "new" oil, or the additional output, was not regulated by government price control. New oil was selling for $6.17 a barrel ($7.17 with the CLC-approved increase). The price of imported crude was about $6 at the end of November.

Tax cut vote reversed. A minor tax bill was rejected by the Senate Jan. 24, 1974 after a major amendment had been attached to increase the personal tax exemption from $750 a person to $850, effective with the 1973 tax year.

The bill, passed by the House, would have provided additional tax breaks to families of prisoners of war and servicemen missing in action. It had been encumbered with amendments for minor tax breaks to various industries and individuals, some unnamed, into a "Christmas tree" bill, so-called because such bills normally gained passage at the end of a session. The defeat in the Senate was unprecedented for such a bill.

During its consideration Jan. 24, Sen. Edward M. Kennedy (D, Mass.), possibly in an attempt to gain at least a committee hearing on the issue, proposed the $100 increase in the personal exemption as a countermove to a recessed economy. Others argued that the $3.5 billion tax revenue reduction involved would be inflationary. The Senate accepted the increase by a 53-27 vote.

The Senate also accepted Kennedy's proposal to attach a provision tightening the minimum income tax and bringing in an additional $860 million in revenue a year.

Then Sen. Russell Long (D, La.), main sponsor of the original bill, suggested the entire package be returned to his Finance Committee for further study. It was so voted 48-27.

'75 Budget Avoids Tax Raise. President Nixon Feb. 4, 1974 submitted his fiscal 1975 budget, which avoided major tax increases. It proposed outlays of $304.4 billion and was the first budget to exceed $300 billion.

The budget did not suggest any increase in basic tax rates, aside from the already proposed plan to tax "windfall" profits of oil firms. The estimate assumed an additional $3 billion collection from the oil industry from the windfall profits tax.

Total corporate income tax revenue was estimated at $48 billion. The total income tax from individuals was expected to be $129 billion. The Social Security tax yield for fiscal 1975 was put at $72.5 billion.

Aides affirm anti-recession intent—At a briefing on the new budget Feb. 4, Frederic Malek, deputy director of the Office of Management and Budget, said the President was not going "to tolerate a recession" and "if we have to bust the budget to prevent it, we'll bust the budget."

Treasury Secretary George P. Shultz, at the same briefing, offered a list of steps the Administration recommended to counter a recession. He stressed that tax reduction was "at the end of the list" because of the necessity to maintain federal revenue. "But if we must, we must," he added.

The Budget Dollar

Where it comes from:

Individual income taxes . . . . .42¢
Social insurance receipts .28¢
Corporation income taxes. . . . . .16¢
Excise taxes . . . . 6¢
Borrowing . . . . 3¢
Other . . . . 5¢

Where it goes:

Benefit payments to individuals . . . . .37¢
National defense . . . . .29¢
Grants to states and localities . . . . .17¢
Other federal operations . . . . .10¢
Net interest . . . . 7¢

Fiscal 1975 receipts were estimated at $295 billion, a $25 billion increase over the previous year. The $9.4 billion deficit was pegged primarily to an anticipated economic slowdown cutting into the normal revenue.

Reform of budget process OKd. A sweeping reform bill, revising the processing of the federal budget through Congress, was cleared and sent to the President June 21. The final votes of approval were 401–6 by the House June 18 and 75–0 by the Senate June 21.

In addition to revising the Congressional budgetary process, the bill, projected for full implementation by 1976, would change the federal fiscal year to begin Oct. 1 (instead of July 1), curb spending programs funded outside the regular budgetary process and restrict impoundment of Congressionally mandated funds by the executive branch.

A Budget Office was to be established in Congress to provide expertise and each chamber would have a budget committee.

A budget resolution would be devised to set target figures for total appropriations, spending and tax and debt levels. The initial resolution, considered a tentative alternative budget to the presidential budget, was to be reported by the budget committees by April 15 and was to be cleared by Congress by May 15.

The resolution would provide a breakdown of appropriations and spending by category—defense, education, health, etc.—within the larger target figures. Any recommended changes in tax revenues or the federal debt ceiling were to be included in the resolution.

Tax cut proposed. At a press conference April 22, 1974, Chairman Arthur F. Burns of the Federal Reserve Board opposed Democratic proposals of a tax reduction to stimulate the economy.

The President defined his budget as one of "moderate restraint" and said special emphasis was put on "the proper fiscal balance to keep the economy on the track to sustain high employment and more stable prices." The budget continued, he said, "a policy of fiscal responsibility as part of a continuing anti-inflation program."

However, the move for a tax cut gained an important advocate the same day when Senate Democratic leader Mike Mansfield (Mont.) issued a statement espousing a tax cut as "something we can do for the average working stiff who's carrying the load in this country."

A call for a tax cut was made by Sens. Edward M. Kennedy (D, Mass.) and Walter F. Mondale (D, Minn.) in a joint statement April 20. The nation was "in the grip of a serious recession," they said, and a tax cut was "the single most important step that Congress can now take for the long-run strength and vitality of the nation's economy." Deploring "the do-nothing siren call of the Administration," the statement advocated a $5.9 billion income tax reduction to inject buying power into the economy. They suggested an increase in the personal exemption for taxpayers from $750 to $825 or the alternative of a $190 tax credit.

A statement advocating a tax cut for low- and middle-income families "to stimulate the economy through consumer demand" was issued by Sen. Hubert H. Humphrey (D, Minn.) April 21. He referred to the long-standing economic theory that "a high rate of inflation could not exist side by side in our economy with a drop in economic activity, high levels of unemployment and high interest rates." "The Nixon Administration has clearly proved that, with its economic policies, you can have all of this bad news at the same time," Humphrey said.

Administration opposition to a tax cut was expressed on NBC's "Meet the Press" April 21 by Kenneth R. Cole Jr., President Nixon's chief domestic affairs adviser. "As far as a tax decrease is concerned," he said, "we have an inflation problem. We have too much of an inflation problem and we think that a tax decrease at this particular point in time will inflame that problem rather than resolve the problems that we have in the economy."

The economic problem was "primarily in the energy-related area," Cole said, and the situation was "picking up" because of the increase in energy supplies flowing from the lifting of the Arab oil embargo and the "picking up" of automobile production and sales. "So I am not so sure that [a tax cut] would solve the problem," he said

White House spokesman Gerald L. Warren said April 22 Cole accurately reflected President Nixon's views on the subject.

Tax-cut effort defeated. A 10-day effort by liberals to attach a tax cut and reform package to a debt-limit bill failed June 26, 1974, and the measure was passed by the Senate 58–37. The bill, which was signed into law June 30, increased the federal debt ceiling $19.3 billion to $495 billion through March 31, 1975.

The tax-cut and reform effort, led by Sens. Edward M. Kennedy (D, Mass.) and Hubert H. Humphrey (D, Minn.), could not gain enough support to break a filibuster launched against it by Sen. James B. Allen (D, Ala.). Allen gained the floor by proposing to make the debt ceiling $490 billion. A move June 19 to cut off debate on the Allen amendment, requiring a two-thirds majority, fell 12 votes short, 50–43. Another vote June 19 to reject the Allen amendment, requiring only a majority, failed, 45–48.

The Kennedy tax package was rejected June 24 by a 65–33 vote. Humphrey offered a scaled-down version June 26 and when a vote to break the filibuster against it lost by a 48–50 vote, the tax effort was dropped.

Kennedy's proposal would have cut individual taxes by raising the personal income tax exemption to $825 a year from $750 and offering taxpayers the option of taking a $190 tax credit instead. It also would have provided a 10% credit on earned income up to $4,000 a year, the credit reduced as income increased until earnings reached $5,600 a year.

The tax revenue loss would be $6 billion. To partially offset it, Kennedy proposed repeal of the 22% oil depletion allowance, accelerated depreciation provisions for new plants and equipment and special tax benefits for domestic international sales corporations. He also proposed tightening the minimum tax applications.

Humphrey's proposal was similar but would have less revenue loss—$4.5 billion a year. The income tax exemption would have been raised to only $800 and the optional tax credit offered only $175.

Nixon, businessmen confer. President Nixon conferred for more than two hours July 11, 1974 at the White House with a group of businessmen and economists in a meeting that was described by a senior official as a "listening exercise" for the President to obtain business views on the Administration's anti-inflation efforts.

Participants said no new economic policy initiatives were announced at the meeting, which had been billed as the start of a "national dialogue" between the Administration and segments of the economy on ways to combat inflation.

The businessmen generally expressed support for the Administration's policies but also presented a "strong demand" that the Administration stimulate industrial expansion by providing more tax incentives. Among the tax preferences suggested were an increase in the investment tax credit, accelerated depreciation allowances and other write-offs against federal income taxes.

President Nixon's chief economic adviser, Kenneth Rush, who also attended the meeting, said in a later briefing that Nixon "didn't volunteer an opinion" on the group's proposals. No final decision on tax matters would be made until a government study on industry's future capital needs was completed, probably near the end of the year, Rush stated, but the proposal was not rejected out of hand.

Rush contrasted the inflationary impact of tax concessions for industry and tax cuts for individuals, which Nixon had already indicated that he opposed. "A tax cut for individuals means increased demand without increased productivity," Rush said. However, tax incentives for business would be "noninflationary" if they spurred output. "We must have heavy investment in new facilities by industry" to overcome shortages, Rush said, adding that current corporate cash flow was not "nearly sufficient" to spur expansion.

Other Developments

Few tax hikes seen. A New York Times survey cited Feb. 27, 1973 found that the governors and legislatures of 39 states had pledged to avoid a tax increase, and about half the states contemplated some tax reductions.

About one third of the states reported surpluses, many of them substantial, which were attributed to federal revenue sharing, higher than expected tax collections, and tax increases passed in recent years.

Most of the tax reductions planned involved property levies, in some cases limited to elderly taxpayers. Recent reductions in federal social spending was not expected by many officials to change the overall tax situation.

California tax credit voided. A three-judge federal panel in San Francisco ruled law allowing up to $125 in personal income tax credits for each child attending private school.

Citing a 1973 U.S. Supreme Court decision involving New York, the panel said the California law had a similarly im-

proper result—"state sponsorship of religious activity."

The court noted that the law would benefit only those taxpayers sending their children to sectarian schools, a "substantial majority" of which were Catholic schools with religious instruction as part of the curriculum. The law's "statistical" assurance that the individual tax savings would not directly reach religious schools invalid Feb. 1, 1974 a 1972 California did not satisfy the U.S. Constitution's prohibition of establishment of religion, the court concluded.

California told to find tax plan—A state superior court judge ruled in Los Angeles April 10 that the district-by-district property tax system of school financing violated equality guarantees of the state constitution, and ordered that alternative methods be found. The ruling, which allowed the current system to remain in effect until a comprehensive new plan could be devised, came in a six-year-old suit which had been sent back to the lower court for trial.

Judge Bernard S. Jefferson ruled that differences in property valuations among poor and wealthy districts had caused substantial differences in per-pupil expenditures. Jefferson also ruled that an attempt by the state legislature to create parity among districts by proportional allocations of state funds had been insufficient.

New Louisiana constitution approved. Louisiana voters approved a new state constitution April 20, 1974.

A major feature of the new charter was elimination from the tax base of homes valued at less than $50,000.

Oil tax breaks called failure. According to a report released Feb. 3, 1974 by Sen. Henry Jackson (D, Wash.), tax breaks granted the oil industry as incentives to promote exploration and development had failed to generate new supplies of domestic oil. The study, prepared by the Library of Congress, put the cost of the tax breaks at $1.5 billion annually. (Another $600 million–$1 billion was lost to the government in tax credits allowed on foreign oil operations, according to the report.)

A tax study prepared by the Petroleum Industry Research Foundation, a trade group, said Feb. 8 that the oil industry bore a larger domestic tax burden per dollar of sales than any other U.S. industry. (Tax payments per dollar of revenue, however, were smaller than most other sectors of U.S. business because of foreign tax credits and other tax breaks.)

In 1971, according to the group, the industry paid 5.59¢ on every dollar of gross revenue, compared with 4.58¢ for other mining and manufacturing firms, and 4.17¢ for other businesses.

As the depletion tax rate dropped, the report continued, the oil industry also increased its effective federal income tax rate on domestic operations; in 1969 it was 19.1%, 1970—22%, 1971—23.5%, and 1972—25.6%.

IRS rescinds ITT tax break. International Telephone & Telegraph Corp. (ITT) announced March 6, 1974 that the Internal Revenue Service (IRS) had revoked its 1969 ruling that had enabled ITT to acquire the Hartford Fire Insurance Co. It was the largest corporate merger in history.

The merger had provoked controversy within the Administration which was divided over whether to press antitrust charges against ITT. The government's final decisions in the case, which had involved President Nixon and other high White House officials, spurred further controversy and prompted Watergate special prosecutor Leon Jaworski to investigate the ITT case.

The IRS ruling was integral to ITT's take-over plans: the 17,000 Hartford shareholders, whose approval of the merger was required, were allowed by the government to exchange their stock for ITT stock without immediately paying capital gains taxes.

With retroactive revocation of that favorable tax ruling, the former Hartford shareholders could be liable for up to $50 million in back taxes, according to the Wall Street Journal.

The IRS confirmed that its 1969 order had been rescinded but refused to disclose the basis for its decision. ITT officials said March 7 that the action stemmed from the government's investigation of another aspect of the tax arrangements involving ITT's sale of a separate block of Hartford shares to Mediobanca, a Milan bank.

A class action suit brought by a former Hartford shareholder had also challenged this preliminary aspect of the merger which was a basis for the tax break given the Hartford group and ultimately for actual take-over approved by the Hartford shareholders.

The suit, brought by Hilda Herbst, alleged that ITT had obtained the IRS ruling by providing the government with false information. Under an agreement concluded by ITT with the IRS, the Hartford shareholders' tax-free arrangement depended upon ITT's pledge to sell a block of Hartford stock obtained earlier in 1969 "unconditionally to an unrelated third party"—Mediobanca. (ITT had bought the Hartford stock for cash, which violated an IRS requirement that the Hartford acquisition be completed only through an exchange of stock.) The Herbst suit charged that the Mediobanca purchase was not unconditional and that the Italian bank was not as "unrelated" as ITT had claimed.

The IRS acted six weeks before the statute of limitations would have precluded recovery of taxes from the original ruling. Rep. J. J. Pickle (D, Tex.), ranking Democrat on the House Commerce Committee's investigations sub-committee, had urged the IRS to act swiftly on a decision made in April 1973 by its New York regional office to rescind the 1969 decision. Pickle's subcommittee had been investigating the ITT case and the Watergate special prosecutor's office had begun a separate investigation of the matter at Pickle's request.

Taxes Linked to Inflation & Government Spending: 1974-76

Ford's Economic Program & the Tax Revolt

Gerald R. Ford, who Nixon had appointed Vice President, succeeded Nixon as President Aug. 9, 1974 on the latter's resignation. The nation was already struggling with what the Congressional Budget Office later described as "the deepest recession in the American economy since the Depression of the 1930s."

In his first major economic act, Ford proposed an anti-inflation program that included a call for a surtax. Despite the smoldering tax revolt, he repeatedly assailed proposed tax cuts that were not balanced by reduced government spending. As the 1976 Presidential election campaign approached, he expressed more sympathy for tax-cutting demands but did not relax his insistence on countervailing reductions in expenditures.

Surtax Proposed in Economic Plan. President Ford presented his anti-inflation program to the nation Oct. 8, 1974 in a televised address before a joint session of Congress.

Included were creation of a board to develop a national energy policy, a proposed cut in foreign oil imports by 1 million barrels a day, a 5% surtax on families earnings more than $15,000 annually and corporations, and measures to help the depressed housing industry.

Ford called on the nation to "enlist" in the fight against inflation. "I concede," he said, "that there will be no sudden Pearl Harbor to shock us into unity and to sacrifice, but I think we've had enough early warning. The time to intercept is right now. The time to intercept is almost gone."

"Inflation, our public enemy number one, will, unless whipped, destroy our country, our homes, our liberty, our property and finally our national pride as surely as any well-armed wartime enemy," Ford said.

The major elements of his remarks on taxes and government spending:

Taxation—Ford asked Congress to approve a "temporary surcharge of 5% on corporate and upper level individual incomes," generally affecting families with gross incomes of $15,000 or more, and individuals earning $7,500. The estimated $5 billion raised from the added taxes would pay for all the new programs mentioned in the Administration anti-inflation

39

package, according to the President.

Ford said he was aware that any request for new taxes made just prior to a Congressional election was "considered politically unwise," but he declared, "I will not play politics with America's future. Our present inflation to a considerable degree comes from many years of enacting expensive programs without raising enough new revenues to pay for them. Nineteen out of the 25 years I served in this [House] chamber the federal government ended up with federal deficits," Ford told the Congress.

Federal spending—The taxation proposal was linked to new austerity measures planned for the federal budget. Ford asked Congress to move quickly before its recess to set a "target spending limit of $300 billion for the federal 1975 budget." If agreement were reached on this ceiling level, Ford said, he would submit a number of "budget deferrals and recissions" to keep expenditures within the new limit. Budget reductions would require "hard choices," Ford said, but he promised that "no federal agency, including the Defense Department, will be untouchable."

Reiterating a constant theme, Ford said "Fiscal discipline is a necessary weapon in any fight against inflation. We cannot ask the American people to tighten their belts if Uncle Sam is unwilling to first tighten his."

Reaction to Ford's proposals—Widespread opposition to several of Ford's economic proposals quickly developed in Congress. Two features of the Administration's anti-inflation plan—the surtax and jobless aid—were attacked by members of both parties during Congressional hearings.

Other elements of the plan, such as the $300 billion spending limit for fiscal 1975 and tax reform measures, were generally endorsed by Democrats and Republicans.

There was no support for the tax surcharge Oct. 9 in the House Ways and Means Committee. Opposition centered on the proposed income cutoffs of $15,000 for a family and $7,500 for an individual—floors that many members of Congress regarded as too low.

Short term seen for surtax—At a press conference Oct. 9, Ford said he thought the surtax would have to last only a year. "We're in a temporary situation," he said, and the tax would provide sufficient income to meet the additional cost of his community improvement program and at the same time help dampen inflation "by reducing the amount of money of 28% of the taxpayers."

Discussing federal aid to private and parochial schools, he said a tax credit approach was "a good proposal." "There's no reason why there should be a monopoly in education just on the public side," Ford said, and he hoped "some constitutional way" could be found to help private schools.

Tax-revision bill killed. Legislation combining some $2.25 billion in personal income tax reductions with a $3 billion tax increase on the oil industry was defeated Dec. 12, 1974 when the House Rules Committee voted, 9–5, not to permit the House to act on it. Opponents called it too late in the session to consider a major tax bill and some preferred to have the more liberal incoming Congress consider tax revision.

Taxes outpaced other 1974 price rises. A survey by the Congressional Joint Economic Committee released Feb. 9, 1975 found that increases in taxes outpaced all other price rises in the average consumer budget of 1974. Moreover, this rise had greater impact on low- and middle-income taxpayers than on the wealthy, the survey indicated.

The survey, entitled "Inflation and the Consumer in 1974," found that for a family with an "intermediate income" of $14,466, personal federal, state and local income taxes rose 26.5%, and Social Security taxes went up 21.6%. This compared to an overall 1974 inflation rate of 10.2%.

Prices for food consumed by low-income families rose faster than food costs for other income groups. Tax collections, swollen by inflation, reduced consumer demand. (In other recessions, the survey noted, tax burdens had declined, providing consumers with more real disposable income.) Real weekly earnings dropped 4.6% in 1974 and real disposable income declined 3%.

As an example of how inflation "perversely" affected the consumer, the survey pointed out that a family of four with an income of $9,320 had to pay taxes in 1974 that were 31% higher than the year before. Yet a family of four with a 1974 income of $20,883 experienced a 26.5% increase in taxes.

Tax avoidance up in 1974. The Internal Revenue Service said May 5, 1976 that 244 persons with 1974 adjusted gross incomes of more than $200,000 paid no federal income taxes for that year. That was .78% of the 31,000 tax returns on incomes exceeding $200,000 filed for 1974. (Five of those paying no federal income taxes had incomes exceeding $1 million.)

The number of persons in the over-$200,000 income bracket paying no federal income taxes had been increasing since 1972 when 108 persons, or .47% of those filing returns, avoided tax payments. (Six of the group were millionaires.)

In 1973, the number rose to 164 (seven millionaires), or .64% of the total filing returns on adjusted gross incomes in excess of $200,000.

The number of high-income recipients who avoided paying federal income taxes had hit a high of 300 of 1969. That year, Congress passed a minimum-tax provision, designed to limit the number of wealthy persons who paid no federal income tax. In 1971, the second year the minimum-tax provision was in effect, the

number of persons who avoided payments dropped to a low of 80.

The IRS said that population growth and inflation accounted for part of the increase in tax avoidance by high-income persons from 1973 to 1974. Officials added, however, that another factor was the high interest rates paid in 1974 which resulted in higher interest deductions claimed on tax returns for that year.

The Senate Finance Committee, which was considering a bill to extend tax cuts enacted in 1975, was under pressure to close the interest rate loophole and tighten the minimum tax-payment provision.

Tax Cut Urged in Recovery Plan. A $16 billion tax cut was proposed by President Ford as part of an economic recovery program previewed in a televised speech to the nation Jan. 13, 1975 and then formally presented to Congress in his State of the Union message Jan. 15. Congressional democrats presented an alternative plan Jan. 13; they proposed a $10-billion-to-$20-billion tax cut.

Part of the trouble, Ford said, was that the nation had been "self-indulgent," voting "ever-increasing levels of government benefits." "And now the bill has come due," he said.

"I must say to you that the state of the union is not good," he told Congress. The economy was beset with unemployment, recession and inflation. Federal deficits of $30 billion in fiscal 1975 and $45 billion in fiscal 1976 were anticipated. The national debt was expected to rise to over $500 billion. Plant capacity and productivity were not increasing fast enough. "We depend on others for essential energy," Ford said, and "some people question their government's ability to make hard decisions and stick with them."

Ford asked Congress to enact a one-year tax reduction of $16 billion. This would be coupled with higher taxes on oil and natural gas. The latter, to encourage conservation, was expected to produce revenues of some $30 billion which would be "refunded to the American people in a manner which corrects distortions in our tax system wrought by inflation." State and local governments would receive $2 billion of this in additional revenue-sharing to offset increased energy costs.

In addition, both corporate and individual income taxes would be reduced in the future. The corporate tax rate of 48% would be reduced to 42%. Individual income taxes would be reduced by $16.5 billion. (Administration officials, in disclosing Ford's plans Jan. 14, said the $16.5 billion reduction was intended to be applied to the tax rates for 1975 and later years.) This would be done by raising the low-income allowance and reducing tax rates, primarily to benefit lower-and-middle-income taxpayers, the President said. He gave these examples: a typical family of four with gross income of $5,600 paying $185 in federal income taxes would, under his plan, pay nothing; a family of four with gross income of $12,-000, paying $1,260, would pay $300 less; families grossing $20,000 would pay $210 less. Those with the very lowest incomes, he said, would receive compensatory payments of $80.

He asked for the following "interim" actions on oil and natural gas, to be enacted by Congress within 90 days:

■ Excise taxes and import fees totaling $2 per barrel on product imports and on all crude oil.

■ Deregulation of new natural gas and a natural gas excise tax.

■ A windfall profits tax. Ford asked for the windfall profits tax by April 1 since he planned to act to decontrol the price of domestic crude oil on that date.

The President said he was prepared to use presidential power to limit imports as necessary to guarantee success of his energy conservation program.

Before deciding on the program, he said, he considered rationing and higher gasoline taxes as alternatives but rejected them as ineffective and inequitable.

For utilities, whose financial problems were worsening, Ford said, he proposed the one-year investment tax credit of 12% be continued in life for an additional two years "to specifically speed the construction of power plants that do not use natural gas or oil."

In his televised preview to the nation Ford said he wanted an income tax cut of

He proposed a federal income tax cut of $16 billion, $12 billion of it to individual taxpayers as a cash rebate amounting to 12% of their 1974 tax, up to $1,000 in rebate. If Congress acted by April 1, Ford said, half the rebate could be paid in May and the rest by September.

The $4 billion remainder of the tax cut was to go to business taxpayers, including farmers, as an increase in the 7% investment tax credit to 12% for one year to promote plant expansion and job creation. He promised "special provisions" to assist public utilities in increasing their energy capacity.

The President also called for higher taxes on oil and natural gas [see above] and for a return of this revenue, estimated at $30 billion, to the economy in the form of additional payments and credits to business, to state and local governments and to individuals, including those who paid no income taxes because of low earnings.

Ford begins bid for support—President Ford met separately Jan. 16 with Congressional leaders and with governors, mayors and other local leaders to seek support for his economic program.

White House Press Secretary Ron Nessen reported that Ford had found "common ground" with the Congressional leaders and that both Democrats and Republicans recognized the urgent need to reach agreement on a program. Ford appealed for support of his total plan and urged quick enactment of it or legislation that resembled it, Nessen said. The Democrats were said to have indicated they planned "some modifications" of Ford's program. There were indications that a tax cut would receive early consideration.

However, criticism of specific sections of the program was widespread. It came from spokesmen from oil-producing states, and oil-consuming states, particularly in the Northeast. Conservatives objected to the huge proposed budget deficits. Liberals insisted on restricting tax rebates to low-income families. New England legislators decried the prospect of even higher prices for petroleum products. Petroleum industry spokesmen warned that the windfall profits tax would dry up the search for new domestic oil supplies. National Association of Manufacturers President E. Douglas Kenna said Jan. 14 his members had "serious reservations" about the program because of its resultant federal deficits. AFL-CIO President George Meany said Jan. 14 the proposed 12% tax rebate for individuals was "peanuts for the poor," and added Jan. 15 that the entire Ford program was "insupportable."

In Congress, Rep. Al Ullman (D, Ore.), incoming chairman of the House Ways and Means Committee, where tax legislation must originate, said Jan. 15 a $17 billion tax cut plan would be prepared for floor consideration by March, "but it's going to be a greatly different plan from the one the President advocated, funneled far more to low-income and middle-income citizens."

House Democrats present plans. The Democratic leadership in the House Jan. 13 presented "emergency" economic and energy proposals designed to halt recession, check inflation and conserve energy. The plan, devised by a 10-member task force of the Democratic Steering and Policy Committee, was introduced by House Speaker Carl Albert (D, Okla.) at a news conference only hours before President Ford presented the Administration proposals in a nationally televised speech.

The Democrats' plan included a $10 billion-$20 billion tax cut for low and middle income persons, elimination of corporate tax loopholes, expanded credit and reduced interest rates, increased public service jobs and more public works projects, and aid to the housing industry.

The Democrats urged a "tough but selective program to halt the current wage-price spiral," one that occupied a middle ground between the policy extremes of the Nixon and Ford Administrations.

Among the energy saving measures offered for consideration by the House Democrats were mandatory allocation of petroleum and other forms of energy, increased gasoline taxes, rationing of gasoline and home heating oil, higher excise taxes on power boats and high powered cars, a ban on weekend sales of gasoline, subsidized loans for home insulation and a redesign of utility rates to discourage excess use.

Albert, Humphrey give Democratic reply. Two prominent Democrats in Congress replied to President Ford's plan for reviving the economy and reducing dependence on foreign oil; both criticized his tax rebate and energy saving proposals.

House Speaker Carl Albert (D, Okla.) Jan. 20 asked, "What conceivable good will it do for a family to receive a $75–$100 tax rebate if the same family is then required to pay $250–$300 more during the year to get to and from work and to heat their home?" According to Albert's calculations, the richest 17% of the population would receive 43% of the refund from 1974 taxes.

Instead, Albert asked for support for the Democrats' tax cut program favoring low and middle income persons. He also warned that the party would seek a progressive tax on interest income if the Administration did not take steps to force a reduction in interest rates and apportion credit toward "productive" uses."

Albert said the Democrats had "serious reservations" about Ford's energy proposals, particularly his plan to tax oil imports, a measure which Albert said would have an "astounding inflationary impact" on the economy. The Democrats favored a "more moderate approach" which combined gasoline rationing, an excise tax on automobiles, gasless days and other measures, he said.

CBS asked Sen. Hubert H. Humphrey (D, Minn.) to deliver a reply Jan. 22 to the President's program. Humphrey rejected Ford's energy proposals as "the least desirable set of alternatives," charging that they would cost consumers $45 billion a year.

Ford's tax rebate plan would not provide the quick remedy that was needed to stimulate the economy, Humphrey charged. Instead, he urged Congress to cut 1975 withholding rates, retroactive to Jan. 1, in order to cut individual income taxes by $18.5 billion and reduce corporate taxes $2.5 billion.

$18 billion tax cut bill introduced. A bill providing for a total $18 billion tax cut was introduced in the House Jan. 28 by Rep. Ullman. The program differed somewhat from Ford's tax proposals; Ullman emphasized tax cuts for lower and middle income persons and called for permanent tax reductions combined with a one time rebate that was smaller than Ford's.

Ullman's bill would cut individual tax payments in 1975 by about $14 billion— through a $6 billion rebate on 1974 taxes and an $8 billion permanent reduction on 1975 taxes. The rebate would apply as a 10% credit against 1974 tax liability up to $300 on persons with gross incomes of less than $30,000. For 1975 taxes, withholding rates would be lowered immediately by increasing standard deductions and establishing a refundable tax credit for lower and middle income taxpayers.

Ullman claimed that 94% of the individual tax relief provided in his bill would go to persons making $20,000 a year or less; 57% of Ford's tax cut would benefit persons earning $20,000 or less.

Economists support $16 million tax cut. Seven economists of varying ideological and political views testifying before the Ways & Means Committee Jan. 27, 1975 agreed that a $16 billion tax cut was the minimum amount needed to provide the economy with sufficient stimulus to bring the nation out of its current recession.

Under the Ullman bill, corporate taxes would be reduced by about $4 billion—the investment tax credit would be increased permanently to 10% for all businesses. Corporations would be able to pay the lower 22% corporate tax rate on the first $35,000 of income a year, an increase over the current limit of $25,000. (The tax rate was 48% on income in excess of that amount.)

(Sen. Edward Kennedy [D, Mass.] Jan. 27 introduced a bill in the Senate that combined three controversial items: an increase in the debt ceiling, legislation that would prohibit the President from increasing oil tariffs for 90 days, and a tax rebate provision providing every person represented on an individual's tax return with a $70 rebate if the taxpayer's income were less than $25,000. Persons with incomes between $25,000 and $40,000 would receive a smaller rebate.)

Ford's program had garnered support Jan. 23 when two Johnson Administration economists, Charles L. Schultze and Gardner Ackley, joined Paul McCracken, an occasional Ford adviser, in endorsing the White House tax rebate plan.

John Sawhill, former administrator of the Federal Energy Administration, and Harvard University professor Hendrik Houthakker, a former Nixon adviser, also supported Ford's tax cut plans and urged Congress to approve the measures quickly. Their testimony was delivered before the Joint Economic Committee of Congress Jan. 29.

Mayors warn of cities' plight— A delegation representing the U.S. Conference of Mayors told the Senate Government Operations Subcommittee on Intergovernmental Relations Jan. 30 that many if not most of the nation's major cities would soon be forced to reduce services, lay off employes and raise taxes.

"Any federal program to cure the ills of the economy by a reduction in federal taxes without some form of direct assistance to the cities will be offset by increases in local taxes," Moon Landrieu, mayor of New Orleans, testified. "What the hand of the Internal Revenue Service puts into the pocket of the taxpayer, the hand of the local tax collector will take out of his other pocket."

San Francisco Mayor Joseph Alioto, current president of the mayors' conference, said that many current anti-recession economic proposals were aimed at aiding the taxpayer in the $8,000-$14,000 income bracket. However, he said, financially strapped local governments would be forced to raise property taxes, which already fell most heavily on middle income groups.

The mayors urged Congressional passage of a one-shot, $5 billion emergency relief act to help balance city and state government budgets and head off tax increases. It should be in addition to the $16 billion tax cut proposed by President

Ford, they said. A survey of 67 cities, the delegation said, had indicated that 42 cities would either raise taxes or reduce services if outside financial aid were not forthcoming.

Tax-cut program budgeted. President Ford sent to Congress Feb. 3, 1975 a $349.4 billion federal budget that envisaged a deficit of $51.9 billion for fiscal 1976. The deficit for fiscal 1975 (July 1, 1974–June 30, 1975) was estimated at a peacetime record of $34.7 billion.

The expenditures budgeted represented a 11.5% increase over the previous year, although Ford proposed $17 billion in spending cutbacks and presented no new programs except in energy. The budget was predicated on the President's previously disclosed antirecession and energy program.

The budget forecast for 1975 was for deep recession—production further ebbing (down 3.3% after adjustment for inflation), double-digit inflation (11.3%), and the highest unemployment rate (8.1%) since 1941. Corporate profits were expected to fall more than 18% to $115 billion, on a pretax basis.

The projected deficit was attributed to the recession. Roy L. Ash, director of the Office of Management and Budget, at a budget briefing Feb. 3, estimated that the fiscal 1976 budget would have showed a small surplus instead of a record deficit if the economy were running at the employment and production levels of 1974.

The budget remained stable as a percentage of the total economy, or GNP—21.9% for both fiscal 1975 and fiscal 1976. The $35.9 billion increase in spending planned in fiscal 1976 was matched almost entirely by inflation and expected inflation. A quarter of the increase, $8.7 billion, was for defense.

Ford's proposals of a $16 billion annual antirecession tax cut became, in final form, a $16.3 billion reduction in the budget—a $6.1 billion reduction in fiscal 1975 and a $10.2 billion reduction in fiscal 1976. The proposed income-tax rebates for individuals—12% of the taxpayer's 1974 payment, up to a $1,000 limit, re-

bated in two installments—would cause a revenue loss of $4.9 billion in fiscal 1975 and of $7.3 billion the next year. The one-year increase in the investment tax credit for business—to 12%—would lower revenues by $1.2 billion in fiscal 1975 and $2.9 billion the next year.

Other tax relief proposed included an increase in the $1,300 minimum standard deduction, retroactive to Jan. 1, 1975, to $2,000 for individuals and $2,600 for families. This would cut tax receipts by $600 million in fiscal 1975 and by $8.1 billion in fiscal 1976.

A reduction in individual tax rates for individuals was to be made retroactive to Jan. 1, 1975, but the change in withholding from paychecks was to be delayed until June, making the projected revenue loss from it only $800 million in fiscal 1975. The loss in fiscal 1976 was estimated at $16.3 billion.

The proposed reduction in the corporate income tax rate to 42%, retroactive to Jan. 1, 1975, was expected to reduce tax revenues $1.8 billion in fiscal 1975 and $6.6 billion in fiscal 1976.

The projected tax credit for home improvements to save energy, such as insulation, of 15% of the cost up to a $150 credit over three years, would cut $500 million from fiscal 1976 tax receipts.

The budget also incorporated the Administration's plans to increase energy taxes by $30 billion annually and return these monies to the economy.

Tax preferences listed. A listing of "tax expenditures" was provided by the budget for the first time, as required under 1974 legislation. The items were tax preferences granted to individuals and corporations that could be viewed as federal spending in that they were revenues lost to the government.

The items listed by the Administration amounted to $81.4 billion in fiscal 1975—$62.1 billion for individuals, $19.3 billion for corporations—and $91.7 billion in fiscal 1976—$70.9 billion for individuals and $20.8 billion for corporations.

Among the items (fiscal 1975): Corporations—Investment tax credit, $4.2 billion. Lower tax rate (22%) on first $25,000 of corporate earnings, $3.6 billion. Tax

The Budget Dollar

Where it comes from:

Individual income taxes 30c
Social insurance receipts 26c
Corporation income taxes 14c
Excise taxes 9c
Borrowing 15c
Other 6c

Where it goes:

Benefit payments to individuals 39c
National defense 27c
Grants to states and localities 16c
Other federal operations 11c
Net interest 7c

exempt status of state and municipal bonds, $3.2 billion. Mineral depletion allowances, such as for oil and gas, $2.2 billion. Tax deferrals for export sales, $1.1 billion. Bad-debt reserve write-offs allowed for financial institutions, $1 billion.

Individuals—Deductions for state and local taxes other than on property and gasoline, $8.8 billion. Mortgage interest payment deductions, $5.6 billion. State gasoline-tax deductions, $850 million. Excluding pension contributions from taxable income, $5.2 billion. Property tax write-offs, $4.7 billion. Deductions for charitable contributions, $4.5 billion. Special rate for capital gains, $3.3 billion. Consumer credit interest deductions, $2.9 billion.

Economic Report. "The economy is in a severe recession," President Ford told Congress in the opening sentence of his Economic Report Feb. 4, 1975. Unemployment, inflation and interest rates were all too high, he said, and the nation faced an energy problem demanding conservation and development of new energy sources.

Ford advocated passage of his tax and energy proposals to help stabilize the economy. Although these proposals "will not produce swift and immediate results," he said, they will be effective and he urged Congress "to adopt them and to help me follow through with further measures that changing circumstances may make desirable."

The President stressed the need to curb the growth of federal spending and to reduce the federal deficit as the economy moved toward recovery and full employment.

Ford emphasized the need for Americans to adjust to higher pricing for energy products and to reduce U.S. dependence on unreliable sources of oil. He reiterated his proposal of permanent tax reductions to compensate consumers for the coming higher costs of energy.

The President conceded that his proposed $16 billion anti-recession tax cut "might delay achieving price stability" but he called the tax cut "essential."

Ford said:

As I proposed to you in my State of the Union Message, the economy needs an immediate one-year tax cut of $16-billion. This is an essential first move in any program to restore purchasing power, rebuild the confidence of consumers, and increase investment incentives for business.

Several different proposals to reduce individual taxes were considered carefully in our search for the best way to help the economy. We chose the method that would best provide immediate stimulus to the economy without permanently exacerbating our budget problem.

Accordingly, I recommended a 12% rebate of 1974 taxes, up to a maximum of $1,000. The rebate will be paid in two large lump-sum payments totaling $12 billion, the first beginning in May and the second by September.

I have also proposed a $4 billion investment tax credit which would encourage businessmen to make new commitments and expenditures now on projects that can be put in place this year or by the end of next year.

The prompt enactment of the $16 billion tax reduction is a matter of utmost urgency if we are to bolster the natural forces of economic recovery. But in recognizing the need for a temporary tax cut, I am not unmindful of the fact that it will increase the size of the budget deficit. This is all the more reason to intensify our efforts to restrain the growth in federal spending.

The only practical and effective way to achieve energy independence, therefore, is by allowing prices of oil and gas to move higher—high enough to discourage consumption and encourage the exploration and development of new energy sources.

I have, therefore, recommended an excise tax on domestic crude oil and natural gas and an import fee on imported oil, as well as decontrol of the price of crude oil. These actions will raise the price of all energy-intensive products and reduce oil consumption and imports. I have requested the Congress to enact a tax on producers of domestic crude oil to prevent windfall profits as a result of price decontrol. . . .

• • •

Taken as a whole, the energy package will reduce the damage from any future import disruption to manageable proportions. The energy program, however, will entail costs. The import fee and tax combination will raise approximately $30 billion from energy consumers.

However, I have also proposed a fair and equitable program of permanent tax reductions to compensate consumers for these higher costs. These will include income tax reductions of $16 billion for individuals, along with direct rebates of $2 billion to low-income citizens who pay little or no taxes, corporate tax reductions of $6 billion, a $2 billion increase in revenue-sharing payments to state and local governments, and a $3 billion increase in Federal expenditures.

Largest Tax Cut to Date

$22.8 Billion Tax Cut Enacted. President Ford March 29, 1975 reluctantly signed a $22.8 billion tax cut bill passed by the House and Senate, but warned the Democratic majority in Congress that tax cuts must be tied to spending cuts. Ford said he would not accept any more Congressional spending initiatives that would raise the federal budget deficit above an estimated $60 billion level, thereby jeopardizing the nation's recovery from recession by spurring inflation.

The bill-signing ceremony was nationally broadcast. Ford told his radio and television audience that the tax relief provisions, which provided for the largest tax cut in the nation's history, represented a "reasonable compromise" between the $16 billion tax cut proposal he had submitted to Congress and the $30.6 billion tax cut and spending bill passed by the Senate.

But Ford also noted his objections to features that had prompted Republican legislators to urge a presidential veto. Chief among the bill's defects, Ford said, were "extraneous changes [made] in our tax laws ... which were adopted in a hectic last-minute session" before Congress broke for its Easter recess. Ford also said he opposed the bill's distribution of tax cuts. The legislation "fails to give adequate relief to the millions of middle-income taxpayers who already contribute the biggest share of federal taxes," he said.

Citing these objections, Ford said he was signing the bill "despite [its] serious drawbacks" because "any damage they do is outweighed by the urgent necessity of an anti-recession tax reduction right now."

(Ford also referred to the "take-it-or-leave-it" position he said he was forced to assume on the bill, noting that if a veto were sustained, there was no assurance that Congress "would send me a better bill—it might even be worse.")

In signing the compromise bill, Ford avoided an open clash with Congress on the politically volatile tax cut issue, but he took a hardline stand on a related issue the burgeoning federal deficit.

Ford reminded the Democratic majority that his $16 million tax cut proposal had been coupled with a plan for cutting spending on existing federal programs by $17 billion and setting a one-year moratorium on all new government spending programs except in the energy field.

If renewed efforts were not made toward reducing the federal budget, Ford warned, "another round of inflation due to giant and growing deficits would cancel out all expected gains on economic recovery."

"If Congress had accepted all my economic recovery proposals, both for tax cuts and spending cuts," Ford said, "the estimated federal deficit for fiscal year 1976 [beginning July 1] would have been about $52 billion." Instead of this, he continued, because of the tax cut bill and "other changes," the projected deficit for fiscal 1976 currently was estimated at $60 billion.

According to Ford, if Congress failed to implement the spending cutbacks requested by the Administration, the deficit could reach $72 billion. New spending proposals under consideration in Congress would add another $30 billion, bringing the deficit to the "enormous total of $100 billion," Ford warned.

"Deficits of this magnitude are far too dangerous to permit. They threaten another vicious spiral of run-away double digit inflation which could well choke off any economic recovery," the President said.

Pointing to a chart to illustrate his message, Ford declared "I am drawing the line right here [at $60 billion], serving notice that this is as high as our fiscal 1976 deficit should go."

"This is as far as we dare go," Ford said. "I will resist every attempt by Congress to add another dollar to this

deficit by new spending programs. I will make no exceptions, except where our long-range national security interests are involved as in the attainment of energy independence."

The tax cut bill would reduce federal revenues by about $20.9 billion with tax cuts for individuals totaling $18.1 billion, business tax cuts of $4.8 billion and an offsetting $2 billion increase in the oil industry's taxes. The bill also increased federal spending by $1.9 billion for the calendar 1975. The $22.8 billion figure represented the bill's net cost. (Actual tax cuts totaled $22.9 billion.)

Several controversial amendments in the House and Senate bills were retained in modified form in the final bill, including repeal of the 22% depletion allowance for major oil and gas producers, restrictions on use of foreign tax credits, $50 bonus payments to Social Security recipients, railroad retirees and those on welfare and disability support, and a 5% tax credit for buyers of new homes.

Among the compromise bill's provisions:

Individual taxes $8.1 billion would be refunded to individuals. Taxpayers would receive a 10% rebate on 1974 individual taxes up to a maximum $200. The minimum rebate was $100 or an individual's total tax payment if it were less than $100. The $200 maximum would be phased downward for taxpayers with income of $20,000 or more. Individuals earnings $30,000 or more would receive a maximum $100 rebate.

The percentage standard deduction on 1975 taxes was increased to 16% of adjusted gross income with a maximum of $2,300 for single persons and $2,600 for joint returns. The previous maximum had been 15% up to $2,000. The low-income allowance— a minimum standard deduction designed to free poverty-level families from paying federal taxes was increased to $1,600 for single persons and to $1,900 for joint returns. The previous maximum had been $1,300 for single and joint returns. Total cost in lost revenue for the

changes in standard deductions— $2.6 billion.

Individuals were allowed a $30 credit against taxes owed in 1975 income for each taxpayer and dependent. Cost $5.2 billion.

A negative income tax provided a refundable 10% tax credit up to $400 on earned income of $4,000 or less for a family with at least one dependent child. The credit would be phased down in higher incomes and eliminated at the $8,000 level. Cost $1.5 billion.

Individuals who purchased a newly built home that was finished or under construction by March 26, 1975 were entitled to a 5% tax credit up to $2,000. The credit was available for principal residences bought between March 13, 1975 and Dec. 21, 1976. Cost $600 million.

The $4,800 limit on itemized deductions for child care or household services was raised from $18,000 to $35,000. Cost $100 million.

The 12-month limit was extended to an 18-month period in which a taxpayer who sold one house after Dec. 31, 1974 must reinvest proceeds in another house to qualify for deferral of taxes on his capital gain. The limit for the purchase of a new house being built by the taxpayers was increased to 24 months from 18 months.

A tax credit for homeowners installing fuel-saving insulation or solar heating devices was omitted from the final bill.

Business taxes—The business investment tax credit was increased to 10% in 1975 and 1976 from the existing levels of 4% for public utilities and 7% for other businesses. Total cost in lost revenue from changes in the investment tax credit—$3.3 billion.

Corporations were allowed to take an 11% credit on investments during 1975 and 1976 provided that benefits from the additional 1% credit were contributed to an employes' stock ownership plan.

The existing $50,000 limit on the amount of used property qualifying for the investment tax credit was increased to $100,000 for 1975 and 1976.

The limit on the amount of investment credit taken by a utility during one year was increased from the existing ceiling of

50% tax liability above $25,000 to 100% of tax liability in 1975 and 1976. After that two-year period, the limit would phase back to 50% over a five year period.

Businesses were allowed to claim the investment credit for progress payments made during one year toward construction of investments taking several years to complete.

Public utilities that had elected immediately to pass along to consumers through lower rates the benefits of the existing 4% credit were allowed to choose to keep for their own purposes the benefit of the additional credit provided by the increase to 10%. If a state regulatory agency required that the benefits be passed on to consumers immediately, the increased credit would be denied.

The amount of corporate income exempt from the 26% corporate tax surcharge was increased from the existing $25,000 level to $50,000 for 1975. Cost—$1.2 billion.

The normal 22% corporate income tax rate was reduced to 20% on the first $25,000 in income during 1975. Cost—$300 million.

(Tax aid for Chrysler Corp. and other financially troubled firms was deleted from the bill.)

Individuals and business—Self-employed persons were allowed to deduct from their 1975 taxable incomes contributions to qualified pension plans made after the end of the year but before their 1975 tax returns were filed.

A tax credit was allowed for 20% of the wages paid between the date of enactment and July 1, 1976 to hire a recipient of federal aid to families with dependent children (AFDC). Individual taxpayers hiring AFDC recipients for personal services rather than for a business were allowed a tax credit limited to $1,000 for each employe hired.

Oil and gas depletion—The 22% depletion allowance on oil and gas production was repealed retroactive to Jan. 1, 1975. However, the allowance was retained until July 1, 1976 for natural gas sold under federal price regulations (or until the con-

trolled price was raised to take account of repeal of depletion). The allowance also was retained for natural gas sold under fixed price contracts until the price was raised.

Small producers were provided a permanent exemption that allowed independent oil companies to continue taking the depletion allowance on a basic daily output of oil and natural gas, averaging 2,000 barrels of oil or 12 million cubic feet of natural gas or an equivalent quantity of both oil and gas.

The daily production eligible for depletion would be reduced by 200 barrels a day for each year between 1976 and 1980, leaving the small-producer exemption at a permanent level of 1,000 barrels of oil per day or 6 million cubic feet of natural gas.

The depletion rate available for the small producers would be reduced to 20% in 1981, 18% in 1982, 16% in 1983, and to a permanent 15% rate in 1984.

The 22% depletion rate would be kept until 1984 for production of up to 1,000 barrels a day through costly secondary or tertiary recovery methods used to extract remaining oil and gas from wells that were mostly pumped out.

The deduction taken under the small-producer exemption would be limited to 65% of the taxpayer's income from all sources. The small-producer exemption would be denied to any taxpayer who sold oil or gas through retail outlets or operated a refinery processing more than 50,000 barrels of oil a day.

Foreign Income—The amount of foreign tax payments on oil-related income that an oil company could take as a credit against U.S. taxes was limited to 52.8% of its 1975 income from foreign oil operations. The limit would be reduced to 50.4% in 1976 and 50% thereafter. Use of excess credits within those limits was allowed only to offset U.S. taxes on foreign oil-related income, not on income from other foreign sources.

After 1975, oil companies were denied the use of the per-country limitation option that allowed a company to compute its maximum foreign tax credits on a country-by-country basis.

It was required that oil companies re-capture foreign oil-related losses that were deducted from income subject to U.S. taxes by taxing an equivalent amount of subsequent foreign oil-related profits as if earned in the U.S. (and therefore not eligible for deferral until transferred to the U.S.). The credit for foreign taxes on the subsequent profits also would be reduced in proportion to the amount treated as U.S. profits.

The foreign tax credit was denied for any taxes paid to a foreign country in buying or selling oil or gas from property that the nation had expropriated. Domestic international sales corporations (DISCs) were denied the deferral of taxes on half of the profits from exports of natural resources and energy products. Effective in 1976, certain existing exemptions were repealed from a 1962 law requiring current U.S. taxation of profits earned by subsidiaries set up by a U.S. corporation in tax haven countries that imposed little or no taxes. Allowance was made for deferral of U.S. taxes on all earnings by a foreign subsidiary if less than 10% of its income was defined as tax haven income.

Non-tax provisions requiring new federal spending—A $50 bonus payment out of general Treasury revenues was granted to each recipient of Social Security retirement, railroad retirement or supplemental security income benefits.

An additional 13 weeks of emergency unemployment benefits was provided jobless workers in nine states that had exhausted their available 52 weeks of regular and extended benefits.

Preliminary action on '75 tax cut. The House Feb. 27, 1975 had voted, 317–97, to approve a $21.3 billion tax cut bill that also included an amendment repealing the 22% oil depletion allowance.

The tax cut provisions were nearly identical to those adopted by the Ways and Means Committee when it took final action on the bill Feb. 19. Rebates to individuals on 1974 income taxes would total about $8.1 billion and 1975 personal

income taxes would be cut by nearly the same amount. Business taxes would be reduced $5.1 billion.

House Republicans offered a substitute plan that more closely resembled President Ford's tax proposal, but the measure, which provided only for 1974 tax rebates totaling $12.4 billion, was defeated 251–160.

The crucial vote on the depletion issue came when the House voted 248–163 to attach the amendment to the tax cut bill, a strategy devised by the House Democratic caucus.

The caucus Feb. 25 ordered the House Rules Committee to send the tax cut legislation to the floor with a resolution allowing the depletion repeal to be offered as an amendment during floor debate. Without the order, it was feared that the Rules Committee would have approved a rule requested by the Ways and Means Committee barring consideration of the depletion amendment with the tax cut measure.

The Ways and Means Committee had refused to allow the depletion measure to be attached to the tax cut bill when the vote was taken to report the bill out of committee. In 1974, the Ways and Means Committee had approved a plan for the gradual phase-out of the tax write-off.

The House-approved repeal amendment, which had been proposed by Rep. William D. Green (D, Penn.), would end the allowance outright for oil and gas producers retroactive to Jan. 1, 1975, with two exceptions. For natural gas sold under fixed contract, the allowance would be available until the price was raised to take account of depletion repeal. For natural gas subject to federal price regulations, the allowance would be available until July 1, 1975, or until federal price ceilings were lifted.

According to the Joint Committee on Internal Revenue Taxation, repeal of the allowance would raise oil and gas industry taxes by nearly $2.5 billion in 1975 and by $2.9 billion in 1976.

The vote was the first ever taken for repeal since the allowance was enacted in 1926. The tax write-off permitted oil and gas producers to ignore the first 22% of their gross income in calculating federal income taxes.

The Senate version of the tax bill, approved by 60–29 Senate vote March 22, called for a $30.6 billion tax cut.

Action on the Senate bill came after several days of parliamentary maneuvering on proposed amendments, including debate over whether to exempt small, independent oil producers from repeal of the 22% oil depletion allowance. Although the issue was resolved when it was decided on an 82-12 vote to grant the exemption to small producers, other procedural problems slowed final consideration of the tax cut bill reported to the Senate floor by the Finance Committee.

Majority Leader Mike Mansfield (Mont.) broke the impasse March 20 when he proposed that the Senate scrap the committee bill and substitute a streamlined compromise version. His proposal was accepted on an 85-11 roll call vote. (The committee bill would have provided a $1 billion tax break to financially troubled corporations and granted a $3 billion reduction to taxpayers buying homes during the remainder of 1975.)

The Senate and House bills were in near agreement on some features. Both chambers voted to repeal the depletion allowance for major oil companies, although the first portion produced by oil and gas firms would remain tax exempt.

In other areas, the Senate version was more generous than the House bill. The Senate's 12% rebate proposal on 1974 taxes would pay most taxpayers a minimum $120 and a maximum $240. The difference in cost between the Senate and the House plan, which called for 10% rebates, was estimated at $1.6 billion. The Senate also was more liberal in several other tax cut areas: taxpayers would benefit from higher personal exemptions under the Senate version and low-income workers with children would receive a 10% payment ($400 maximum) from the government on the first $4,000 in earned income. The House version of this negative income tax plan would pay a 5% bonus to the working poor with or without children. The Senate also would increase the investment tax credit to 12% for 1975 and 1976 and reduce it thereafter. The House would increase the tax credit from 7% to 10% for 1975.

Other tax cut provisions of the Senate bill were not included in the House-passed legislation. Among the Senate features: tax rates would be lowered for all taxpayers on the first $4,000 in income— estimated cost in lost revenue $2.3 billion; a 5% ($2,000 maximum) credit was voted for consumers purchasing new housing during the last nine months of 1975—cost $1 billion; the cost of child care could be claimed as a tax deductible business expense by working parents—cost $800 million; tax savings were provided the financially troubled Chrysler Corp. and other major companies cost $500 million (a similar bailout provision providing tax aid to Pan American World Airways and Lockheed Corp. was rejected); a tax credit up to $1,000 was voted to partially reimburse householders for the cost of installing fuel-saving insulation—cost $500 million; repeal was authorized of the 10% excise tax on trucks and buses—cost $700 million.

Two new programs requiring additional outlays of funds also were voted by the Senate. (The House bill included plans for no new expenditures.) A 13-week extension in unemployment benefits was voted at a cost of $200 million to aid workers who had exhausted their current 52 weeks of support. A one-time payment of $100 also was approved for each of the nation's 30 million Social Security recipients, railroad retirees and those on federal welfare and disability support. The cost of this program was estimated at $3.4 billion.

Compromise achieved—The compromise bill, as adopted by both houses and signed by President Ford, was worked out by Senate and House conferees in sessions ending March 25. Over protests of outnumbered Republicans, the conference report was rushed to the floor for a final vote March 26 so that Congress could begin its Easter recess.

The House vote in favor of the bill's final version was 287 125 (232 D & 55 R vs 43 D & 82 R). In subsequent Senate action, the vote in favor of adopting the conference report was 45 16 (34 D & 11 R vs 2 D & 14 R).

Tax Reduction & Spending Reduction

Later in 1975 Ford called for permanent reductions in taxes and government spending. When Congress passed a tax-cut extension without conditioning it on reduced spending, Ford vetoed the tax bill. Two days later Congress repassed the measure, this time combining it with a spending limitation, and Ford signed the tax-cut extension bill into law.

Ford requests tax cuts. President Ford Oct. 6, 1975 proposed enacting permanent reductions in current federal tax rates coupled with a reduction in federal spending.

In a televised speech from the White House, Ford emphasized that the tax and spending reductions "must be tied together in one package. It would be dangerous and irresponsible to adopt one without the other."

The President proposed that the $17 billion in tax reductions enacted in March be made permanent with some changes, and he proposed enactment of an additional $11 billion in tax reductions for next year. The temporary tax reductions enacted in March were due to expire Dec. 31.

This would make a $28 billion reduction from the permanent tax rates established in 1972.

He proposed to reduce federal spending by the same amount, $28 billion, to a total of $395 billion for the next fiscal year, ending Oct. 1, 1977. Ford said the $28 billion represented a reduction from "what we will spend if we just stand still and let the train run over us." The growth of spending, which he described as "horrendous," could "easily jump to more than $420 billion" next year without a single new federal program.

The President pointed out that the proposed reduction in taxes and spending was almost on "a dollar-for-dollar" basis. "For every dollar that we return to the American taxpayer," he stressed, "we must also cut our projected spending by the same amount."

The overall goal was to balance the budget. "I want these actions to be a first step—and they are a crucial first step," Ford said, "toward balancing the federal budget within three years."

Individual taxpayers were to receive three-quarters of the proposed permanent tax reductions, Ford said, and "the chief benefits will be concentrated where they belong: among working people."

Ford's proposal would increase the personal income tax exemption from $750 to $1,000, make the standard deduction for single taxpayers a flat $1,800 and for married couples $2,500, and would lower basic personal income rates.

As an example, the President said a typical family of four earning $14,000 a year "would get a permanent tax cut of $412—a 27% reduction." The reduction quoted was from the 1972–1974 tax rates, before this year's temporary reduction. In tables issued by the White House Oct. 6, a family of four earning $5,000 a year would have a $98 reduction from the 1972–74 tax rates, but no reduction from tax rates currently in effect. A family of four earning $50,000 a year would be getting a $510 reduction from the 1974 rate, a $390 reduction from the current rate.

The other quarter of the proposed tax cut was for business. A 2% reduction in corporate tax rates was proposed, from a 48% maximum to 46%, and the increased temporary investment tax credit would be made permanent. This would raise the credit from 7% to 10% for most businesses and from 4% to 10% for utilities. The President also planned a special tax relief program for electric utilities.

"If we allow politics as usual to prevail in the Congress," Ford cautioned, "there will be a temptation to overwhelmingly approve the tax cuts and do nothing on the spending cuts. That must not happen. I will go forward with the tax cuts that I am proposing only if there is a clear, affirmative decision" by Congress to hold federal spending to $395 billion. He would "not hesitate to veto any legislation . . . which violates the spirit of that understanding," he said.

In his visits across the country, Ford said, he found many people "believe that what the government puts in your front pocket, it slips out of your back pocket through taxes and inflation. They are figuring out that they are not getting their money's worth from their taxes. They believe that the politics of federal spending has become too much of a shell game. And I must say that I agree with them.

"America's greatness was not built by taxing people to their limits but by letting our people exercise their freedom and their ingenuity to their limits. Freedom and prosperity go hand in hand. . . . Only by releasing the full energies of our people—only by getting the government off your back and out of your pocket—will we achieve our goals of stable prices and more jobs."

'Neutral' impact on economy—Alan Greenspan, chairman of the Council of Economic Advisers, said Oct. 6 that the President's program would have an essentially "neutral" impact on the economy in terms of promoting an upturn.

Prior to the President's proposals, Labor Secretary John T. Dunlop was the only member of his cabinet to take a firm public stand in favor of continuing the anti-recession tax reductions enacted in March. An economist, Dunlop noted Sept. 30 that the reductions for individuals would have to be increased, rather than just extended, or taxpayers would experience an increase in their withholding rates in the new year because the current temporary reduction was concentrated into eight months.

Congressional views on tax policy—Rep. Al Ullman (D, Ore.), chairman of the House Ways and Means Committee, said Oct. 6 he favored a simple extension of the current tax reductions adjusted to avoid withholding increases. The President's proposals could be analyzed after that, he said, but he added that he considered the proposals a "mirage." "There is no way we can enact a tax based on a spending ceiling," he said.

The Democratic majority of the Joint Economic Committee, in the panel's mid-year report released Oct. 1, advocated an additional tax reduction of $8 billion to $10 billion in 1976, as well as extension of the 1975 law. If present policies were continued, it said, there was "little prospect" that the current "strong recovery path will be sustained in 1976."

The panel's Republican minority said "a reasonable case can be made for a simple extension" of the current tax reductions and it warned against any further reductions.

Simon's, Burns' views—Treasury Secretary William E. Simon told reporters Oct. 8 that restricting the growth of federal spending was "the most important political choice of my lifetime" and it would be a major political issue in 1976. Congress and the country, he said, were facing "a classic choice between freedom and socialism—ultimately, that is what is involved here."

Simon told the Ways and Means Committee Oct. 7 that Ford's tax and spending cut plan was supported by Federal Reserve Board Chairman Arthur Burns. Burns explained to a reporter later Oct. 7 that his support for a tax reduction in 1976, which he had opposed in testimony before Congress recently, was conditioned to a "concurrent and equivalent" expenditure reduction. According to the Wall Street Journal, Burns said, "I like the President's proposal, which I interpret to mean that a tax reduction will be accompanied by a concurrent and equivalent expenditure reduction."

Ford stumps for tax plan. President Ford sought support for his tax and budget reduction plan in an appearance at a White House regional conference on domestic problems in Knoxville, Tenn. Oct. 7.

"It can be done," he asserted to participants in the conference, drawn from six states in the Appalachian area. He "specifically" disagreed with the members of Congress "who say they can't do it. I think they can. I believe Congress can handle the program of spending restraints and tax reductions."

One Congressional critic, Rep. Al Ullman (D, Ore.), chairman of the House Ways and Means Committee, described Ford's plan Oct. 7 as "totally preposterous." Ullman's objection focused on Ford's requirement that a ceiling be put then on a budget that the Administration would not present in detail to Congress until January of 1976.

The same criticism had been sounded by Rep. Brock Adams (D, Wash.), chairman of the House Budget Committee, and Sen. Russell B. Long (D, La.), chairman of the Senate Finance Committee. Adams said Oct. 6 that the President's plan was "simply not realistic," that it would be impossible to reduce spending on the scale proposed by Ford without cutting into social programs as well as the defense budget. Long said Oct. 10 there was "no way" Congress could pledge in advance to cut spending by $28 billion, as proposed by Ford, "without knowing who it is they are cutting."

Ford met with reporters Oct. 14 to emphasize that the public was "very disturbed" about the escalation of federal spending and was willing to accept "some tightening up" in spending on social programs. While there would not have to be fixed reductions in spending for medical programs, he explained, for example, "there would have to be some 'caps' " on expenditures for these programs.

Ford scores House panel's tax cut. A $12.7 billion tax reduction plan approved by the House Ways and Means Committee was criticized by President Ford Oct. 24 as "too small."

The committee's plan, adopted Oct. 23 by a 21–16 vote, called for continuing into 1976 the $8 billion in 1975 tax reductions for individuals, scheduled to expire with the year. An additional $4.7 billion reduction would be granted for 1976, with 75% of the additional benefit going to taxpayers with incomes of from $10,000 to $30,000 a year.

In the vote, the committee's 12 Republicans voted in opposition to the plan, joined by Democrats Joe D. Waggonner Jr. (La.), Wilbur D. Mills (Ark.), Omar Burleson (Tex.) and Andy Jacobs Jr. (Ind.).

The plan consisted of a $2.8 billion tax cut through extension of the 1975 changes in the standard deduction and a $9.9 billion reduction through a 2% tax credit up to $240 for each taxpayer and dependent. The latter would replace the temporary $30 credit Congress enacted for 1975.

In adopting the plan, the committee rejected several proposals to join the tax cut with a requirement for an equivalent cut in federal spending. The decision was based largely on parliamentary technicalities to avoid jurisdictional infringement on other committees responsible for budgetary matters.

President Ford, who had proposed a $28 billion tax reduction tied, as a condition, to a $28 billion spending cut, made clear his opposition to the committee plan the next day. His spokesman, Ron Nessen, said the President was convinced that "the American people want a bigger tax cut" and thought the public would let Congress know about it. "The President believes that the American people deserve and want a bigger tax cut," Nessen said, adding that the committee's Democrats "who share the view that the American people only deserve a smaller tax cut" were bound to "get the word from their constituents and will end up voting for the bigger tax cut that the President proposed."

House votes tax cut measure. The House Dec. 4, 1975 approved, 257–168, a bill expanding and extending through 1976 antirecession tax cuts Congress had enacted in March. As passed, the bill called for reductions of $13.4 billion in individual and business taxes, about $2.6 billion more than under the 1975 tax cut measure.

Before taking a final vote on the measure, the House passed three amendments closing tax loopholes contained in the bill reported by the Ways and Means Committee. Two other amendments to the committee version that would have curbed tax breaks for the real estate industry and exporters were defeated, however.

In addition, the House rejected, 220–202, an amendment proposed by Republicans linking continuation of tax cuts to passage of a $395 billion budget ceiling for fiscal 1977. Prior to the vote, Rep. John Rhodes (Ariz.), the Republican minority leader, announced he had spoken to President Ford by overseas telephone and that Ford had affirmed his intention to veto the tax cut bill if a spending ceiling were not attached.

The Democratic leadership had opposed enactment of a spending limit for fiscal 1977 before the President presented his budget message to Congress.

The three reform amendments adopted were expected to yield an additional $706 million in revenue for the Treasury in calendar 1976:

One amendment eliminated a committee provision permitting individuals to carry back capital losses for three years and apply them against capital gains. This provision, which was deleted by a 379–24 vote, would have benefited H. Ross Perot, the Texas businessman, who would have stood to gain $15 million. Perot had made sizable contributions to the campaigns of some of the members of the Ways and Means Committee. The committee members denied they had initially known the provision would aid Perot. But Rep. Fortney Stark (D, Calif.), sponsor of the amendment against the provision, labeled it "somewhat of an embarrassment to the committee."

A second amendment, passed by a 314–107 margin, would increase the minimum tax on preference income, the most important of which was the half of capital gains income not subject to ordinary taxation.

The third amendment, approved on a 301-119 vote, eliminated a Ways and Means provision that would have exempted foreign citizens from having to pay U.S. taxes on dividend and interest income.

The amendments that were defeated would have reduced existing tax breaks for exporters and curbed the use of real estate tax shelters by wealthier individuals to reduce taxes.

Among the bill's other provisions:

Increases in the minimum standard deduction and the regular standard deduction that were part of the 1975 tax cut bill would be made permanent. As in the 1975 measure, the House bill contained a $30 per person tax credit, but it also alternately gave taxpayers a 2% tax credit on taxable income up to $12,000.

The 1975 provision assessing the first $25,000 of business income at a 20% tax rate and the next $25,000 at a 22% rate would continue in effect.

Individuals who did not itemize deductions would benefit from a provision that would in effect offer a partial tax credit for child care expenses. Alimony payments would also be made deductible by those who did not itemize deductions.

Ford vetoes tax cut extension. Congress Dec. 17 completed action on the bill extending antirecession tax cuts for six months, and President Ford promptly vetoed it.

The President, in a statement on his veto, reiterated his assertion that Congressional failure to link the tax cut to a budgetary spending ceiling for fiscal 1977 would bring the risk of a "new round of double digit inflation" that would "invisibly tax every dollar" earned by taxpayers at "a much higher figure than any relief the bill" offered.

However, Ford added that his veto did not mean that taxes would have to go up Jan. 1, 1976 when the current tax cut expired. Congress need only approve a tax cut extension for 1976 "coupled with a clear commitment to cut the growth of federal spending," he said.

Ford said he would propose to Congress in January 1976 a $395 billion budget for fiscal 1977. Since this figure represented a $28 billion reduction from the $423 billion present government programs were expected to cost in fiscal 1977, he argued, "we can have a $28 billion tax cut without adding to inflation."

The bill, which was passed by voice vote in both chambers of Congress, extended, with some adjustments, tax cuts enacted in March. Over the six months covered by the bill, individuals would pay about $7.4 billion less in taxes and businesses nearly $1 billion less than they would have without the legislation. The bill's specific provisions represented a compromise between the versions originally passed in the House and Senate.

The minimum standard deduction, or low-income allowance, was boosted to $1,-700 for one individual and $2,100 for a couple. This was an increase over the $1,-600 for individuals and $1,900 for couples permitted in 1975, and the $1,300 for both in prior years. In addition, the regular standard deduction was increased to 16%

Trends in personal income and tax capacity of the representative tax system, by State, 1960-1975

(Indexes per Capita as a Percent of the National Average)

	1960		1962		1967		1969		1972		1975	
	Tax capacity	Personal income	Tax capacity	Personal income	Tax capacity	Personal income	Tax capacity	Personal income	Tax capacity	Personal income	Tax capacity	Personal income
United States	100	100	100	100	100	100	100	100	100	100	100	100
Alabama	66	68	68	68	70	71	70	73	76	77	78	79
Alaska	69	126	88	113	99	115	104	114	131	115	143	162
Arizona	99	91	101	90	95	86	99	90	107	95	93	90
Arkansas	69	63	76	65	77	70	77	70	81	74	78	78
California	126	122	128	120	124	115	122	114	112	111	110	112
Colorado	114	101	104	100	104	94	103	95	106	102	104	102
Connecticut	112	128	111	129	117	127	117	126	112	119	113	118
Delaware	112	125	128	123	123	117	120	117	122	115	122	114
Dist. of Columbia	126	134	138	132	121	128	120	125	126	131	120	131
Florida	101	88	105	85	104	88	109	92	112	99	98	96
Georgia	69	74	75	75	80	82	81	84	93	87	88	86
Hawaii	76	107	90	108	99	108	99	111	116	113	109	113
Idaho	108	83	93	85	91	82	88	82	88	83	87	88
Illinois	116	119	116	119	114	117	112	115	110	113	114	115
Indiana	101	98	95	99	99	99	97	99	97	96	98	96
Iowa	114	89	96	92	104	95	100	94	99	95	103	103
Kansas	113	97	103	97	105	97	105	96	101	100	105	102
Kentucky	74	71	76	74	80	77	81	78	84	79	90	83
Louisiana	88	75	84	75	94	80	94	78	93	79	103	83
Maine	78	84	79	81	81	81	82	82	84	81	74	81
Maryland	93	105	98	108	101	105	103	107	101	110	102	109
Massachusetts	96	111	98	111	98	108	99	109	98	107	94	103
Michigan	99	106	101	105	104	108	105	110	100	109	101	105
Minnesota	103	93	95	93	95	95	95	96	97	95	98	99
Mississippi	57	55	61	56	64	63	65	64	71	70	70	69

(Indexes per Capita as a Percent of the National Average)

	1960		1962		1967		1969		1972		1975	
	Tax capacity	Personal income	Tax capacity	Personal income	Tax capacity	Personal income	Tax capacity	Personal income	Tax capacity	Personal income	Tax capacity	Personal income
Missouri	99	95	96	96	97	97	97	95	96	94	94	93
Montana	129	92	107	95	105	86	101	85	106	90	98	92
Nebraska	119	95	109	94	110	95	108	96	106	98	103	103
Nevada	146	126	155	131	171	110	173	114	156	113	151	113
New Hampshire	98	96	99	96	110	95	109	94	115	93	97	91
New Jersey	105	123	111	123	107	119	106	118	112	117	111	114
New Mexico	102	83	98	83	94	77	92	76	92	78	93	81
New York	105	123	119	123	108	120	108	120	106	116	102	111
North Carolina	72	72	74	74	78	79	80	81	87	85	84	83
North Dakota	108	77	88	92	92	80	91	80	86	88	99	98
Ohio	103	106	101	103	100	102	100	103	96	101	102	99
Oklahoma	84	84	98	82	102	85	102	84	98	85	102	89
Oregon	103	100	105	99	106	96	104	95	106	95	98	97
Pennsylvania	91	102	91	101	91	101	91	100	95	100	94	101
Rhode Island	87	100	90	102	91	103	92	100	88	99	86	100
South Carolina	60	63	64	66	64	72	66	74	74	7,	77	78
South Dakota	107	80	90	82	91	80	90	79	89	84	91	83
Tennessee	71	71	73	73	78	77	78	78	84	82	82	83
Texas	120	87	94	86	98	89	101	89	99	90	113	95
Utah	101	89	95	91	87	82	84	80	83	82	86	84
Vermont	85	83	81	83	88	87	88	87	102	86	84	84
Virginia	81	84	86	86	86	90	87	92	92	97	93	98
Washington	102	106	106	109	112	109	110	107	101	100	100	106
West Virginia	74	73	78	73	75	76	74	74	81	79	90	84
Wisconsin	97	98	91	98	94	97	93	95	95	95	93	96
Wyoming	161	101	137	100	141	92	137	92	125	94	147	103

Source: Tax Wealth in 50 States (National Institute of Education)

of adjusted gross income, with a maximum of $2,400 for a single person and $2,800 for a couple. In 1975, the standard deduction had been 16% up to a maximum of $2,300 for an individual and $2,600 for a couple. Before that, the standard deduction had been 15% up to $2,000 for singles or couples.

The bill also established a tax credit of $35 for each exemption listed on a return or a 2% credit on taxable income up to $9,000. A provision in the measure extended the so-called earned-income credit for the working poor. A family with children earning up to $4,000 would receive a 10% tax credit, with those not owing taxes getting cash payments. The "work bonus" credits would be extended to incomes above $4,000 and be phased out, ending at $8,000.

As a whole, 13.3% of the cuts would go to individuals with adjusted gross incomes of less than $5,000, 27.4% would go to individuals with incomes between $5,000 and $10,000 and more than 95% to individuals with incomes less than $30,000.

The bill's corporate provision extended for six months the 20% tax rate for the first $25,000 of business income and the 22% rate for the next $25,000 of income. The regular 48% rate continued to apply to amounts over $50,000. Without the extension, business taxes would revert to 22% of the first $25,000 of income and 48% thereafter.

Senate action—The Senate Dec. 15 had passed, by 73–19, legislation extending the tax reduction that was somewhat different than that approved by the House. Before taking a final vote, the Senate rejected, 66–27, an amendment by Sen. Roman Hruska (R, Neb.) to set a $395 billion spending limit for fiscal 1975. A Senate provision that would have extended the tax credit for purchasers of new homes was subsequently dropped by House-Senate conferees.

Tax cuts extended in compromise. Congress Dec. 19 passed compromise legislation extending antirecession tax cuts for the first six months of 1976. The

bill, identical to the measure vetoed by President Ford Dec. 17 except for a non-binding provision limiting government spending, was approved by the House, 372–10, and by the Senate on a voice vote.

Ford signed the $8.4 billion tax-cut extension bill into law Feb. 23, 1975.

Action on the compromise bill followed by one day the House's failure to override the President's Dec. 17 veto. The House vote Dec. 18 to override was 265–157, 17 votes short of the two-thirds majority needed.

According to published reports, the compromise bill was the product of negotiations initiated by Sen. Russell Long (D, La.), chairman of the Senate Finance Committee, who, along with other members of Congress and the President, was concerned that a stalemate over the measure would result in the expiration of the 1975 tax cut Dec. 31.

Working with Sen. William Roth (R, Del.), a senior member of the Finance Committee, and Reps. Barber Conable (R, N.Y.) and Joe Waggoner (D, La.), Long was able to obtain a compromise amendment to the bill acceptable to Ford and Congressional Democrats.

The compromise provision, later rewritten somewhat by the House Democratic leadership, stated that Congress was determined to continue the tax cut and "to control spending levels in order to reduce the national deficit."

If "economic conditions warranted" extending the tax cut past June 30, 1976, the amendment said, Congress would agree to provide "for reductions in the level of spending in the fiscal year 1977 . . . equal to any additional reduction in taxes (from the 1974 tax rate levels)" for fiscal 1977. However, the amendment also stated that Congress was not to be precluded from passing a budget resolution "containing a higher or lower expenditure figure if Congress concludes that this is warranted by economic conditions or unforeseen circumstances."

At a press conference Dec. 20, Ford said that the bill was "a good bill under the circumstances" because it stated the "fundamental principle that the growth of spending must be limited." "I won that 100%," he remarked in reference to the struggle with Congress over tax reduction combined with reduced federal spending.

The President said he would propose to the next session of Congress to add $10 billion to the $18 billion tax reduction approved at the end of this session.

Panel contradicts Ford on economy. A study by the staff of the Joint Economic Committee of Congress, reported Dec. 21, said that implementation of President Ford's budget and tax proposals would lead to economic stagnation in 1977. The study said that in order not to restrain economic recovery, the government would have to effect a combination of spending increases and tax reductions totaling $12 billion.

Ford and the committee staff agreed that spending of approximately $420 billion would be necessary to maintain government services at their 1976 level. But Ford had said he would submit a $395 billion budget to Congress in January, 1976. The committee study said Ford's proposed cuts would push unemployment up to 9% in 1977 and recommended expenditures of $420 billion to keep the economy on its current course.

Contrary to the Administration's assertions that spending was out of control, the staff report maintained that if no new policies were adopted, there would be substantial surpluses in the federal budget by 1981.

State Tax Operations

Capacity, Effort & Distribution. The following tables summarize the capacity, effort and percent distribution for taxes of state and local governments in 1975 (from "Tax Wealth in 50 States," the National Institute of Education):

	Cap.	Eff.	Dist.
Colorado	106	103	15.9%
Connecticut	132	3	18.3%
Delaware	118	212	15.2%
District of Columbia	130	183	17.0%
Florida	96	0	15.4%
Georgia	77	98	13.6%
Hawaii	108	179	15.6%
Idaho	80	139	14.5%
Illinois	125	81	17.2%
Indiana	99	80	15.8%
Iowa	101	124	15.2%
Kansas	105	71	15.6%
Kentucky	78	124	13.6%
Louisana	80	35	12.1%
Maine	72	58	15.3%
Maryland	124	192	19.0%
Massachusetts	102	166	16.9%
Michigan	104	104	16.1%
Minnesota	94	217	15.0%
Mississippi	55	71	12.4%
Missouri	92	87	15.4%
Montana	86	137	13.7%
Nebraska	100	50	15.3%
Nevada	122	0	12.7%
New Hampshire	92	11	14.8%
New Jersey	125	5	17.6%
New Mexico	73	67	12.2%
New York	109	226	16.7%
North Carolina	73	138	13.6%
North Dakota	98	103	15.5%
Ohio	103	85	15.9%
Oklahoma	84	71	12.8%
Oregon	96	193	15.4%
Pennsylvania	100	119	16.7%
Rhode Island	92	92	16.8%
South Carolina	67	111	13.7%
South Dakota	75	0	13.0%
Tennessee	80	5	15.2%
Texas	103	0	14.4%
Utah	75	116	13.7%
Vermont	75	155	13.9%
Virginia	102	107	17.2%
Washington	116	0	18.3%
West Virginia	84	78	14.7%
Wisconsin	90	211	15.1%
Wyoming	118	0	12.6%
U. S.			15.7%

CORPORATION NET INCOME

	Cap.	Eff.	Dist.
Alabama	54	95	3.4%
Alaska	217	70	7.4%
Arizona	51	141	2.7%
Arkansas	52	158	3.2%
California	99	191	4.4%
Colorado	89	83	4.1%
Connecticut	142	102	6.1%
Delaware	164	59	6.5%
District of Columbia	81	0	3.3%
Florida	55	128	2.7%

INDIVIDUAL INCOME

	Cap.	Eff.	Dist.
Alabama	71	80	14.3%
Alaska	217	110	23.8%
Arizona	84	84	14.2%
Arkansas	63	95	12.5%
California	107	107	15.2%

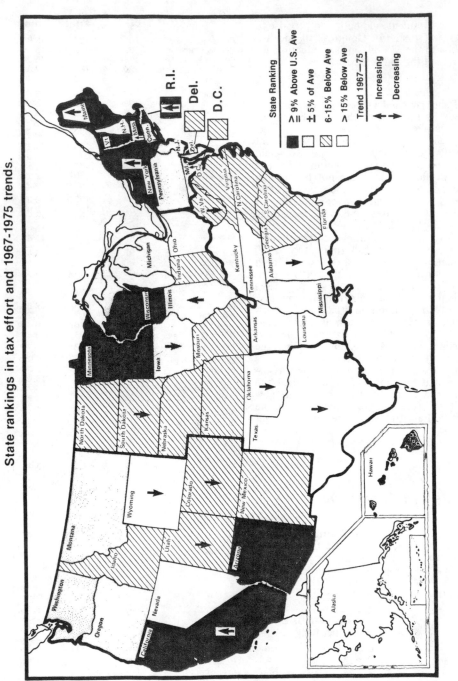

State rankings in tax effort and 1967-1975 trends.

Source: Tax Wealth in 50 States (National Institute of Education)

	Cap.	Eff.	Dist.		Cap.	Eff.	Dist.
Georgia	60	130	3.3%	Iowa	112	66	38.4%
Hawaii	55	212	2.4%	Kansas	110	77	37.1%
Idaho	59	189	3.3%	Kentucky	92	89	36.5%
Illinois	135	65	5.7%	Louisiana	91	118	31.2%
Indiana	79	59	3.9%	Maine	91	115	43.5%
Iowa	58	124	2.7%	Maryland	103	79	35.9%
Kansas	95	128	4.4%	Massachusetts	95	58	35.7%
Kentucky	91	121	5.0%	Michigan	98	94	34.4%
Louisana	172	39	8.1%	Minnesota	98	86	35.4%
Maine	46	132	3.0%	Mississippi	81	136	41.3%
Maryland	57	125	2.7%	Missouri	104	86	39.3%
Massachusetts	76	194	3.9%	Montana	95	41	34.4%
Michigan	97	81	4.7%	Nebraska	118	71	40.6%
Minnesota	87	185	4.3%	Nevada	216	80	50.6%
Mississippi	53	88	3.7%	New Hampshire	128	36	46.6%
Missouri	74	51	3.8%	New Jersey	99	97	31.4%
Montana	63	151	3.1%	New Mexico	100	120	38.0%
Nebraska	59	91	2.8%	New York	93	138	32.4%
Nevada	46	0	1.5%	North Carolina	93	93	39.3%
New Hampshire	53	198	2.6%	North Dakota	114	86	40.7%
New Jersey	105	85	4.6%	Ohio	99	77	34.4%
New Mexico	84	62	4.3%	Oklahoma	96	81	33.3%
New York	157	109	7.5%	Oregon	110	27	39.7%
North Carolina	67	146	3.9%	Pennsylvania	91	98	34.2%
North Dakota	46	218	2.3%	Rhode Island	93	102	38.3%
Ohio	100	80	4.8%	South Carolina	86	107	39.8%
Oklahoma	188	27	8.9%	South Dakota	114	83	44.5%
Oregon	73	174	3.6%	Tennessee	92	114	39.3%
Pennsylvania	108	151	5.5%	Texas	105	86	32.8%
Rhode Island	66	191	3.7%	Utah	89	110	36.9%
South Carolina	51	185	3.2%	Vermont	109	70	45.9%
South Dakota	33	27	1.8%	Virginia	92	98	35.0%
Tennessee	62	156	3.7%	Washington	96	172	34.2%
Texas	185	0	8.0%	West Virginia	88	142	34.9%
Utah	71	68	4.0%	Wisconsin	99	82	37.6%
Vermont	42	160	2.4%	Wyoming	115	108	27.8%
Virginia	57	132	3.0%	**U.S.**			**35.4%**
Washington	67	0	3.3%				
West Virginia	80	43	4.3%				
Wisconsin	79	136	4.1%				
Wyoming	268	0	8.9%				
U. S.			**4.9%**				

SALES AND GROSS RECEIPTS

	Cap.	Eff.	Dist.
Alabama	87	122	39.7%
Alaska	113	60	28.0%
Arizona	105	126	40.1%
Arkansas	91	94	41.3%
California	107	111	34.4%
Colorado	109	96	37.1%
Connecticut	93	119	29.2%
Delaware	120	45	34.8%
District of Columbia	125	85	36.8%
Florida	111	108	40.4%
Georgia	98	99	39.2%
Hawaii	109	177	35.4%
Idaho	92	82	37.6%
Illinois	107	108	33.1%
Indiana	103	96	37.3%

PROPERTY

	Cap.	Eff.	Dist.
Alabama	73	30	35.3%
Alaska	125	69	33.0%
Arizona	86	112	34.9%
Arkansas	75	50	35.9%
California	119	130	40.4%
Colorado	99	89	35.6%
Connecticut	123	118	40.9%
Delaware	124	43	38.3%
District of Columbia	122	67	38.2%
Florida	89	76	34.3%
Georgia	89	75	37.9%
Hawaii	122	51	42.2%
Idaho	82	82	35.5%
Illinois	119	97	39.1%
Indiana	98	98	37.6%
Iowa	103	106	37.5%
Kansas	99	105	35.4%
Kentucky	82	48	34.6%
Louisiana	94	37	34.3%
Maine	62	155	31.4%

	Cap.	Eff.	Dist.
Maryland	101	86	37.4%
Massachusetts	95	188	37.9%
Michigan	106	114	39.6%
Minnesota	101	95	38.7%
Mississippi	66	61	35.5%
Missouri	88	86	35.2%
Montana	99	127	38.1%
Nebraska	95	122	34.8%
Nevada	118	89	29.5%
New Hampshire	79	166	30.6%
New Jersey	123	139	41.4%
New Mexico	77	51	31.0%
New York	104	147	38.6%
North Carolina	83	59	37.3%
North Dakota	89	89	34.0%
Ohio	107	78	39.3%
Oklahoma	97	50	35.8%
Oregon	92	125	35.2%
Pennsylvania	94	72	37.4%
Rhode Island	78	142	34.2%
South Carolina	76	55	37.3%
South Dakota	81	137	33.5%
Tennessee	77	63	35.3%
Texas	105	75	35.2%
Utah	81	78	35.5%
Vermont	68	181	30.5%
Virginia	95	68	38.4%
Washington	103	92	38.7%
West Virginia	79	53	33.3%
Wisconsin	93	121	37.5%
Wyoming	127	92	32.6%
U. S.			**37.6%**

Tax Cuts Deepen in 1976

President Ford opened the 1976 Presidential election year with calls for deeper reductions in taxes. A major tax revision bill was passed by Congress less than two months before the election.

State of the Union. President Ford Jan. 19, 1976 said it was time "for a fundamentally different approach for a new realism that is true to the great principles upon which this nation was founded."

His approach, as outlined in his second State of the Union message, delivered before a joint evening session of Congress, was to reduce taxes and federal spending; secure the financial base of the Social Security system; consolidate federal education, health and social-services programs for more flexible application by the state and local governments.

"And in all that we do," Ford said in his address, which was broadcast nationally, "we must be more honest with the American people, promising them no more than we can deliver, and delivering all that we promise."

The state of the union at the moment, he said, was "better" than a year ago "but still not good enough."

Much of Ford's message was about the economy. "My first objective is to have sound economic growth without inflation," he said. Although inflation was slowing, "we must stop it cold." To do this, "the government must stop spending so much and stop borrowing so much of our money; more money must remain in private hands, where it will do the most good. To hold down the cost of living, we must hold down the cost of government."

On taxes, he proposed to add $10 billion of federal income tax reductions, effective July 1, to the $18 billion in tax cuts enacted in December 1975 for the first six months of 1976.

Ford also proposed:

■ A business tax incentive to speed up plant expansion and equipment purchase in areas of high unemployment.

■ A change in estate taxes to help preserve the family farm and family-owned small business.

■ A tax change to give "moderate income families income benefits if they make long-term investments in common stock in American companies."

Another tax proposal—for a .3% increase in both employer and employe Social Security taxes, effective Jan. 1, 1977—was made because the Social Security trust fund was "headed for trouble" and needed replenishment.

Tax cuts budgeted. Ford Jan. 21, 1976 submitted a $394.2 billion budget for fiscal 1977. Revenues were estimated at $351.3 billion, the deficit at about $43 billion.

The growth rate of the total outlay was 5.5%, about half the average growth rate for the past 10 years. About half that increase came from defense, where spending was projected over the $100 billion mark for the first time, or 25.4% of the total federal budget.

Outlays for domestic programs fell below the inflation line of growth. The budget's total of $394.2 billion, in fact, was about $20 billion less than the budget would have increased through built-in growth even without new programs.

The reductions imposed by the President were exacted from Social Security, Medicare, food stamps, housing subsidies, child nutrition and veterans benefits, among others.

A new $10 billion tax cut for individuals and corporations was scheduled in the budget for mid-year. Other new tax provisions requested included a credit for middle-income investment in stocks and a credit for firms to expand in high-employment areas.

In his budget message, Ford said that the combination of tax and spending changes he proposed "will set us on a course that not only leads to a balanced budget within three years, but also improves the prospects for the economy to stay on a growth path that we can sustain."

The 1977 budget reflected plans for a $28 billion-a-year permanent tax reduction, about 75% of which would go to individuals, the rest to businesses. Of the $22.2 billion scheduled to take effect in calendar 1976, about $9 billion had been enacted already for the first six months.

For individuals, the personal exemption of $750 would go to $875 for calendar 1976. A $17.50 tax credit would be allowed for each exemption or, as an alternate, a 1% credit on taxable income up to $9,000.

The Budget Dollar

Where it comes from:

Individual income taxes .... 39¢
Social insurance receipts .... 29¢
Corporation income taxes .... 13¢
Borrowing .... 11¢
Excise taxes .... 4¢
Other .... 4¢

Where it goes:

Benefit payments to individuals .... 40¢
Military .... 26¢
Grants to states and localities .... 15¢
Other federal operations .... 11¢
Net interest .... 8¢

The low-income allowance of $1,700 would go to $1,750 for one person and from $2,100 to $2,300 for a couple. The regular standard deduction would remain at 16% of adjusted gross income, but the maximums would drop to $2,100 (from $2,400) for one and to $2,650 (from $2,800) for couples.

The special "work bonus" for poor families would be retained at 5% of earned income, with a maximum of $200 in cash payments to families not owing any taxes.

For corporations, the basic tax rate for income over $50,000 would drop a point to 47% in calendar 1976. The President requested a new faster amortization for electric utilities and an investment tax credit of 12%.

For calendar 1977, the personal exemption was scheduled to rise to $1,000 and a single standard deduction was planned of $2,500 for couples and of $1,800 for single taxpayers. A reduction in individual income-tax rates also was envisaged but not specified in the budget. The regular 10% business investment tax credit on purchases of machinery and equipment was to be made permanent.

Businesses in areas with unemployment of 7% or more would receive an accelerated depreciation rate for new equipment and plant expansion.

In other special provisions, the President proposed a tax deferral for investment by individuals in stocks or mutual funds, the investment lasting at least seven years. Some limits were planned although not set as yet, such as a maximum on the amount of taxes deferred and a maximum on personal income level. The proposal was to become effective July 1 with full deduction allowed for calendar 1976.

An estate-tax change for small businessmen and small farmers would permit heirs to defer the initial estate-tax payments for five years, thereafter payable over the next 20 years at 7% annual interest. The qualification was the first $300,000 in value of the estate. The deferral also could be claimed in part for estates up to $600,000 in value.

A .3% increase in the Social Security payroll taxes for both employers and employes was scheduled to become effective Jan. 1, 1977. The new 6.15% rate would make the maximum payment by workers about $1,014.75 a year. Currently, it was $895.05.

A rise in the federal unemployment-insurance tax rate paid by employers also was planned, effective Jan. 1, 1977. The rate would go from .5% to .65% and the wage base upon which it was paid would be increased also from $4,200 to $6,000.

The President repeated his 1975 proposal to eliminate the "double taxation" on income as it was earned by corporations and again as it was received by stockholders in dividends.

Moderate recovery pace advocated. President Ford and his economic advisers Jan. 26 urged a moderate and steady pace of recovery for the economy with a wary eye on the inflation factor.

In his Economic Report to Congress, President Ford said the "underlying fact about our economy is that it is steadily growing healthier."

The President told Congress "another major tax cut will be feasible by 1979" if proper budgetary restraint were exercised. This would be in addition to the $28 billion-a-year tax reduction proposed by the President in his State of the Union Message.

The message on moderation and caution against inflation was the same in the annual report of the Council of Economic Advisers, which accompanied the President's report to Congress. It said:

The budget which the President has proposed provides for a marked deceleration in the growth of Federal spending, as outlays are to be held to $394 billion in fiscal 1977, which ends in September of next year. Starting in July 1976, taxes are to be cut by about $28 billion relative to what they would be under

Budget Receipts and Outlays

In millions of dollars

Receipts by Source	1975 actual	1976 estimate	TQ* estimate	1977 estimate
Individual income taxes	122,386	130,822	40,003	153,641
Corporation income taxes	40,621	40,056	8,416	49,461
Social insurance taxes and contributions	86,441	92,571	25,174	115,052
Excise taxes	16,551	16,901	4,371	17,806
Estate and gift taxes	4,611	5,100	1,400	5,800
Customs duties	3,676	3,800	1,000	4,300
Miscellaneous receipts	6,711	8,284	1,530	7,202
Total receipts	**280,997**	**297,534**	**81,894**	**351,262**

Outlays by Function	1975 actual	1976 estimate	TQ* estimate	1977 estimate
Military	86,585	92,759	25,028	101,129
International affairs	4,358	5,665	1,334	6,824
General science, space, and technology	3,989	4,311	1,157	4,507
Natural resources, environment, and energy	9,537	11,796	3,289	13,772
Agriculture	1,660	2,875	742	1,729
Commerce and transportation	16,010	17,801	4,819	16,498
Community and regional development	4,431	5,802	1,529	5,532
Education, training, employment, and social services	15,248	18,900	4,403	16,615
Health	27,647	32,137	8,291	34,393
Income security	108,605	128,509	32,742	137,115
Veterans benefits and services	16,597	19,035	4,362	17,196
Law enforcement and justice	2,942	3,402	914	3,426
General government	3,089	3,547	961	3,433
Revenue sharing and general purpose fiscal assistance	7,005	7,169	2,046	7,351
Interest	30,974	34,835	9,769	41,297
Allowances**	....	200	175	2,260
Undistributed offsetting receipts	− 14,075	− 15,208	− 3,589	− 18,840
Total outlays	**324,601**	**373,535**	**97,971**	**394,237**
Budget surplus or deficit (−)	**− 43,604**	**− 76,001**	**− 16,077**	**− 42,975**

*The period July 1, 1976–Sept. 30, 1976 is a "transitional quarter" resulting from the change in the government's fiscal year. The old fiscal year started July 1. Starting this year fiscal years will begin Oct. 1.

**Includes allowances for civilian agency pay raises and contingencies.

Source: Office of Management and Budget

1974 law. Because of the recovery, Federal receipts are then expected to grow over three times as fast as outlays between fiscal 1976 and fiscal 1977 causing the deficit to fall by more than $30 billion.

However, the full-employment balance, on a national income accounts basis, will show little change during calendar 1976 from the $6-billion deficit estimated for the second half of last year. In this way of the fiscal policy stimulus will be maintained throughout 1976. It will then be reduced in 1977 because of the proposed increase in Social Security tax rates and the much faster rise in individual income tax receipts than Federal expenditures. . . .

. . .

To avoid inducing a policy and output mix that is incompatible with the requirements of long-term economic growth, fiscal stimulus must be diminished gradually during coming years. Without greater fiscal restraint, the saving flows available for private capital formation might eventually become too small. Furthermore the danger of intensifying inflationary pressures under such conditions would preclude expanding the money supply sufficiently to finance both the Government deficits and the needed improvements and growth in our industrial capacity.

It is this public-versus-private allocation problem to which the President's program tying a $28 billion cut in the growth of Federal outlays to a comparable cut in taxes is addressed. . . .

Congressional groups score Ford economic proposals. In separate appraisals, the Democratic-controlled Joint Economic Committee of Congress and the independent Congressional Budget Office criticized President Ford's economic proposals as too restrictive.

The Democratic majority of the House-Senate panel warned Congress March 10 that Ford's proposed $394.2 billion budget for fiscal 1977, beginning Oct. 1, was a "blueprint for recession-level unemployment and high inflation for several years to come."

The panel contended that the Administration's proposed limit on expenditures was too restrictive. Unless more stimulative measures were adopted, the panel said, the "recovery could founder in 1977."

The Democrats called for a spending ceiling of $412-$418 billion in fiscal 1977, an expanded emergency federal jobs program and an extension of the current personal-income tax cuts, due to expire at mid-year, through calendar 1977.

The committee claimed that its "recommendations, after counting additional tax revenues from higher income and employment, wouldn't materially enlarge the deficit," which was projected at $61 billion. Ford had estimated a $43 billion

deficit if his budget were adopted. The committee termed this an overly optimistic assessment and placed the actual deficit resulting from his budget plan at "nearly $60 billion."

The committee charged that the sharp restrictions on government expenditures called for by Ford would result in an average unemployment rate of 7.9% in 1977 and an inflation rate of 6.3%. Their own stimulative policies would create 1.5 million jobs, raise real gross national product by 4%, reduce the inflation rate to 4.3% by 1977 and cut unemployment to 6.4%, according to the Democrats.

The panel urged Congress to reject Ford's proposed tax increases for social security and federal unemployment insurance. In addition to recommending an extension of the current tax through the end of 1977, the committee also asked Congress to consider expanding the tax reductions if the nation's real growth rate fell below 7% during 1976.

2-month tax-cut extension. The Senate, by voice vote June 28, 1976, approved a two-month extension of federal income-tax cuts that had been due to expire June 30. The measure, freezing withholding rates at their 1975 levels until Sept.1, was tacked onto a minor tax-revision bill passed earlier by the House.

President Ford signed the bill June 30. The Senate took the stopgap action when it became apparent after two weeks of debate that no final action would be taken before the June 30 deadline on a major tax-revision bill under consideration. That bill would extend most of the 1975 tax cuts permanently.

Members' tax exemption vetoed. Legislation exempting members of Congress from the Maryland state income tax—unless the members represented Maryland—was vetoed Aug. 3 by President Ford. The veto, Ford's 54th, criticized the legislation as "federal interference" in state affairs. Ford also said that the bill violated "equity and fairness" by singling out members of Congress from all those obliged to take up temporary residence in the Washington area.

The District of Columbia and the State of Virginia had, of their own initiative, exempted members of Congress from their taxes. The bill, in addition to its Maryland provision, would have embodied those exemptions into federal law. The bill had cleared Congress July 20. Most of the members representing Maryland opposed it.

Tax reform enacted. Congress Sept. 16, 1976 cleared the long-pending income-tax revision bill. It had been worked on for three years. The bill extended anti-recession tax cuts that had been enacted in 1975, made substantial changes in the treatment of estates and gifts, raised the taxes of the very rich, curbed the use of tax shelters and imposed penalties on countries that complied with the Arab boycott of Israel.

In signing the tax bill Oct. 4, the President reaffirmed his intention to seek $10 billion in additional personal and corporate tax cuts in 1977, matched by dollar-for-dollar cuts in federal spending. "The best kind of tax reform is tax reduction," he observed.

Both houses passed the bill Sept. 16. The House passed the bulk of the bill 383–26, after splitting off the section dealing with estate and gift taxation. That action was taken after House Republicans had disagreed with one provision of the estate section of the bill as it had been reported from the House-Senate conference committee. A 229–181 vote on a procedural question showed that the conference committee version had a majority behind it; the conference version of the estate and gift section was then formally adopted by a 405–2 vote. The Senate approved the estate section of the bill 81–3, and the rest of the bill 84–2.

(The disputed provision dealt with the taxation of capital gains on inherited property. Under current law, the only appreciation in value that was taxed was that which occurred between the date the owner died and the date the property was sold. A capital gain that occurred between the time of original purchase and the death of the purchaser escaped taxation.

Under the new provision, all future gains on inherited property would be taxed. Dec. 31, 1976 would be the "basis" date—the starting date for figuring the appreciation in value—for property already owned. The "basis" date for property purchased after Dec. 31, 1976 would be the actual purchase date.)

It was estimated that tax revisions in the bill as a whole would increase the government's revenue by $1.6 billion in fiscal 1977. Since the original Senate version of the bill would have resulted in an estimated revenue loss of $300 million, the final figure was viewed as a triumph for the House delegation to the conference committee. The bill as it finally emerged was also seen as testimony that Congress could abide by its new budget system: the estimated revenue gain promised by the tax bill matched that called for by the binding budget resolution passed by Congress Sept. 16.

The tax bill's major provisions:

■ Made permanent 1975 changes that raised standard personal deductions to 16% of adjusted gross income with minimum deductions of $1,700 for single persons and $2,100 for joint returns and maximums of $2,400 for single persons and $2,800 for joint returns.

■ Extended through 1977 the tax credit of $35 a person or 2% of the first $9,000 of taxable income.

■ Extended through 1977 a tax credit for individuals with children amounting to 10% of the first $4,000 of income. The credit would be phased out as income rose from $4,000 to $8,000, and would be refundable so that low-income families who paid no tax could benefit from it.

■ Simplified and made more widely available the 15% tax credit for persons over 65. The credit—which was extended to include earned income—would apply to the first $2,500 of a single person's income, including pensions, and the first $3,750 of income from a couple filing a joint return. The credit would be reduced by $1 for every $2 of income over $7,500 for a single person and over $10,000 for a joint return.

■ Repealed the sick-pay tax exemption except for persons under 65 who were permanently and totally disabled. Such persons could exclude $5,200 a year from their taxable income. The exclusions would be reduced dollar-for-dollar for income in excess of $15,000.

■ Made various other revisions affecting individual tax returns, including changes in the treatment of child-care costs, retirement accounts, rental of second homes, gambling profits, alimony, moving expenses, income from employment by a U.S. company located abroad and use of the home for business purposes.

■ Limited deductible losses from "tax shelter" investments to, in most cases, the amount an investor had risked.

■ Raised the minimum tax (a tax designed to prevent wealthy individuals from avoiding payment of virtually all taxes through the use of tax shelters and other devices) rate from 10% to 15% and tightened the rules so that the tax would include more people. The revised minimum tax was expected to be paid by 300,000 persons, compared with 30,000 under current rules. The bill also tightened the regulations governing the 50% maximum tax.

■ Extended the time for which property would have to be held to qualify for capital-gains treatment to nine months in 1977 and 12 months in 1978 and thereafter. The existing six-month qualification period would be left in effect for agricultural commodity futures.

■ Permitted persons eligible to set up individual retirement accounts to set up pension accounts for their unemployed spouses.

■ Extended the 1975-76 corporation investment tax credit of 10% through 1980.

■ Expanded, for most businesses, the length of time that net operating losses could be carried forward. For most businesses, the period would be lengthened from five to seven years; for regulated industries, it would be increased from seven to nine.

■ Provided a credit—growing from $30,000 in 1977 to $47,000 in 1981—to be counted against gift or estate taxes. The credit would have the effect of increasing the amount of money—from $120,000 in 1977 to $175,000 by 1981—that could be given or willed tax free.

■ Increased the amount that a person could leave or give to a spouse tax free to $250,000 or half of the estate, whichever was greater.

■ Required private foundations to pay out to charities all of their income or 5% of their assets, whichever was greater. The 5% requirement, established as permanent by the bill, replaced a scheme whereby the percentage varied from year to year, and was currently 6.25%.

■ Denied various tax benefits to U.S. companies complying with the Arab boycott of Israel.

■ Required immediate—rather than deferred—payment of taxes on bribes given by U.S. companies to foreign officials.

■ Tightened prohibitions against unauthorized disclosure of tax-return data by the Internal Revenue Service to the White House, Congress or government agencies.

■ Increased the legal liability of individuals or businesses preparing tax returns for profit.

■ Required the IRS to notify taxpayers when it was seeking to examine their financial records in banks or in the hands of other third parties. The taxpayer could then legally challenge the IRS request for or subpoena of the records. Notification would not be required, however, when it would impede an investigation.

■ Allowed state and local governments to require use of social security numbers by taxpayers, welfare recipients, car owners and drivers.

The Tax Revolt & the 1976 Presidential Campaign

Election years are periods during which political parties and their candidates pay particular attention to voters' grievances, among which complaints about taxes may rank high.

Party platforms. The Democratic Party platform, adopted at the national convention July 13, 1976, had this plank:

Tax reform. Economic justice will also require a firm commitment to tax reform at all levels. In recent years there has been a shift in the tax burden from the rich to the working people of this country. The Internal Revenue Code offers massive tax welfare to the wealthiest income groups in the population and only higher taxes for the average citizen. In 1973, there were 622 people with adjusted income of $100,-000 or more who still managed to pay no tax. Most families pay between 20 and 25 percent of their incomes in taxes.

We have had endless talk about the need for tax reform and fairness in our federal tax system. It is now time for action.

We pledge the Democratic Party to a complete overhaul of the present tax system, which will review all special tax provisions to ensure that they are justified and distributed equitably among our citizens. A responsible Democratic tax reform program could save over $5 billion in the first year with larger savings in the future.

We will strengthen the internal revenue code so that high income citizens pay a reasonable tax on all economic income.

We will reduce the use of unjustified tax shelters in such areas as oil and gas, tax-loss farming, real estate, and movies.

We will eliminate unnecessary and ineffective tax provisions to business and substitute effective incentives to encourage small business and capital formation in all businesses. Our commitment to full employment and sustained purchasing power will also provide a strong incentive for capital formation.

We will end abuses in the tax treatment of income from foreign sources; such as special tax treatment and incentives for multinational corporations that drain jobs and capital from the American economy.

We will overhaul federal estate and gift taxes to provide an effective and equitable structure to promote tax justice and alleviate some of the legitimate problems faced by farmers, small business men and women and others who would otherwise be forced to liquidate assets in order to pay the tax.

We will seek and eliminate provisions that encourage uneconomic corporate mergers and acquisitions.

We will eliminate tax inequities that adversely affect individuals on the basis of sex or marital status.

We will curb expense account deductions.

And we will protect the rights of all taxpayers against oppressive procedures, harassment and invasions of privacy by the Internal Revenue Service.

At present, many federal government tax and expenditure programs have a profound but unintended and undesirable impact on jobs and on where people and business locate. Tax policies and other indirect subsidies have promoted deterioration of cities and regions. These policies should be reversed.

There are other areas of taxation where change is also needed. The Ford Administration's unwise and unfair proposal to raise the regressive social security tax gives new urgency to the Democratic Party's goal of redistributing the burden of the social security tax by raising the wage base for earnings subject to the tax with effective exemptions and deductions to ease the impact on low income workers and two-earner families. Further revision in the Social Security program will be required so that women are treated as individuals.

The Democratic Party should make a reappraisal of the appropriate sources of federal revenues. The historical distribution of the tax burden between corporations and individuals, and among the various types of federal taxes, has changed dramatically in recent years. For example, the corporate tax share of federal revenue has declined from 30 percent in 1954 to 14 percent in 1975.

The Republican Party platform, adopted Aug. 18, included this plank:

The Republican Party recognizes that tax policies and spending policies are inseparable. If government spending is not controlled, taxes will inevitably rise either directly or through inflation. By failing to tie spending directly to income, the Democrat-controlled Congress has not kept faith with the American people. Every American knows he cannot continually live beyond his means.

The Republican Party advocates a legislative policy to obtain a balanced federal budget and reduced tax rates. While the best tax reform is tax reduction, we recognize the need for structural tax adjustments to help the working men and women of our nation. To that end, we recommend tax credits for college tuition, post-secondary technical training and child-care expenses incurred by working parents.

Over the past two decades of Democrat control of the Congress, our tax laws have become a nightmare of complexity and unfair tax preferences, virtually destroying the credibility of the system. Simplification should be a major goal of tax reform.

We support economic and tax policies to insure the necessary job-producing expansion of our economy. These include hastening capital recovery through new systems of accelerated depreciation, removing the tax burden on equity financing to encourage more capital investment, ending the unfair double taxation of dividends, and supporting proposals to enhance the ability of our working and other citizens to own "a piece of the action" through stock ownership. When balanced by expenditure reductions, the personal exemption should be raised to $1,000.

Carter pledges cautious tax move. Democratic presidential nominee Jimmy Carter pledged July 22 to take a cautious approach to tax reform. "I would not make any substantive change in our tax law, or propose any as president," he told a group of business executives in New York, "until at least a full year of very careful analysis."

"I'll do everything I can as president to keep the American people acquainted with the facts that relate to the advantages of international trade, that relate to the fairness or unfairness of specific tax regulations and the importance of the free-enterprise system within our societal structure."

On specific tax items, Carter indicated he favored retention of the foreign tax credit that allowed multinational corporations to subtract foreign taxes from their U.S. tax liability.

On the matter of tax deferrals for multinational firms, or deferral of the U.S. taxes on foreign earnings of American firms until that income was brought into the U.S., Carter said that was a matter he would "have to address." At a news conference later, he said his "inclination would be to remove tax deferral."

Ford for education aid. President Ford launched his campaign Sept. 15 with an attack on Carter and a promise to provide tax relief for middle-income families bearing the expense of a private-college education for their children.

In an address to 15,000 students at the University of Michigan in Ann Arbor, signaling the official start of his campaign, Ford focused primarily on Carter.

On education, Ford said that ways must be found "through the tax system to ease the burden on families who choose to send their children to non-public schools and to help families cope with the expenses of a college education."

"In my administration, the education needs of America's middle-income families will neither be forgotten or forsaken," he said. (There was already a proposal in a pending tax-reform bill that would provide some relief for those faced with tuition costs.)

Taxes argued during debate. President Ford and Jimmy Carter asserted their opposing views on economic policy and, at times, their uncomplimentary views of each other's stands in their nationally televised debate from the Walnut Street Theater in Philadelphia Sept. 23.

One question directed to Ford was how it was possible to promise tax cuts and balance the budget in view of the "very large" deficits being accumulated.

Ford stressed the necessity "to hold the lid on federal spending." Tax reduction must be offset by "an equal reduction in federal expenditures," on "a one-for-one" basis, Ford said, noting:

". . . I recommended . . . [to Congress] . . . a budget ceiling of $395 billion and that would have permitted us to have a $28-billion tax reduction.

"In my tax reduction program for middle-income taxpayers, I recommended that the Congress increase personal exemptions from $750 per person to $1,000 per person. That would mean, of course, that for a family of four that that family would have a $1,000 more personal exemption—money that they could spend for their own purposes, money that the government wouldn't have to spend.

"But if we keep the lid on federal spending, which I think we can with the help of the Congress, we can justify fully a $28-billion tax reduction.

"In the budget that I submitted to the Congress in January this year I recommended a 50% cutback in the rate of growth of federal spending. For the last 10 years the budget of the United States has grown from about 11% per year. We can't afford that kind of growth in federal spending. And in the budget that I recommended we cut it in half, a growth rate of 5 to 5½%.

"With that kind of limitation on Federal spending we can fully justify the tax reductions that I have proposed, and it seems to me with the stimulation of more money in the hands of the taxpayers and with more money in the hands of business to expand, to modernize, to provide more jobs, our economy will be stimulated so that we'll get more revenue and we'll have a more prosperous economy."

Ford indicated that he intended to sign the tax reform bill just passed by Congress although he preferred "an additional tax cut and a further limitation on federal spending."

Carter said that Ford was "changing considerably his previous philosophy" and called the tax structure "a disgrace" and "a welfare program for the rich."

Carter said that 25% of tax deductions went to only 1% of the richest persons in the country, over 50% of the tax credits to 14% of the richest persons. Carter said:

"The whole philosophy of the Republican Party, including my opponent's, has been to pile on taxes for low-income people to take them off on the corporations. As a matter of fact, since the late sixties when Mr. Nixon took office, we've had a reduction in the percentage of taxes paid by corporations from 30% down to about 20%. We've had an increase in taxes paid by individuals, payroll taxes from 14% up to 20%. And this is what the Republicans have done to us. And this is why tax reform is so important."

Carter suggested revising some tax provisions of multinational corporations. "When they don't pay their taxes," he said, "the average American pays the taxes for them." Another area for change, he said, was in business deductions—"jet airplanes, first class travel, the $50 martini lunch." Carter said he would not end all business deductions. That would be a "very serious mistake," he said.

Ford said he believed in "tax equity for the middle-income taxpayers, increasing the personal exemption" and that Carter had "indicated publicly in an interview that he would increase the taxes for roughly half of the taxpayers." The President also recalled to Carter that "the Democrats have controlled the Congress for the last 22 years and they wrote all the tax bills."

Later in the debate, Carter came back to the charge that he said he would raise taxes for half the taxpayers.

"... Mr. Ford has misquoted an AP news story that was in error to begin with. That story reported several times that I would lower taxes for low- and middle-income families and that correction was delivered to the White House and I am sure that the President knows about this correction, but he still insists on repeating an erroneous statement."

Carter held that there could be $60 billion in additional revenue available to the government by fiscal 1981, assuming both a growth rate for the economy equivalent to that of the Johnson and Kennedy years and a reduction in the jobless rate to a 4-4½% level. That $60 billion would accommodate the programs he promised, Carter said.

If those goals could not be reached, he said, "and I believe they're reasonable goals," he would "cut back on the rate of implementation of new programs in order to accommodate a balanced budget" by fiscal 1981.

Ford replied that any $60-billion surplus should be returned to the taxpayer via a tax reduction, but that "there isn't going to be any $60 billion dividend." He added:

"I've heard of those dividends in the past . . . We expected one at the time of the Vietnam war, but it was used up before we ever ended the war and taxpayers never got the adequate relief they deserve."

Paying for Ford's new programs—Ford was asked how he intended to pay for his recent proposals on jobs, housing, health, parks, crime and education in light of the $50 billion deficit in the budget and his suggestion that night to return as tax reductions any future surpluses.

Ford replied that some of the areas cited did not involve funding. He said:

"We believe that you can revise the federal criminal code, which has not been revised in a good many years. That doesn't cost any more money.

"We believe that you can do something more effectively with a moderate increase in money in the drug-abuse program. We feel that in education we can have a slight increase   not a major increase. It's my understanding that Governor Carter has indicated that he approves of a $30-billion expenditure by the federal government as far as education is concerned. At the present time we're spending roughly $3.5 billion. I don't know where that money would come from.

"But as we look at the quality-of-life programs job, health, education, crime, recreation we feel that as we move forward with a healthier economy, we can absorb the small necessary cost that will be required."

Asked specifically if he would try to reduce the deficit, spend money for his programs or return any surplus in tax relief, Ford expressed confidence that an improved economy—"and it is improving," he said—could accommodate his programs, a tax cut, "moderate" increases in the quality-of-life areas plus a balanced budget. He added:

"Now I cannot, and would not endorse the kind of program that Governor Carter recommends. He endorses the Democratic platform which, as I read it, calls for approximately 60 additional programs. We estimate that those programs would add $100 billion minimum and probably $200 billion maximum each year to the federal budget."

Carter replied:

"Mr. Ford takes the same attitude that the Republicans always take. In the last three months before an election, they're always for the programs that they always fight the other 3½ years."

Tax-relief proposals aired. President Ford and Jimmy Carter engaged in a long-distance debate over their tax proposals Sept. 17-20.

An Associated Press interview distributed Sept. 17 for use in Sunday (Sept. 19) newspapers, quoted Carter as saying that he would shift the tax burden to "those who have the higher incomes" and as defining "higher" to be anything above the "mean or median level of income."

Reminded by the interviewer that the median family income was "somewhere around $12,000 (it was $12,836 in 1974 and rose slightly in 1975), Carter said he could not answer the question. "I don't know how to write the tax code now in specific terms," he said. "It is just not possible to do that on a campaign trail. But I am committed to do it. . . ."

Carter said in the interview that his policy would mean that taxes for "the average American family . . . are going to be no higher or perhaps even lower in some instances, depending on their income, and . . . their taxes as levied will be fair."

He would try to shift the tax burden, he said, "toward those who have the higher incomes and reduce the income [tax] on the lower-income and middle-income taxpayers."

During initial transmittal of the article, the AP erroneously omitted the words "and middle-income."

The Republicans seized on the remarks as an issue. Sen. Robert J. Dole, the GOP vice-presidential nominee, said Sept. 18 that he was "astounded to read that he [Carter] is going to raise taxes for half the American families—anyone over the median income."

Dole stressed the issue while campaigning in Ohio and Florida Sept. 19. "If he's going to raise my taxes if I make over $14,000 that's the part he better explain to the American people," he remarked in Medina, Ohio. "He's going to lead America" and "he doesn't know after three years of campaigning what the median income for a family in America is," he told a Republican group in Panama City, Fla. "I suggest, if that's the case, that he ought to get out of the race now."

Ron Nessen, White House press secretary, Sept. 18 characterized Carter's remark as "a major blunder." Nessen recanted Sept. 20. "My saying that it was a major blunder was a minor blunder," Nessen told reporters.

The Carter camp protested that Carter's remarks were being distorted. At a rally Sept. 19 in Kansas City, Mo., Carter denied the GOP charges. "I would never increase taxes on the working people of our country in the lower- and middle-income groups," he said, "but we will shift the burden of taxes to where the Republicans have always protected—onto the rich, the big corporations and the special interest groups."

President Ford touched upon the topic during a televised talk to farm credit bank executives in the White House rose garden Sept. 20. "This Administration will give you tax relief because it is good for America," he promised.

"Those who advocate additional expenditures have now suggested," he said, "that in order to pay for those new programs and added expenditures, there should be an additional tax levy on the middle-income people, which is approximately 50% of the taxpayers in the country."

"We should go in the opposite direction," Ford said. "We should give them tax relief, not additional taxes."

By coincidence, Ford was quoted in a Reader's Digest article published Sept. 19 as defining "middle-income" as in the $8,000 to $30,000 a year bracket. (Not more than 5% of American families had income of more than $30,000 a year and fewer than 10% had incomes of more than $25,000.) "I favor giving greater tax relief to the so-called middle-income taxpayers—those in the earning brackets of $8,000 to $30,000 a year," Ford said in the interview.

Carter's tax views, given in response to an interview, also were published by the Reader's Digest in the same issue. Carter told the magazine he favored a "truly progressive tax rate" in which the higher-income families would pay a higher portion of their income in taxes.

Sen. Walter F. Mondale (Minn.), Carter's running mate, made his views on the subject known Sept. 20. Campaigning in Binghamton, N.Y. and Lewiston, Me., Mondale said: "The Republican administration's efforts to paint itself as the champion of fair tax treatment for the average family is sheer hypocrisy. The record shows that they have consistently fought to preserve tax breaks for big business, and to shift tax relief, not to the average family, but toward those making $50,000, $100,000 and more."

In an interview printed in the October issue of Liberty magazine, a journal of the Seventh Day Adventist Church, Carter was asked his views on the taxation of "the church building and subsidiary things such as publishing houses, church institutions, et cetera." Carter's answer was that he would "favor the taxation of church properties other than the church building itself."

Sen. Robert J. Dole, Ford's Vice Presidential running mate, criticized Carter in New Haven, Conn. Oct. 2 for his answer. Dole told Republicans: "I find it incredible that Mr. Carter wants to impose taxes on church-owned hospitals, schools, senior citizens homes and orphanages."

The subject also was brought up at a White House meeting of Republican ethnic leaders. "Nothing could be worse," Ford said in response to a query, than to impose taxes on "church-operated schools, hospitals and orphanages, many of which face constant financial struggles to make ends meet."

Carter riposted later Oct. 2 while cam-

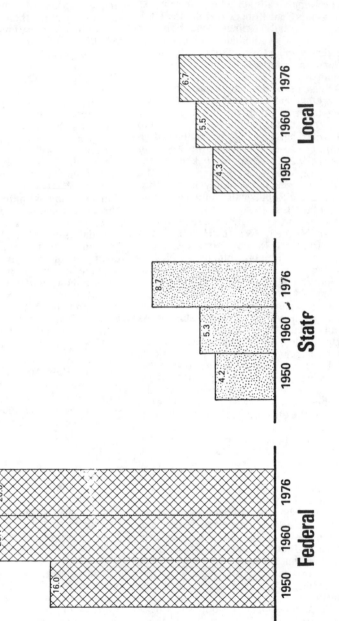

From Joint Economic Committee of Congress

paigning in Maryland. Ford's interpretation of his stand, Carter said, represented a "conscious, willful, disgraceful effort at misinterpreting" his position.

Carter said that the only tax he advocated on church properties was that on profits from any business operation of the church, a position taken by the Supreme Court. He said he had always favored tax exemption for church-owned properties used for religious, cultural, education or charitable purpose, such as church-run hospitals and schools. He cited his record as governor of Georgia in advocacy of exemption for nonprofit hospitals and nursing homes from the sales tax. They were already exempt from property taxes.

Speaking in Rochester, N.Y. Oct. 14, Carter told a noontime crowd: "Anyone who works for a living and who reports all their income for tax purposes will never have their income taxes raised under my administration. I'm not going to raise taxes, I'm going to cut out loopholes, and that will help all of you, and you can depend on it."

Carter spokesman Jody Powell, who admitted to reporters that it was "a pretty flat promise," checked with Carter and reported back that Carter anticipated no tax increases "barring unforeseen developments, crises and so forth" of the magnitude of war. "What he should have said," Powell explained, "is, 'no tax increase under my tax-reform plan.'" Powell said that this meant there was no intention to raise taxes for working people under Carter's tax-reform plan for shifting the tax burden more to the wealthy.

Carter hints at tax cut. Two days after being elected President, Carter said at a news conference in Plains, Ga. Nov. 4 that he thought that a tax cut was a "strong possibility" if the economy remained "as stagnant" as it was currently. Warning that he was "not qualified to be specific" about the details, Carter said a possible tax cut would be targeted at stimulating purchasing power and "oriented toward payroll deductions" for working Americans.

The President-elect had another press conference Nov. 15. He did not reject a tax cut at the outset of his administration, as a stimulant to the economy, but he emphasized that no final decision had been made.

Carter said that he would meet soon with Arthur F. Burns, chairman of the Federal Reserve Board, to get Burns's assessment of economic prospects. Carter said that he had received a pledge of cooperation from Burns and that he expected that he and Burns would "find a substantial degree of compatibility." If there were "differences," Carter said, he would make his own decisions about increasing the supply of money, through such devices as tax rebates or budget moves.

Burns then warned the Senate Banking Committee Nov. 11 that inflation might worsen if "traditional policies" were used to stimulate the current sluggish pace of economic recovery in an effort to reduce unemployment.

Since most definitions of traditional stimulative policies included tax cuts as well as increases in federal spending, many analysts believed that Burns's warning was directed at Carter.

The day after his Senate appearance, Burns took steps to counter the impression of a possible conflict between the Fed and the incoming Carter administration. A Fed spokesman called some of the nation's major newspapers Nov. 12 to say that Burns had intended only to warn Congress against voting major new spending increases, not to warn Carter against use of a tax cut.

Ford's Final Tax Proposals

Tax cut urged. Early in 1977, outgoing President Ford proposed a $12.5-billion tax reduction program to Congress Jan. 4.

The primary purpose of the proposals was said to be tax relief for middle-income taxpayers. Ford recommended that Congress "periodically counteract the growing burden imposed by the tax system by providing offsetting tax cuts while continuing to restrain the rate of growth of federal spending."

At a White House briefing, Treasury Secretary William Simon made the point that the tax program "should be viewed as part of an overall approach which includes restraint on the growth of federal spending." Stressing that the tax reductions were not planned as an economic stimulant, Simon said an "additional stimulus at this time is unwise, unnecessary and undesirable."

Ford's program called for $10 billion in individual tax cuts and $2.5 billion in business tax cuts. In addition, he urged an increase in the Social Security tax rates to prevent depletion of the system's funds.

Specifically, Ford requested a 1.1 percentage point increase in the combined employer-employe payroll tax over a three-year period. This, plus a previously scheduled increase in the rate, would take the tax to a 13.2% level in 1980 from its existing 11.7% level.

For individuals, the President asked Congress to increase the personal income tax exemption from $750 to $1,000. This would replace the temporary tax credit of $35 per exemption and the alternative credit of 2% of taxable income up to $9,000.

The low-income allowance for single persons would be raised from $1,700 to $1,800 and for joint returns from $2,100 to $2,500. Tax rates would be lowered slightly for lower-income and middle-income individuals, but the current earned-income credit for poor families, providing a refundable tax credit of up to $400, would be eliminated.

For business, the President requested a reduction in the basic corporate tax rate from 48% to 46%. He asked Congress to make permanent a 20% tax rate on the first $25,000 of corporate income and a 22% rate on the second $25,000. These provisional rates were scheduled to expire by 1978.

Ford also asked Congress to permanently extend the 10% investment tax credit for business equipment. This was scheduled to revert to 7% by 1981.

An accelerated depreciation rate was requested for new equipment in areas with unemployment rates of 7% or higher.

Congress was asked to end authority for certain practices, such as the funding of employe stock-ownership plans through supplemental investment tax credits and the double taxation of corporate dividends. For the latter, Ford suggested a deduction at the corporate level for part of the dividend paid and an adjustment at the shareholder level for the remaining tax due on dividend distribution.

Budget predicts end to deficits. Ford Jan. 17, 1977 submitted to Congress a budget calling for a gradual slowdown in the growth of federal spending and permanent income tax reductions for individuals and businesses.

The budget contained, for the first time, detailed projections for the year beyond the proposed 1977–78 budget year, which would begin Oct. 1. "Our only real hope of curbing the growth of federal spending," Ford said in his budget message, "is to plan further in advance and to discipline ourselves to stick to those plans."

For fiscal 1978 (Oct. 1, 1977–Sept. 30, 1978), Ford estimated outlays of $440 billion for a deficit of $47 billion. For fiscal 1979, spending would rise to $466 billion, but the deficit would decline to $11.6 billion because of a boost of $61.4 billion in anticipated receipts. Ford projected a balanced budget by fiscal 1980.

Then, "with restraint on the growth of federal spending," he declared in his message, "we can begin to provide permanent tax reductions to ease the burden on middle-income taxpayers and businesses. For too long government has presumed that it is 'entitled' to the additional tax revenues generated as inflation and increases in real income push taxpayers into higher tax brackets. We need to reverse this presumption. We need to put the burden of proof on the government to demonstrate the reasons why individuals should not keep the income and wealth they produce. Accordingly, my long-term budget projections assume further tax relief will be provided, rather than presuming, as has been the practice in the past, that positive margins of receipts over expenditures that show up in projections are 'surpluses' or 'fiscal dividends' that must be used primarily for more federal spending, on existing or new

The Budget Dollar

Where it comes from:

Individual income taxes ....39¢
Social insurance receipts ....29¢
Corporation income taxes ....13¢
Borrowing...11¢
Excise taxes .... 4¢
Other .... 4¢

Where it goes:

Benefit payments to individuals ....38¢
Military ....26¢
Grants to states and localities ....16¢
Other federal operations ....13¢
Net interest .... 7¢

---

programs or both."

In addition to his call for a $12.5-billion reduction in income taxes in 1977, Ford recommended further tax cuts for individuals—$7.3 billion in fiscal 1980, $19.6 billion in fiscal 1981 and $30.6 billion in fiscal 1982. Such cuts would keep the rate of income allotted to federal taxes at about 1979 levels.

Ford's economic report to Congress. In a report to Congress Jan. 18, the President's Council of Economic Advisers said that the pace of economic recovery had "re-accelerated" after several months of pause, but contended that a pickup in business spending, rather than an increase in government spending, was the key to a sustained recovery.

At a press conference Jan. 18, council chairman Alan Greenspan said the Ford Administration's report was not "specifically critical of [President-elect Jimmy] Carter's programs." However, the

Administration stated its economic policies in a set of "general principles" that were implicitly critical of Carter's plan to stimulate the economy through the combined use of increased public spending and a temporary tax rebate.

"Economic stimulus, where needed," the report said, "should be provided by reduction rather than by increases in government spending. Tax reduction should be permanent rather than in the form of a temporary rebate. Policy initiatives should be balanced between measures directed toward consumption and those aimed at increased business fixed investment."

Greenspan said that in the "short-run" the economic impact of Carter's still-formulative program "isn't significantly different" from Ford's budget proposals. The central point of difference between the two positions involved policies on business fixed investment (spending on plant and equipment).

The Ford Administration believed that the most important task facing the Carter Administration was the "restoration of business confidence" so that business leaders would be encouraged to launch long-term expansion projects. A permanent tax cut was the best means to rebuild this confidence, the report said.

Tax reductions for individuals would "yield a sustained rise in consumer spending," which in turn would prompt business leaders to increase their capital investment, the report said.

Although a temporary tax rebate might

Budget Receipts

in billions of dollars

Receipts by Source	Estimate			Projection		
	1977	1978	1979	1980	1981	1982
Individual income taxes	153.1	171.2	205.3	234.1	252.3	267.7
Corporation income taxes	56.6	58.9	63.7	69.7	74.7	78.0
Social insurance taxes and contributions	108.9	126.1	146.2	164.8	182.6	196.5
Excise taxes	17.9	18.5	19.1	19.6	20.0	20.1
Estate and gift taxes	5.9	5.8	6.3	6.9	7.3	7.9
Customs duties	4.7	5.3	5.9	6.5	7.0	7.5
Miscellaneous receipts	6.9	7.2	7.7	8.5	9.1	9.7
Total receipts	**354.0**	**393.0**	**454.4**	**510.0**	**553.1**	**587.3**

COMPARATIVE TAXATION OF INDIVIDUALS IN 8 MAJOR WESTERN COUNTRIES

Country	Per capita tax in 1975 (1)	Personal income tax (2)	Social security payment (3)	VAT/sales taxes (4)	Specific goods taxes (5)	IND. property taxes (6)	Regressivity indexes (percent) $\frac{4}{2+3}$	$\frac{5}{2+3}$	$\frac{4+5}{2+3}$
U.S. dollars:									
United States	$2,044	¹$644	$202	¹$137	¹$192	$154	16	23	39
United Kingdom	1,495	565	113	117	218	73	19	32	51
France	2,348	¹291	201	548	215	23	111	44	155
West Germany	2,420	722	353	356	253	16	33	23	56
Italy	997	¹150	90	136	134		57	56	113
Switzerland	2,494	¹870	347	194	¹265	14	16	22	38
Sweden	3,890	¹1,783		464	442		26	25	51
Japan	919	¹230	85		¹145			46	46
Percentages:									
United States	100	31.5	9.9	6.7	9.4	7.5			
United Kingdom	100	37.8	7.6	8.7	14.6	4.9			
France	100	12.4	8.6	23.4	9.2	1.0			
West Germany	100	30.1	15.0	14.7	10.5	.7			
Italy	100	15.1	9.0	13.7	13.5				
Switzerland	100	34.9	13.9	7.8	10.7	.6			
Sweden	100	45.9		11.9	11.4				
Japan	100	25.0	9.2		15.8				

¹ Including State and local taxes.

NOTES

The per capita tax is the total tax revenue of the country divided by the population. The other items are their respective contributions to total tax revenue on a per capita basis. The regressivity indexes show the extent to which total per capita tax revenue comes from indirect taxes felt by individuals (VAT or sales taxes and other indirect taxes of specific goods and services, excise taxes, etc.).

Despite the fact that the United States allows resident citizens to deduct State sales taxes from their gross taxable income, it denies this same possibility to those American citizens living abroad. Thus, those living abroad in highly regressive tax countries are faced with tax credit (or deduction) losses that can exceed what they pay in direct income tax. (See France above.)

Source: OECD Revenue Statistics of OECD Member Countries 1965-75, OECD 1977.

be "useful in bringing about a reversal of generally declining demand during a recession," the report said, a rebate was not "consistent with the maintenance of an expansion of demand that is already underway."

Among the objections to stimulative government-spending plans was the long start-up date required for most federal programs. As a result of this delay, the report said, "the economic impact of new spending programs won't be felt when it is needed most and will then outlast the need for stimulus."

Other Developments

Black leaders offer tax proposals. Representatives of more than 50 black professional, business, religious, civil rights and community organizations Sept. 23, 1974 ended the first national black economic meeting, calling on the Administration to establish a public service work program that would provide a million jobs as a means of easing the "depression" that inflation had produced among blacks.

In a position paper issued at the close of the two-day meeting in Washington, the group also called for sharp tax increases on excess profits, a surtax on upper income persons, direct tax relief for the poor, substitution of cash for federal food stamps, and direct price controls.

The group opposed Administration plans to cut domestic spending levels. "Social programs have traditionally enhanced the participation of blacks in America's economy. It is imperative that these programs not be cut," the paper stated.

Mayors focus on federal dollar. A bigger share of the federal dollar was a major topic at the 51st annual convention of the National League of Cities held in Miami Beach Nov. 30–Dec. 4, 1975.

New York Mayor Abraham Beame told the convention Dec. 1 that "perhaps the single most progressive federal effort to help our cities" would be renewal of the general revenue-sharing program by Congress. Beame said he thought New York's desperate fight to avoid financial default had spotlighted urban problems and "reawakened a sense of urgency in dealing with them."

Countercyclical aid, or federal aid that was increased in bad times and cut in good times, was endorsed by Democratic mayors meeting in caucus at the convention Nov. 30. The Democrats adopted and issued a major urban policy statement declaring that cities could maintain fiscal health and offer citizens an improved quality of living only through new federal help and a drastic revision of federal spending priorities. It urged increased federal funding of health, transportation, housing, energy and criminal justice programs. Among other things, it called for a full employment policy, federal takeover of welfare costs, a national health insurance program, revision of the local property tax structure and a national ban on handguns. It suggested the creation of regional tax bases as a way to sustain the big cities drained of tax revenue because of the middle-class flight.

Social Security panel rejects tax rise. The Social Security Advisory Council Jan. 19, 1975 reversed its earlier call for financing Medicare hospital benefits through an increase in payroll taxes for upper income workers, and voted instead to finance the program with general federal tax revenues.

The council, a government-appointed panel of 13 private citizens, initially had recommended that Congress finance retirement benefits for more than 30 million persons by levying new Social Security taxes on the first $24,000 a worker earned each year. The current upper limit on the wage base was $14,000. The action, if adopted by Congress, would have meant a 70% boost in payroll taxes on workers in the top income range.

The council warned Jan. 24 that benefits would exceed receipts by $3 billion-$4 billion by 1976. To overcome

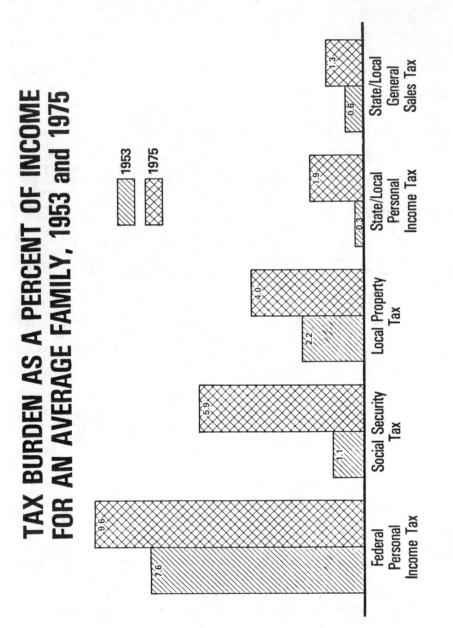

TAX BURDEN AS A PERCENT OF INCOME FOR AN AVERAGE FAMILY, 1953 and 1975

1953
1975

Federal Personal Income Tax — 7.6 / 9.6

Social Security Tax — 1.1 / 5.9

Local Property Tax — 2.2 / 4.0

State/Local Personal Income Tax — 0.3 / 1.9

State/Local General Sales Tax — 0.6 / 1.3

From Joint Economic Committee of Congress

the expected deficit, the group said it would urge Congress to use general tax revenues to finance more than half of Medicare, rather than authorize further increases in the payroll tax. (Employes and employers currently were assesed 5.85% of annual income up to $14,000.)

The council's proposals, embodied in its final report, went to Congress and the President March 7.

In a statement March 7, President Ford applauded the council's confidence in the system but flatly rejected the recommendation to transfer Medicare financing to the general tax revenues.

Eight former officials involved with Social Security Feb. 10 had issued a "white paper" scoring "attacks on the system designed to create doubts of its soundness and durability."

The system would require "some additional financing" once benefits began to outrun tax receipts, the white paper said, adding that the "size of the problem over the next 25 years is easily manageable and certainly does not constitute a financial crisis."

As to the contention that the system was a poor bargain for contributors who could do better with private investments, the white paper pointed out that such investments often ended in losses. The statement also denied that the system was regressive because lower-income workers paid higher proportions of their wages as taxes than did higher-income persons. Lower-paid workers received proportionately higher benefits, said the report, which noted that "the net effect of the system is to transfer some income from the more affluent as a group to the less affluent."

Signatories of the paper were five former secretaries of health, education and welfare—Elliot L. Richardson, Robert H. Finch, John W. Gardner, Wilbur J. Cohen and Arthur S. Flemming—and three commissioners of Social Security, Robert M. Ball, William L. Mitchell and Charles I. Schottland.

Despite an impending $3 billion Social Security deficit in 1975, the Ford Administration opposed an increase in payroll taxes until 1977, Caspar W. Weinberger, secretary of health, education and welfare, told the House Ways and Means Social Security subcommittee May 19.

Weinberger, who denied the system was in "dire peril," said the Administration would not suggest what action should be taken to lessen the projected deficit. The Administration, he said, had already proposed a $2.2 billion savings by limiting benefit increases to 5% instead of the 8% rise scheduled for July 1. But, since Congress did not want to curtail benefits, it, not the President, should propose the necessary tax increases to keep the system solvent, Weinberger said.

Weinberger said that the Administration felt that a recession was not the proper time to raise taxes and reduce consumer purchasing power. Deficits over the next few years would easily be covered by the existing $46.1 billion trust fund, he said. The secretary also reiterated the Administration's strong opposition to financing of any Social Security benefits from general government revenues.

Trustees urge tax raise—In their 1976 report, issued May 24, the trustees of the Social Security System urged Congress to boost the program's payroll tax (paid by both employes and employers) to 6.15% from 5.85%. The report presented the increase as a short-term remedy for the ailing benefits program for which continuing deficits were forecast.

Social Security income and expenses were estimated under a variety of assumptions about the economy—optimistic, pessimistic and intermediate. The report concluded that the multibillion dollar Social Security trust fund would be exhausted by the early 1980s if the tax increase were not enacted or if some other form of additional financing were not found.

Projecting the system's income and payments over the next 75 years, the report predicted deficits for every year. The long-term prospects would necessitate substantial tax increases, the report said.

1976 state tax referenda. In balloting Nov. 2, 1976: Massachusetts voters rejected a proposed graduated state income tax; New Jersey voters approved a constitutional amendment providing that net proceeds of the state income tax go to property tax relief. Michigan voters rejected a state income tax and a state constitutional amendment that would have limited state taxes and spending to 8.3% of total state personal income.

New Jersey adopts income tax. New Jersey Gov. Brendan Byrne July 8, 1976 signed legislation that made the state the 43rd in the nation to have a personal income tax. The state Senate had approved the measure, which called for a graduated 2%-2.5% tax, earlier in the day on a 22-18 vote, one more than the minimum necessary for passage.

Enactment of the bill ended a legal dispute over the financing of the state's public schools. The State Supreme Court had ruled that New Jersey's reliance on property taxes to finance school budgets was unconstitutional and had ordered the state to consider more equitable means of paying for its school systems. A court injunction had shut New Jersey's public schools July 1.

A year later (Nov. 8, 1977) Byrne was relected governor by winning a 300,-000-vote victory over state Sen. Raymond H. Bateman (R).

Byrne had been 10-12 points behind Bateman in public opinion polls only two months before the vote. He had been counted an extremely unpopular governor because of the state income tax enacted under his prodding. As a candidate in 1973, he had discounted the income tax as a possibility.

The issue dominated the campaign. Bateman was forced to produce an alternative to the income tax, which brought in $900 million annually for use largely as school aid and property tax rebates to homeowners.

Bateman's plan featured budget tightening, a possible increase in the sales tax and an underlying dependency on an improved business climate.

11 big firms paid no '75 U.S. income taxes. Eleven major corporations, with combined earnings of more than $1 billion in 1975, paid no federal income taxes for

that year, according to Rep. Charles Vanik (D, Ohio), a senior member of the House Ways and Means Committee.

Vanik identified the 11 as Ford Motor Co., Delta Air Lines Inc., Northwest Airlines Inc., Chemical New York Corp., Manufacturers Hanover Corp., Western Electric Co. (a subsidiary of American Telephone & Telegraph Co.), Bethlehem Steel Corp., Lockheed Aircraft Corp., National Steel Corp., Phelps Dodge Corp. and Freeport Minerals Co.

Vanik's data, issued Oct. 2, 1976, were based on corporate taxes reported in public records filed with the Securities and Exchange Commission.

For 1974, Vanik said, eight major firms had paid no federal income taxes. They were Ford, Lockheed, Honeywell Inc., U.S. Industries Inc., American Airlines Inc., Eastern Air Lines Inc., American Electric Power Co. and Allstate Insurance Co., a subsidiary of Sears Roebuck & Co.

Vanik said that another 27 major corporations paid less than 10% of their pretax profits in federal income tax for 1975. Among them were: AT&T, which Vanik said paid 2.4%; Mobil Oil Corp. (1.8%); Gulf Oil Corp. (6%) and Texaco Inc. (9.2%); holding companies for the nation's second and third largest commercial banks, Citicorp (6.7%) and Chase Manhattan Corp. (3.4%); two large railroads, Chessie System Inc. (9.5%) and Burlington Northern Inc. (8.4%); Aluminum Co. of America (less than 1%); Allied Chemical Corp. (less than 1%); Weyerhaeuser Co. (5%); Xerox Corp. (8.7%), and Colgate-Palmolive Co. (9.7%).

Based on his five years of studying the SEC reports, Vanik said, corporate contributions to U.S. tax revenues were declining.

The maximum corporate tax rate was 48% of earnings, but Vanik's report showed that the effective tax rate paid by the nation's 148 largest corporations was 21.6%. Tax Analysts and Advocates, a Washington-based public interest law firm, provided a breakdown of weighted average tax rates—U.S. taxes on worldwide earnings—paid by the largest companies in different industries. The figures, published in the Washington Post Oct. 14, showed that the largest oil companies paid 10%, chemical companies 24%, steel firms

11.7%, timber firms 17.6%, utilities 15.3% and railroads 5.3%.

Of the nation's 10 largest airlines, four were profitable in 1975 and none paid federal income taxes. The eight largest banks showed a profit that year and none paid taxes.

The Post said corporations chiefly used two provisions in the Internal Revenue Service Code to reduce their taxes. One, the foreign tax credit, permitted U.S. companies to subtract from U.S. taxes on foreign income any income taxes paid to foreign governments. (That was an important provision, particularly in 1975, when many companies reported losses in domestic operations but showed profits abroad.)

The other, the investment tax credit, permitted companies to subtract from their taxes 10% of the cost of most machinery they bought. Extra investment tax credit could be applied against any taxes paid in the preceding years or held in reserve for the next seven years.

Ford Motor Co., which paid 30% in foreign taxes on its worldwide income for 1975 and applied investment tax credits for 1975 and 1974 to U.S. taxes paid in 1973, used these options not only to reduce its U.S. income-tax liability for 1974 and 1975 to zero but also to win a $189 million refund from the government for those years.

In his report, Vanik said that the nation's 148 largest corporations paid about $20 billion in foreign taxes in 1975, and that their U.S. income taxes for that year were $10 billion. "It is preposterous that American-protected corporations are currently paying more than twice as much to foreign governments in taxes as they pay to our own government in federal income tax," Vanik said.

230 rich persons paid no '75 federal taxes. The Treasury Department said March 3, 1977 that 230 persons with adjusted gross incomes above $200,000 had paid no federal income tax in 1975, compared with 244 in 1974.

Officials said the 34,121 persons who had reported incomes in the $200,000-plus bracket had paid an average of 42.9% of their incomes in taxes in 1975. Fewer than 15% of persons in that bracket had paid less than 20% in taxes. A family of four with the 1975 median income of $13,719 had paid about 10% in taxes, officials said.

Annual disclosure of these figures was required by the 1976 Tax Reform Act.

Per capita tax burden rose in 1975. Per-capita taxes paid to state and local governments increased in every state but Maine during the 1975 fiscal year, Commerce Clearing House reported Oct. 12, 1976. For the 10th consecutive year, New Yorkers carried the heaviest tax burden—$1,025 in fiscal 1975. Ranking second was California ($869), replacing Massachusetts which had held the second spot for fiscal 1974.

Arkansas replaced Alabama as the state with the lowest per-capita tax burden—$405 in fiscal 1975.

The average U.S. tax burden rose $46 in fiscal 1975 to $664. The median tax burden was $612, up $39 from fiscal 1974.

State, local tax revenue sets mark. State and local governments collected a record $165.7 billion in taxes in calendar year 1976, according to U.S. Census Bureau data May 4, 1977. The figure was $18.8 billion, or 12.8%, more than the 1975 total.

State tax collections totaled $94.5 billion, up from $82.9 billion in 1975. Local revenues rose to $71.3 billion from the 1975 total of $64.1 billion.

The breakdown by taxes was as follows: Property taxes—$60.2 billion, up 10.9% from 1975; gross receipts and general sales taxes—$34.3 billion, up 14.2%; individual income taxes—$26.8 billion, up 17.5%; fuel taxes—$9 billion, up 6.2%; corporate net income taxes—$8.03 billion, up 18.9%; motor vehicle and operator's license fees—$4.8 billion, up 11.3%.

Taxes collected by counties, municipalities and townships totaled $41.1 billion in fiscal 1976, according to U.S. Commerce Department reports July 7, 1977. Municipal taxes accounted for $23.3

Per-Capita Figures for Personal Income and Tax Burden*

STATES AND REGION	Personal Income AMOUNT	PERCENTAGE CHANGE FROM 1975	RANK (in income)	Tax Burden
United States	$6,399	9.3		
New England	6,573	9.2		
Connecticut	7,356	8.1	4	778
Maine	5,366	12.6	43	671
Massachusetts	6,588	9.0	15	903
New Hampshire	6,010	10.9	30	571
Rhode Island	6,331	10.4	21	711
Vermont	5,411	10.4	40	742
Mideast	6,924	8.4		
Delaware	7,030	8.4	9	768
District of Columbia	8,067	9.0	2	924
Maryland	6,880	8.6	11	814
New Jersey	7,381	9 1	3	793
New York	7,019	7.3	10	1,140
Pennsylvania	6,439	9.7	18	684
Great Lakes	6,687	10.6		
Illinois	7,347	8.5	5	769
Indiana	6,222	11.7	24	588
Michigan	6,754	13.0	13	749
Ohio	6,412	11.0	19	586
Wisconsin	6,117	9.5	27	791
Plains	6,105	7.0		
Iowa	6,245	6.4	23	701
Kansas	6,469	8.6	16	651
Minnesota	6,183	7.3	26	823
Missouri	5,963	9.2	31	570
Nebraska	6,086	3.7	28	658
North Dakota	5,846	-1.5	32	667
South Dakota	5,120	2.2	48	596
Southeast	5,526	10.1		
Alabama	5,106	10.6	49	455
Arkansas	4,934	9.5	50	454
Florida	6,020	7.6	29	566
Georgia	5,548	10.6	37	549
Kentucky	5,379	10.4	42	549
Louisiana	5,405	11.6	41	610
Mississippi	4,529	12.0	51	486
North Carolina	5,453	10.7	39	527
South Carolina	5,147	10.7	47	489
Tennessee	5,364	10.7	44	493
Virginia	6,341	9.8	20	609
West Virginia	5,460	10.8	38	584
Southwest	6,024	10.4		
Arizona	5,799	8.5	33	731
New Mexico	5,322	10.2	46	598
Oklahoma	5,707	8.8	34	530
Texas	6,201	11.0	25	581
Rocky Mountain	6,010	8.7		
Colorado	6,440	8.5	17	728
Idaho	5,640	9.3	36	590
Montana	5,689	5.7	35	709
Utah	5,350	10.5	45	593
Wyoming	6,642	9.6	14	847
Far West	7,033	9.2		
California	7,151	9.3	7	964
Nevada	7,162	8.6	6	820
Oregon	6,261	9.9	22	703
Washington	6,802	8.4	12	728
Alaska	10,415	10.3	1	1,896
Hawaii	7,080	6.2	8	935

*Income figures are for calendar year 1976. Tax-burden figures are for the fiscal year that ran from July 1, 1975 through June 30, 1976

Source: Commerce Department and Commerce Clearing House

billion of the total, county taxes $14.1 billion and township taxes $3.7 billion.

The major source of local revenue was the property tax, which provided $29.1 billion in fiscal 1976. This was a $2.6 billion (9.8%) increase over the previous year. Municipalities collected $14.1 billion in property taxes, counties $11.6 billion and townships $3.4 billion.

The $12 billion in nonproperty taxes taken by the local governmental units represented a 12.1% increase over the previous year's total.

The major components of the nonproperty taxes were $6.9 billion from sales and gross receipts taxes, $3.1 billion from income taxes and $300 million from motor vehicle license taxes.

Revenue received by local governments from federal and state sources amounted to $35.9 billion in fiscal 1976, a $1.3 billion (3.7%) increase over the fiscal 1975 figure. The federal portion, 26.4%, represented almost double the federal contribution before revenue sharing was instituted.

In fiscal 1972, state governments contributed 86.1% of the intergovernmental revenue of counties, cities and townships while the federal government supplied 13.9%.

In fiscal 1973, reflecting the beginning of federal revenue sharing in October 1972, the federal share was 22.4%, the state share 77.6%.

State governments' general revenue increased 13% during fiscal 1976 to $152.1 billion, and general expenditures rose 11.1% during the same period to $153.7 billion, according to the Commerce Department Sept. 2.

(Comparisons with previous years were not exact because the 1976 data did not include unemployment compensation funds.)

Tax revenue rose 11.4% to $89.3 billion. This meant that taxes provided the bulk, 58.7%, of the states' general revenue.

Americans paid an average of $731 in taxes to state and local governments in fiscal 1976, according to Commerce Clearing House Oct. 18. That was $67 per person more than in fiscal 1975.

The tax burden increased over the year for residents of every state. The increases ranged from a high of $1,054 for Alaska to $8 in Indiana. Alaska collected the highest taxes ($1,896 per person), replacing New York, which had led the list for 10 years. (Alaska's property taxes, alone, rose to $400 million from $76 million.) New York, with a per capita tax burden of $1,140, was the only other state to pass the $1,000 mark. Arkansas had the lowest tax burden—$454 per person.

State and local tax collections totaled $156.8 billion in fiscal 1976. That was 10.9% higher than in fiscal 1975 and more than double the 1969 level. California's tax revenues were the highest—$20.75 billion—followed by New York, with $20.61 billion.

Carter Administration & the Tax Revolt: 1977-78

Tax Cuts & Federal Spending Proposed to Stimulate Economy

Jimmy Carter succeeded Gerald Ford as President of the United States Jan. 20, 1977. His early economic policies seemed to suit the widespread mood of "tax revolt" as Carter Administration spokesmen explained the President's plans for stimulating the lagging economy by means of tax reductions, incentives to business and job-creating government programs.

Congress gets economic plan. A $31.2-billion package of tax cuts and spending to stimulate the economy was outlined to Congress by Carter Administration officials Jan. 27, 1977.

The officials—Treasury Secretary Michael Blumenthal, Budget Director Bert Lance and economic adviser Charles Schultze—testified on the economic plan before the House Budget Committee. Lance had disclosed some details to the press Jan. 25. The plan was larger than previous versions and contained increased incentives for capital spending by business.

The package would cover two years. In fiscal 1977, $15.5 billion of stimulus would be applied—tax cuts of $13.8 billion and spending of $1.7 billion on jobs programs. In fiscal 1978, the tax cuts would total $8.1 billion, spending $7.6 billion.

In the first year, $11.4 billion would be provided in rebates on individual income taxes and in payments to Social Security recipients and poor families with little or no tax liability.

The plan included a $50 rebate for each taxpayer, spouse, child and other dependent included on an income-tax return. The same rebate also would be paid to poor families filing for the federal earned-income credit. The $50 payments also would be sent to beneficiaries of Social Security, supplemental security income and railroad retirement programs.

A permanent tax reduction, $4 billion a year, was proposed for individuals in the lower-income brackets. It would come from a change in the standard deduction to $2,400 for single persons and $2,800 for married couples. Currently, the deduction ranged from $1,700 to $2,400 for individuals and from $2,100 to $2,800 for couples.

For business, the package would provide $2.6 billion a year in permanent tax cuts. An option was offered: a new credit against income tax equal to 4% of an employer's share of Social Security payroll taxes (which totaled 5.85% of taxable payrolls); or a 12% investment tax credit for equipment purchases (currently 10%). The option selected would be binding upon a business for a minimum of five years.

The spending on jobs programs would consist of $1.7 billion in fiscal 1977 and $7.6 billion the next year. The public-service jobs programs under federal financing would receive a $715-million boost the first year and $3.39 billion the following. The goal was to expand the program from the current level of 310,000 jobs to 600,000 by Sept. 30 and to 725,000 by 1978.

President Carter told Congress Jan. 31 that his economic stimulation program "will not aggravate current levels of inflation in any significant way."

One of his economic proposals, for a credit against payroll taxes, Carter said, would tend to reduce labor costs and thus "help hold prices down." The credit against income taxes, equal to 4% of payroll taxes, was proposed as an option for businesses. They could take that or an additional 2% investment tax credit.

Carter visited employes of the Treasury Department and Housing and Urban Development Department Feb. 10. At HUD, Carter disclosed that part of his tax-revision plan would be to replace the existing $750 personal exemption and $35-per-person credit with a standard credit in the range of $240–$250 per person. The change would have an effect of raising taxes on persons in the upper income brackets and lowering taxes on those in the lower and middle brackets.

Economic stimulus plan debated. President Carter's two-year $31.2-billion plan of tax reduction and economic stimulus was the subject of congressional hearing in late January and early February.

Some congressmen urged a phasing out of the proposed tax rebates for persons in the higher income brackets. A number of Democrats argued that a greater share of the stimulus should come in the form of federal spending on job-creating projects.

Most Republicans expressed the view that permanent, rather than one-time, tax cuts would give the best chance for economic growth. The harsh winter of 1976–77 also entered into the debate, with some businessmen saying that economic losses inflicted by the cold had persuaded them to favor federal economic stimulus.

The chief spokesmen for the Administration were W. Michael Blumenthal, secretary of the Treasury; Bert Lance, director of the Office of Management and Budget, and Charles L. Schultze, chairman of the Council of Economic Advisers. Starting Jan. 27, one or more of them had testified before various congressional committees, including the Budget committees of both chambers, the House Ways and Means Committee and the Joint Economic Committee.

Among the viewpoints expressed:

Rep. Al Ullman (D, Ore.), chairman of the House Ways and Means Committee, Feb. 1 urged that the proposed tax credit for businesses be limited to an "employment tax credit" for businesses adding to their 1976 payrolls. The credit would partially offset the cost of hiring new workers. The idea had the support of the ranking Republican on the Ways and Means panel, Rep. Barber B. Conable Jr. (R, N.Y.).

An AFL-CIO spokesman Feb. 1 told the House Public Works Committee that the funding proposed by Carter for public works—$4 billion—was "too little" and should instead be $10 billion. (Commerce Secretary Juanita Kreps Feb. 3 said the public works funds should go only to areas suffering most from the recession. She specifically criticized an existing funding formula that would allow 30% of the public works money to go to communities with unemployment less than the national average.) An AFL-CIO economist said Feb. 4 that all economic stimulus should be concentrated in increased federal spending on public works, housing and public service jobs, with no stimulus in the form of tax cuts or rebates.

Republican senators Feb. 2 announced an alternative stimulus plan with an overall projected cost of $26.2 billion over two years. Among the features of the plan, which was approved by the 38 GOP senators in caucus, were: a tax credit for employers who hired persons jobless for six months or longer; a program for training and employing young persons; a permanent tax cut for small businesses; new or increased tax exemptions for dividends and earnings on savings accounts; a permanent reduction in personal income tax covering the first $18,000 of adjusted gross income (the average reduction would be about 7.5%, but there would be a graduated scale giving proportionately larger tax cuts to low-income persons). The GOP senators said 1.8 million to 2.3 million new jobs would be created by their plan.

Federal Reserve Board Chairman Arthur Burns told the House Banking Committee Feb. 3 that Carter's stimulus plan was not required at present because "the economy is improving on its own." Burns particularly criticized Carter's proposed tax rebates, which Burns said would have "a transitory effect on retail trade" but would not stimulate business investment leading to long-term growth. However, Burns praised Carter for having "put together a fiscal package smaller and more prudent than many had urged upon him." Burns said he did not "quarrel" with the Administration's proposed increases in public works spending, public service employment and countercyclical aid to hard-hit localities, nor with the proposed permanent tax cut for lower- and middle-income taxpayers. Speaking in response to fears that the Federal Reserve Board might implement monetary policies that would undercut the stimulative effort, Burns promised that "the monetary growth rates we have projected will be sufficient to finance significantly faster [economic] growth rates."

A number of Democrats on the House Ways and Means panel wanted to alter the proposed tax rebate scheme from an across-the-board plan benefiting all taxpayers to a plan favoring low- and middle-income taxpayers, according to the Feb. 3 Washington Post. The revised rebate would not go to upper-income taxpayers.

Carter submits budget revisions. President Carter sent Congress Feb. 22 his proposed changes in the fiscal 1978 budget submitted by the Ford Administration in January.

Carter proposed sizeable increases in federal spending and deficits for fiscal years 1977 and 1978.

For fiscal 1977, Carter called for outlays of $417.4 billion, or $6.2 billion more than in the Ford budget. The deficit would be $68 billion, up from Ford's $57.2 billion. In fiscal 1978, the spending would total $459.4 billion, up $19.4 billion from Ford's plan; the deficit would be $57.7 billion, compared to $47 billion in his predecessor's version.

The budget revision incorporated Carter's previously submitted package of $31.2 billion in tax cuts and spending to stimulate the economy.

Carter retained only five of Ford's tax proposals. One was to give state and local governments an option to continue sales of tax-exempt bonds or to receive a subsidy in return for selling taxable bonds.

The other proposals retained would require restaurant owners to pay Social Security taxes on tip income of waiters; authorize the Nuclear Regulatory Commission to collect fees to cover the cost of research on reactor safety and licensing services; levy user charges on federal waterways, and increase the migratory bird-hunting stamp to $10 from $5.

The economic underpinning of the revised budget was similar to that projected by the Ford Administration, although Carter's advisers envisioned faster growth and lower unemployment.

The Carter estimates (Ford estimates in parentheses): "real" growth of gross national product, or the total output of goods and services adjusted for inflation—5.4% in calendar 1977 (5.2%), 5.4% in calendar 1978 (5.1%).

Unemployment rate—7.1% in calendar 1977 (7.3%), 6.3% in calendar 1978 (6.6%). The current rate was 7.3%.

Increase in consumer price index—5.1% in calendar 1977 and 5.4% in calendar 1978, the same as Ford projections.

In his message to Congress, Carter described the fiscal 1978 budget as "still President Ford's budget." His own changes, Carter said, represented "important first steps toward a federal government that is more effective and responsive to our people's needs."

New budget levels cleared. Congress March 3 gave final approval to a budget resolution providing for increased federal spending, decreased tax revenues and a larger federal deficit for fiscal year 1977.

The resolution was binding in that any legislation that promised to cause the government to exceed the spending limit or fall short of the revenue floor would be ruled out of order. A binding resolution for fiscal 1977 had been passed in September 1976. The new resolution, not part of Congress' normal budget-setting process, had been made necessary by President Carter's proposal to stimulate the economy through tax cuts and increased federal spending.

The budget resolution did not specify what shape the tax cuts and spending increases should take. Those matters would be resolved in separate legislation written by committees other than the House and Senate budget panels—the committees with jurisdiction over the budget resolution. However, the figures arrived at in the budget resolution reflected assumptions about specific stimulus programs.

The total for the new spending programs was about $3.7 billion, almost twice what Carter had proposed in stimulative outlays for fiscal 1977. The budget resolution assumed a package of tax cuts totaling $13.8 billion in fiscal 1977, the full amount proposed by Carter.

The resolution passed the Senate by voice vote and the House, 226–173, March 3.

Carter drops tax rebate plan. President Carter said April 14, 1977 that he no longer favored providing a $50 tax rebate for individuals. Carter said he had decided to abandon the rebate—the centerpiece of the fiscal 1977 part of his two-year $31.2-billion stimulus plan—because the economy was showing clear signs of picking up without need of the rebate and because there was danger that the rebate would fuel inflation.

At the same time, Carter withdrew his support for the proposed tax benefits for business that had figured in his stimulus plan. One of the proposals would have raised the investment tax credit available to business; the other would have provided a tax credit calculated against an employer's Social Security payroll taxes.

Although Carter pictured the reversal in policy as primarily a response to altered economic circumstances, it was generally thought that the lack of enthusiasm in Congress for the rebate plan must have weighed in the decision. The House of Representatives had passed a tax bill incorporating the rebate plan (in a form somewhat, but not unacceptably, altered from the original Administration proposal), but the rebate and tax credits faced stiff opposition in the Senate when Carter decided to drop them. Administration officials said they believed the rebate plan could have been pushed through the Senate but that the all-out effort necessary might have weakened the Administration later in pressing other controversial legislation.

In announcing the decision, Carter said he would "strongly oppose" any attempts by Congress to divert the money that would have gone for the rebate into new spending programs. As originally proposed, the rebate would have amounted to $11.4 billion, providing more than two-thirds of the stimulus in the first year of Carter's plan.

Administration officials denied that the decision to abandon the proposed business tax benefits was a political move aimed at defusing consumer resentment at loss of the rebate. Treasury Secretary W. Michael Blumenthal April 14 termed the decision not to go forward with the business tax benefits "proper." However, Blumenthal said that tax benefits for business would "be taken up in the context" of the Administration's tax revision program, scheduled to be announced in the fall.

Carter said the remaining portions of his stimulus package would "guarantee a durable growth" in the economy.

There were various reactions on Capitol Hill to Carter's announcement. Senate Majority Leader Robert Byrd (D, W.Va.) said Carter had made a "wise decision." He said "the justifications that seemed apparent for the rebate last December have less validity at this time." Senate Majority Whip Alan Cranston (D, Calif.) also approved of the President's decision, and Sen. Jacob Javits (R, N.Y.) called the action "prudent and courageous." Senate Budget Committee Chairman Edmund Muskie (D, Me.) was critical of the decision, terming it "a disappointment [and] breach of his promise to the people." House Ways and Means Committee Chairman Al Ullman (D, Ore.) said he might still press for an employment tax credit for businesses, and Senate Finance Committee Chairman Russell Long (D, La.) said Congress should hold "in abeyance," rather than kill entirely, the rebate plan.

Carter made the decision to cancel the rebate the evening of April 13. Blumenthal and Budget Director Bert Lance had been the chief critics in the Administration of the rebates, while Charles Schultze, Chairman of the Council of Economic Advisers, had been their primary supporter. Schultze April 14 said he "fully concur[red]" with Carter's decision, adding, "I don't think any of us are keeping box scores [on whose views prevailed with the President]."

Carter and Administration spokesmen, including Blumenthal had defended the rebates vigorously in public up until Carter finally made the decision to drop them. Blumenthal, in an April 13 speech to the National Press Club, had supported the rebates. Earlier, on April 7, Carter had stressed the "need for continuing emphasis" on passage of his stimulus plan, including the rebates. However, Carter had resisted suggestions that he might win support in Congress for the rebates by dropping his opposition to a number of water projects.

(The rebate had been attacked sharply in Congress. A number of legislators supporting the rebate while it was still an Administration objective had indicated they were doing so chiefly out of loyalty to the Administration, not because they were convinced of the wisdom of rebates.)

Reaction of business community—The nation's business community was surprised and pleased by President Carter's decision to drop his proposal for a $50 tax rebate. Businessmen expressed some regret at Carter's decision also to withdraw his proposed increase in the investment tax credit, but most agreed that political factors made the tax-credit decision inevitable.

For many persons in the financial and business communities, the rebate had become a symbol of economic stimulus that was unnecessary and possibly inflationary.

The rebate proposal had been designed early in the Administration when the economy appeared to have run out of steam and the recovery from the recession of 1974-75 faced new threats because of severe winter weather and fuel shortages.

The rebate was intended as an immediate stimulus for demand, one that was aimed primarily at boosting consumer spending. When the economy rebounded quickly and strongly from the winter doldrums, opposition began to develop against the rebate. Many persons in the financial and business communities argued that inflation posed a greater threat to the economy than did a slowdown.

When the trend toward renewed economic growth was established, two of Carter's closest economic advisers began pressing the President to reassess the rebate's economic and political implications. Both men—Bert Lance, director of the Office of Management and Budget, and Treasury Secretary W. Michael Blumenthal—also were anxious to create a good relationship between the Administration and the business community.

Several analysts believed that an upsurge in retail sales provided the final proof that consumer spending was rebounding strongly without the aid of a rebate boost. (Retail sales, which had declined 2.1% in January from the previous month, surged 2.7% in February and rose 2.4% in March.)

Carter's decision to drop the rebate appeared to produce the desired psychological effect. Many bankers and businessmen questioned by the major newspapers said the President's abandonment of the rebate proposal had increased their confidence in Carter. "It illustrates that the man is flexible, that he's willing to change when conditions change," said Norman Robertson of Pittsburgh's Mellon Bank.

The financial community responded to the White House announcement with an overwhelming vote of approval. Stock prices, which had been in sharp decline since the beginning of the year, rose strongly April 14 on heavy trading. On the New York Stock Exchange April 4, the Dow Jones industrial average had had fallen to a 1977 low of 915.56, down almost 90 points, or 9%, from the year-end high. Carter's announcement touched off a rally April 14 that lifted the Dow to 947 at the close, bringing the cumulative gain over five sessions to nearly 32 points.

The new strength in the stock market stemmed from a perception that inflationary pressures had lessened and also from a drop in interest rates. The interest-rate decline was linked to the President's decision to drop his rebate proposal, which analysts had estimated would cost the Treasury more than $10 billion in lost revenues.

Elimination of the rebate plan, the analysts said, would mean that the government would not have to borrow as heavily in the credit markets to finance the federal deficit. This easing of credit conditions April 14 sent bond prices up and interest rates down.

The President's action also had a positive effect on trading in the dollar on foreign exchange markets. The dollar, which had been declining recently as inflation heated up, April 14 halted its slide against major European currencies.

National debt to be reduced—In a later announcement April 27, the Treasury Department said it would pay back $2 billion of the $668.9-billion national debt during the third fiscal quarter.

Officials said they would be able to reduce the debt because President Carter's withdrawal of the proposed $50 tax rebate had left the government with an unexpected "cash surplus." Instead of borrowing heavily to cover the shortfall between reduced tax revenues and rising expenditures, the Treasury would be able to redeem some of its securities.

Anti-inflation program outlined. President Carter April 15 outlined a coor-

dinated program of attack against "the very difficult and pernicious problem of inflation." His goal was to reduce the annual inflation rate by two percentage points to a level of about 4% by the end of 1979.

The President outlined the program at a news conference and statement.

The President stressed that steady business expansion and "discipline" over the growth of federal spending were keys to the overall anti-inflationary effort. He reiterated his commitment to reduce the huge federal deficits and achieve a balanced budget by fiscal year 1981.

Carter said "inadequate tax revenues from a stagnant economy—not legitimate federal spending programs—are the principal source of the deficits. We have large budget deficits today because recovery from the worst recession in 40 years is still incomplete. As the recovery proceeds, the deficits must shrink and eventually disappear. The combined total of private and public demands on the economy must not be allowed to exceed our productive capacity, or inflation will surely be rekindled."

Responding to a query about his withdrawal of the $50 tax rebate, Carter said he would veto the Republican alternative of an across-the-board permanent tax cut. Such an approach, he said, would impose a barrier to comprehensive tax reform and would be "permanently inflationary."

Carter stresses fiscal restraint. Congressional Democratic leaders were told by President Carter May 2 that a balanced budget by 1981 was his highest priority.

The primary message was that federal spending must be restrained and new programs planned in the context of that restraint. Deferral of costly new social programs during that period was not ruled out.

Also attending the meeting, which was held at the White House, were members of the Cabinet, the President's chief economic advisers and Federal Reserve Board Chairman Arthur Burns.

There were reports afterward of

concern among the Democratic leaders that Carter's message sounded conservative enough to be Republican. At a follow-up meeting next day, the congressional contingent reportedly spoke up for a cause more traditionally tied to the Democrats—economic stimulus to reduce the nation's high unemployment, along with its contingent costs and loss of tax revenue.

Stimulus tax cuts enacted. Congress May 16, 1977 passed a bill providing a package of tax cuts proposed by Carter as a stimulus to the economy. The bill did not include the $50-a-person tax rebate, which the President had dropped from his plan. Carter signed the Tax Reduction & Simplification Act of 1977 May 23.

Both chambers passed the bill May 16, the House of Representatives by 383–2, and the Senate by voice vote.

Among the major provisions:

—Flat standard deductions were set to take effect with the 1977 tax year. For single persons, the deduction was set at $2,200 (replacing the standard deduction that ranged from $1,700 to $2,400 under existing law) and for joint returns, the deduction was put at $3,200 (replacing a deduction that ranged from $2,100 to $2,800).

—The general tax credit of $35 per person, or 2% of the first $9,000 of taxable income, was extended through 1978. The $35 credit also was made available for age and blindness exemptions.

—The earned income credit for low-income persons was extended through 1978.

—The corporate tax rate reductions enacted in 1975 were extended through 1978. Under those rates, corporations paid 20% taxes on their first $25,000 of taxable income, 22% taxes on the next $25,000, and 48% on taxable income over $50,000.

—An employment tax credit of $2,100 for each new worker hired was provided for businesses in 1977 and 1978. (A business first had to achieve a "normal" payroll expansion of 2% over the previous year before it was eligible for the tax credit. The maximum an employer could claim in employment credits in one year was $100,000.) The provision was opposed by President Carter, who had withdrawn his support for several proposed tax breaks for businesses at the same time he dropped his $50 rebate plan.

The employment tax credit had been added by the House, which had passed its initial version of the bill by 232–131 vote March 8. This credit replaced a provision, eliminated by the House, that would have let businesses to choose instead a 2% increase in the investment tax credit.

The elimination of the investment tax credit option for businesses was vigorously opposed by the Administration. Treasury Secretary W. Michael Blumenthal said March 8 that the investment credit was "in itself important in achieving more investment, but the psychological impact on investment decisions [in private industry] is probably still more important."

The bill delayed for one year (to the tax year beginning Jan. 1, 1977) the effective date of a number of provisions of the 1976 tax revision act. In consequence, various items—among them, sick pay, income earned abroad, and oil and gas producers' deductions for intangible drilling costs—would be treated under the (usually more generous) tax code provisions that predated the 1976 act.

The bill extended through fiscal 1978 a program of countercyclical aid to state and local governments. The aid was tied to the national unemployment rate, with a certain amount of funds to be released quarterly if the jobless rate were 6%, and additional aid provided for each one-tenth of a percentage point increment above 6%. Up to $1 billion in additional countercyclical aid was authorized for fiscal 1977, and up to $2.25 billion for fiscal 1978.

The bill also authorized an additional $435 million in each of fiscal years 1978 and 1979 for employment and support services for welfare recipients.

The bill provided an estimated overall reduction in tax payments of $34 billion for the three years fiscal 1977–79. In fiscal 1977, the bill's tax cuts came to an estimated $2.6 billion. In fiscal 1978 the figure was $17.75 billion, and in fiscal 1979 it was $13.8 billion.

Carter asks Social Security tax hike.
The President told Congress May 9, 1977 that swift action was needed to "restore the financial integrity of the Social Security system." He urged a substantial increase in the Social Security taxes paid by employers, coupled with a lesser increase in employe tax contributions. Carter also proposed on an experimental basis that general tax revenues be used to shore up the Social Security system in times of high unemployment.

If no action were taken, Carter cautioned, the Disability Trust Fund would be exhausted in 1979 and the Old Age and Survivors Insurance Trust Fund would "run out in 1983."

The Social Security Administration currently paid benefits to more than 33 million persons—retired and disabled workers and their dependents and survivors. Payroll taxes on employed (and self-employed) persons were supposed to finance those benefits: currently, 5.85% of an employe's earnings up to a certain amount (the wage base, currently set at $16,500) went to Social Security, and employers contributed an equal share. (The wage base and the tax rate were scheduled to rise under current law.) In the early decades of the Social Security system, the payroll tax had more than covered the pay-out in benefits, providing a surplus. Since 1975, benefits had exceeded payroll taxes.

High inflation (because benefits were increased to offset price rises) and unemployment (reducing the amount of payroll taxes going into the system) had combined to cause the recent deficits in the system. Also, the number of persons claiming disability benefits had far exceeded expectations.

Other factors threatened the long-term fiscal health of the system. One was a formula, enacted in 1972, for calculating benefits. The formula tied future benefits to increases in prices and wages, and was considered potentially overly generous. The second factor was related to population trends. If those trends continued in their present direction, the ratio of persons drawing Social Security benefits to those working would increase considerably by the next century.

Carter's primary proposal for raising Social Security revenues concerned the wage base. For employers, the amount of salaries on which taxes would be assessed would increase to $23,400 in 1979 and $37,500 in 1980. After 1980, employers would pay taxes on the entire salary (in effect, eliminating the wage-base ceiling for employers). Carter also called for increases in the wage base on which employes paid taxes, but the increases would not be so sharp as for employers, nor would the ceiling on the wage base be eliminated. The Carter plan sought increases in the employe wage base of $600 in 1979, 1981, 1983 and 1985, in addition to the increases already mandated by current law.

Besides using revenue from increased wage bases, Carter proposed to divert on a trial basis, "only through 1982," general Treasury funds into the Social Security system. Treasury funds would become available, under Carter's proposal, only if the national unemployment rate exceeded 6% and Social Security financing were inadequate. If those conditions were met, general Treasury funds would be contributed to the Social Security system equal to what would have been the Social Security taxes on those unemployed workers in excess of 6% of the workforce. The general Treasury transfers, the Administration proposed, would be retroactive to 1975.

Carter also proposed raising the tax rate on self-employed persons to 7.5% from 7%.

The Administration estimated the wage base revisions would cost employers an additional $30 billion from 1979 through 1982, while employe tax payments for the same period would be $4 billion more than under current law. An increase in the wage base, the Administration argued, was preferable to increasing the tax rate, since it would not hurt low- and middle-income workers. The Administration also contended that employers would fare better under the proposals than with a simple increase in the tax rate because the use of general Treasury funds would reduce the amount of extra funds that would have to be generated by the Social Security taxes.

For the long-term problems facing the Social Security system, Carter urged that the 1972 formula for calculating benefits be revised. In addition, a one percentage point hike in the tax rate, scheduled to take effect in 2011, should be moved up to 1990, Carter said.

There was a mixed response to the Carter proposals in Congress, with opinion sharply divided, in particular on the question of the use of general Treasury funds. George Meany, president of the AFL-CIO, praised Carter's plan. An early response from business interests, voiced by a spokesman for the U.S. Chamber of Commerce, was critical of the plan's reliance on general revenue funds and the proposed wage-base increases for employers.

Tax Policy & U.S. Economic Health

Carter plans 1978 tax cuts. President Carter told reporters Oct. 13, 1977 that he expected tax reductions to be effected in 1978 but that the timing would depend on the state of the economy.

The major unresolved question, he said, "is how much impact this year's stimulus package is going to have in a beneficial way to keep our economy moving."

In any event, any tax reductions "will be tied intimately with an overall tax reform package," he said. Tax reform was "long overdue."

Carter then told reporters Oct. 27 that he would not submit his planned tax-reform proposals to Congress until legislative action was completed on two other major measures—energy conservation and financing of the Social Security system. Both programs involved complex tax proposals, Carter noted.

Carter said another factor in his decision to delay sending the tax-revision program to Congress was uncertainty about the state of the economy. "By the end of the year," Carter said, the Administration would have more information on "how much of our tax reform proposals should be devoted to stimulating the economy."

The delay also would allow the tax package to be "carefully integrated" with the fiscal 1979 budget, which would be submitted to Congress in January 1978, Carter added.

(In questioning afterward, Carter was asked whether he might give higher priority to tax cuts that would stimulate consumer spending rather than seek action on broad overall reform. Carter replied, "No," and then outlined the shape his tax reform proposals would take. The package would have "three basic elements. One is improved equity, which means more progressivity and an end to many of the unnecessary tax incentives and loopholes. Second, to create investment capital. And third, greatly to simplify the entire tax structure.")

There had been considerable criticism in recent weeks by business leaders and private economists that the Administration lacked a coherent economic policy. Arthur Burns, chairman of the Federal Reserve Board, had joined in the criticism Oct. 26. He called for a "bold tax policy" that would restore business confidence and spur investment.

Burns also said that the Administration's flurry of legislative proposals for overhaul of taxes, welfare reform, energy and the Social Security system had made it difficult for business to evaluate possible policy changes and incorporate them in their future plans.

In response to questions at the press conference, Carter said he shared Burns's concern "that we have created uncertainty in the business community by our major proposals," but he said Burns's criticism represented "just honest differences of opinions."

Carter said, "I think we had delayed too long the addressing of the energy crisis, and this particularly, in these weeks when there is a time of uncertainty, creates a dampening effect on the economy and on the attitude of businessmen toward future investments. But the alternative was to ignore the energy problem for months and perhaps years. The same thing applies to welfare reform. The same thing applies to tax reform."

Carter said at his news conference Nov. 30 that "there will be substantial tax reductions" in 1978 "and combined with that will be an adequate proposal for tax reform."

He did not want to separate tax reductions from tax reform, he said. "They will be together." But, he added:

"Some of the more controversial items on tax reform. . . ,that would be very time consuming and have very little monetary significance, might be delayed until later on, because I feel that it's necessary to expedite the effectiveness of substantial tax reduction."

"I'm committed, and the Democratic Congressional leaders, at least, are committed," he stressed, "to substantial tax reduction in 1978, as soon as we can put it through."

Carter referred to 1977 as the year when major legislation would be passed, "hopefully," to increase Social Security taxes and energy taxes.

Because of their "high impact on the tax structure," Carter said in reference to the pending legislation, the Administration could not work out final details of its 1978 tax program until it knew what would be done on energy and Social Security taxes.

Carter plans $25-billion tax cut. President Carter's decision to seek a $25-billion tax cut in 1978 was made known by Administration officials Dec. 20, 1977.

Most of the reduction—about $23 billion -would come from income-tax cuts. Of that, $16 billion to $17 billion was slated for individuals, $6 billion to $7 billion for business. The remaining tax reductions would come from excise and employer payroll tax cuts.

Some tax reform proposals were built into the tax package, which would be presented to Congress early in 1978, but they were of a modest scale.

Carter said he did not plan to make at that time some controversial reform proposals that had been under consideration by the Administration, such as reducing the special tax breaks for capital gains.

The proposed program also would feature specific measures to help restrain inflation.

The tax cut planned for individuals would be across-the-board. The lowest tax rate would drop to 12% of income from 14% and the highest rate would drop to 68% from 70%.

Other changes called for replacing the existing $750 personal exemption and the $35-per-person credit with a personal credit of $240 or $250. (Analysts said this would be more advantageous to lower-income persons.)

While everyone's taxes would be reduced, a substantial portion of the reductions would benefit persons earning up to $20,000 annually.

A four percentage point reduction was planned in the corporate income tax rate, to a 44% level. The existing 48% rate would drop to 45% on Oct. 1, 1978. The 44% rate would become effective on Jan. 1, 1980.

As a special boon to small businesses, their tax rate on the first $25,000 of income would be reduced to 18% from 20%, and the rate on the second $25,000 of income would be reduced to 20% from 22%. (Income above $50,000 was subject to the maximum corporate rate.)

Another major tax break for business was planned on the investment tax credit. The President proposed that the existing 10% level be made permanent, that the credit be allowed to offset up to 90% of a company's taxes and that it be allowed for "structures."

As the law stood, the investment tax credit was scheduled to drop to 7% at the end of 1980, and the credit could be applied to offset only 50% of a firm's taxes above $25,000. The existing credit also covered only machinery and equipment purchases, not structures.

To help curb inflation, the President planned to propose elimination of the 5% excise tax on telephone bills. Under existing law, the tax was scheduled to drop to 4% on Jan. 1, 1978 and not to be phased out until Jan. 1, 1982.

A reduction in the tax paid by employers to finance the federal unemployment insurance trust fund to .5% of taxable payroll from .7% was another anti-inflationary item in the tax package.

The reform elements of the package included:

■ A phase-out over three years of the tax breaks granted domestic international sales corporations, or DISCs. Under DISC treatment, companies were allowed to consolidate all their income from exports and to defer taxes on part of that income.

■ To phase out or limit tax breaks on income earned by foreign subsidiaries of American corporations. Under existing law, the tax was due only when the income was repatriated. An end to this tax deferral was one of the President's proposals.

■ To halve—to 50%—the deduction permitted for business lunches.

■ To eliminate the deduction allowed companies for the cost of country club memberships related to their business.

Former President Gerald Ford called Dec. 20 for a $68-billion tax reduction by 1981.

Ford recommended that middle-income families receive a major portion of the tax relief, and that business also receive "a healthy proportion."

The economy was "stumbling along" and public confidence in the future was "dangerously fragile," Ford said. Restoration of a strong, growing economy should be a top priority of the government, he added.

Ford made the remarks in a speech in Washington to the American Enterprise Institute for Public Policy Research. Ford had conferred with President Carter earlier in the day.

Carter, at his first press conference of 1978, was asked Jan. 12 about his tax-cut plans in view of signs that the economy was improving.

Carter said the tax proposal he intended to make to Congress would have an effective date of Oct. 1, when it was expected there would be "a need to sustain the economic growth" anticipated for the first two quarters of the year.

"We're not trying to deal with an economy that's tottering or on the verge of collapse or in any danger," he said. "We have basically a very strong national economy."

Poll finds economic problems are top worries. Economic concerns over making ends meet were American families' most frequent cause for worry, according to a Gallup poll reported Aug. 10, 1977.

When more than 1,500 persons were asked to name the "most important problem" facing their family, the responses they most often gave were the high cost of living, inflation, taxes and unemployment, followed by illness, educating children and retirement plans. The energy shortage ranked eighth.

Carter's '78 Messages Reaffirm Tax Plans

Focus Is on Economy. "Militarily, politically, economically and in spirit, the state of the union is sound," President Carter said in his first State of the Union Message, which he delivered over national television Jan. 19, 1978.

Carter said he would seek a $25-billion tax cut: $17 billion in income tax reductions for individuals, a $2-billion cut in excise taxes and cuts in the corporate tax rate, as well as improvements in the investment tax credit for business.

The budget deficit for fiscal 1979, Carter said, would be "only slightly less than this year." Carter reiterated his commitment to balancing the federal budget, but he said that for fiscal 1979 the priority must be "to reduce the burden on taxpayers and provide more jobs for our people."

Carter said his economic policy "is working because it's simple, balanced and fair." He said it was based on these four principles:

First, the economy must keep on expanding to produce new jobs and better income, which our people need. The fruits of growth must be widely shared, more jobs must be made available to those who have been bypassed until now. And the tax system must be made fairer and simpler.

Secondly, private business and not the government must lead the expansion in the future.

Third, we must lower the rate of inflation and keep it down. Inflation slows economic growth, and it's the most cruel to the poor and also to the elderly and others who live on fixed incomes.

And fourth, we must contribute to the strength of the world economy. I will announce detailed proposals for improving our tax system later this week.

We can make our tax laws fairer. We can make them simpler and easier to understand and at the same time we can and we will reduce the tax burden on American citizens by $25 billion.

The tax reforms and the tax reduction go together. Only with the long overdue reforms will the full tax cut be advisable.

Almost $17 billion in income tax cuts will go to individuals. Ninety per cent of all American taxpayers will see their taxes go down. For a typical family of four this means an annual savings of more than $250 a year, or a tax reduction of about 20%. A further $2-billion cut in excise taxes will give more relief and also contribute directly to lowering the rate of inflation.

And we will also provide strong additional incentives for business investment and growth through substantial cuts in the corporate tax rate and improvement in the investment tax credit.

Now these tax proposals will increase opportunity everywhere in the nation, but additional jobs for the disadvantaged deserve special attention.

Economic Message: *Price-Wage Restraint.* An Economic Message to Congress from President Carter Jan. 20 called for voluntary restraint by business and labor in their price and wage decisions.

The President said that "every effort" should be made to reduce the rate of wage and price increases in 1978 to below the average rate of the past two years.

The President stressed that he was working to reduce the federal deficit and balance the budget "as soon as the strength of the economy allows." He cautioned that the goal to balance the budget by 1981 might have to be "deferred."

"With unusually strong growth in the private economy," he said, a balanced federal budget would be needed. "In an economy growing less strongly. however, balancing the budget by 1981 would be possible only by forgoing tax reductions needed to reach our goal of high employment. In those circumstances, the date for reaching the goal of budget balance would have to be deferred."

Carter stressed that the tax reduction he was proposing for 1978 had been designed "to maintain economic growth at a steady pace" by taking into account "the effects of the growing tax burden and of other factors at work in the economy."

Large increases in the Social Security tax had been enacted in 1977 and a further rise in the tax burden was anticipated from energy legislation pending in Congress. Principal among the "other" factors at work was inflation with its bite on income and its push on income into higher tax brackets.

The possibility of further tax cuts in the future was not ruled out.

"If strong expansion is to be maintained in the face of these major drains on the economy," Carter said, "additional tax reductions may be necessary beyond those I have proposed for 1979. But we will be better able to judge this question in a year or two, and we should not prejudge it now."

Carter said in his economic message:

I propose to rely principally upon growth in the private sector of the economy to reduce unemployment and raise incomes. Special Federal efforts will, of course, be necessary to deal with such problems as structural unemployment, but tax reductions will be the primary means by which Federal budget policy will promote growth. Careful management of budget outlays and a growing economy should permit substantial reductions in the years ahead. Tax reductions will be needed to strengthen consumer purchasing power and expand consumer markets. Stable growth in markets, together with added tax incentives for business, will lead to rising business investment and growing productivity.

As inflation and real economic growth raise the incomes of most Americans, they are pushed into higher income tax brackets. The tax burden on individuals is raised just as if higher rates had been enacted. The payroll taxes levied on workers and business firms for social security and unemployment insurance will also increase substantially over the years ahead. These are very large increases, but they are needed to keep our social security and unemployment insurance systems soundly financed.

Between 1977 and 1979, taxes on businesses and individuals will rise very sharply as a result of these several factors. Even though our economy is basically healthy, this increasingly heavy tax burden would exert a mounting drag on economic growth. It must, therefore, be counteracted by tax reductions. The magnitude and timing of the reductions should be designed to maintain economic growth at a steady pace, taking into account the effects both of the growing tax burden and of other factors at work in the economy.

Consistent with this strategy, I am proposing a $25 billion program of net tax reductions accompanied by substantial tax reforms.

Individual income taxes will be reduced primarily through across-the-board reductions in personal tax rates, with special emphasis on low- and middle-income taxpayers. Personal taxs also will be simplified by my proposal to replace the existing personal exemption and credit with a tax credit of $240 for each person in the taxpayer's family.

There also will be important reforms that will improve the individual income tax system and raise substantial revenues, enabling me to recommend larger personal tax reductions.

Overall, I am proposing personal tax reductions of $24 billion, offset by $7 billion in tax reforms. These tax cuts, which will take effect next October 1, will significantly improve the progressivity of the tax system. The typical four-person family with $15,000 in income will receive a tax cut of $258—or more than 19 percent. As a result of the changes I am recommending, filling out tax returns will be simpler for many people.

Individuals also will benefit from reductions I have proposed in the Federal excise tax on telephone bills, and in the Federal payroll tax for unemployment insurance. These two proposals will add about $2 billion to consumers' purchasing power that will be realized principally through lower prices.

Business taxes will be reduced by more than $8 billion in 1979 under my tax program, offset partially by more than $2 billion in business tax reforms for a net tax reduction of nearly $6 billion. I have recommended that the overall corporate tax rate be reduced on October 1 from the current 48 percent to 45 percent, and be cut further to 44 percent in 1980. I also recommend that the existing 10-percent investment tax credit be made permanent, and that the benefits of this credit be extended to investments in industrial and utility structures. My proposal will enable businesses to use the investment tax credit to offset up to 90 percent of their Federal tax liability, compared with the 50-percent limit now imposed.

Important new tax reforms also will affect business. I am, for example, proposing to reduce the deductibility of a large class of business entertainment expenses. I have also proposed changes in the tax status of international business transactions that are of significant cost to taxpayers but that benefit the public insufficiently.

Because tax reform measures will raise $9 billion in revenue, it has been possible for me to recommend $34 billion in overall tax reductions while keeping the net loss revenues to $25 billion, the level I believe is appropriate given the state of our economy and the size of the budget deficit.

These proposals do not include any adjustment to take account of congressional action on my energy proposals. I proposed last April that the Congress pass a wellhead tax and rebate the proceeds of that tax directly to the American people. This is the best course to follow because it protects the real incomes of consumers and avoids a new source of fiscal drag. If the final energy bill includes a full rebate of the net proceeds of the wellhead tax, no further action on my part will be necessary. However, if the final bill allows for a rebate only for 1978—as provided in the House version—I will send a supplemental message to the Congress recommending that the individual tax reduction I am now proposing be increased by the amount of the net proceeds of the wellhead tax.

These tax reductions are essential to healthy economic recovery during 1978 and 1979. Prospects for continuation of that recovery in the near term are favorable. Consumers have been spending freely, and many other economic indicators recently have been moving up strongly. Without the tax reductions I have proposed, however, the longer-term prospects for economic growth would become increasingly poor. Because of the fiscal drag imposed by rising payroll taxes and inflation, economic growth would slow substantially in late 1978, and fall to about 3½ percent in 1979. The unemployment rate would stop declining and might begin to rise again, and the growth of investment outlays for new plant and equipment would slow significantly.

With the reductions in taxes I have proposed, on the other hand, the economy should grow by 4½ to 5 percent in both 1978 and 1979. Nearly one million new jobs would be created. Unemployment would therefore continue to fall and by late 1979 should be down to

FEDERAL GOVERNMENT RECEIPTS & EXPENDITURES, 1948-77

Year	Billions of dollars [1] Receipts	Expenditures	Surplus or deficit (—)	Billions of constant 1972 dollars [2] Receipts	Expenditures	Surplus or deficit (—)
1948	43.2	34.9	8.3	81.3	65.6	15.6
1949	38.7	41.3	-2.6	73.6	78.6	-5.0
1950	50.0	40.8	9.2	93.2	76.1	17.1
1951	64.2	57.7	6.5	112.2	100.8	11.3
1952	67.3	71.0	-3.7	116.0	122.5	-6.4
1953	70.0	77.1	-7.0	118.9	130.9	-12.0
1954	63.7	69.7	-6.0	106.7	116.8	-10.1
1955	72.5	68.1	4.4	118.9	111.7	7.2
1956	77.9	71.9	6.0	123.9	114.3	9.6
1957	81.9	79.6	2.2	125.9	122.4	3.5
1958	78.6	88.9	-10.2	119.0	134.6	-15.5
1959	89.8	90.9	-1.1	133.0	134.7	-1.6
1960	96.1	93.1	3.0	140.0	135.5	4.4
1961	98.0	101.9	-3.8	141.5	147.1	-5.6
1962	106.1	110.4	-4.2	150.5	156.5	-6.0
1963	111.4	114.1	.2	159.8	159.4	.3
1964	114.9	118.1	-3.2	158.0	162.5	-4.4
1965	124.3	123.8	.5	167.3	166.5	.7
1966	141.8	143.6	-1.7	184.7	187.1	-2.3
1967	150.4	163.6	-13.1	190.4	207.1	-16.6
1968	174.7	180.5	-5.8	211.6	218.6	-7.0
1969	196.9	188.4	8.5	217.1	217.3	-.8
1970	192.0	204.1	-12.1	210.2	223.5	-9.8
1971	198.6	220.6	-21.9	206.8	229.7	-13.3
1972	227.4	244.7	-17.2	229.7	244.7	-22.8
1973	258.2	264.9	-6.7	227.4	250.4	-17.2
1974	288.6	299.3	-10.5	224.1	258.0	-6.3
1975	286.2	356.9	-70.5	248.7	280.6	-9.2
1976	331.4	385.2	-53.8	225.1	280.6	-55.5
1977	374.4	422.5	-48.1	247.7	288.0	-40.2
1978	----	----	-59.3	264.4	298.4	-34.0

[1] Source: Department of Commerce, Bureau of Economic Analysis.
[2] Calculations by CRS.

around 5½ to 6 percent. Capacity utilization and after-tax business profits would both improve, and thus the rate of investment in new plants and equipment should increase significantly.

Success in keeping a firm rein on spending will permit further tax reductions in years to come. Our ability to foresee the future course of the economy is not good enough, however, to enable us to know when additional reductions will be needed or how large they should be. It would therefore be imprudent to plan specific policy measures now for more than the current and the next fiscal year. But I will make recommendations for budget and tax policies for 1980 and beyond that are in keeping with our objectives of steady growth in the economy, more stable prices, and principal reliance on the private sector to achieve economic expansion.

Tax-cut Plan Sent to Congress. President Carter submitted to Congress Jan. 21 his plans for a net $25-million tax reduction and for a "fairer and simpler" tax system.

The President said his plan would lower taxes for individuals with incomes of less than $100,000 and raise them for those earning higher incomes. Almost all, 94%, of the reduction would go to those earning $30,000 or less a year.

For individuals and businesses, the taxes would be reduced a total of $33.9 billion. Other changes would increase taxes on individuals and businesses by $9.4 billion for a net reduction of $24.5 billion.

$500.2 billion budget. President Carter Jan. 23, 1978 sent Congress a half-trillion-dollar fiscal 1979 budget that he described as "restrained."

Federal outlays of $500.2 billion were proposed. Revenues were estimated at $439.6 billion, and a deficit of $60.6 billion was anticipated.

This was close to the $61.8-billion deficit expected for fiscal 1978 from outlays of $462.2 billion and revenues of $400.4 billion.

Much of the projected 8% rise of $38 billion in spending between fiscal 1978 and

1979 came from so-called uncontrollable items already built into the budget, such as increased interest on the national debt and the massive Social Security program. The Social Security program alone represented more than one-fifth of the federal budget, with costs of $103.7 billion.

The net increase in spending attributed to Carter totaled only $7.8 billion, or only 1.6% more than the year before.

Aside from a $25-billion net tax reduction sought by the Administration, there were no large new initiatives in the Carter budget.

GOP Attacks Carter's Budget. House Republican leaders assailed President Carter's new budget Jan. 31 as "a fiscal time bomb set to explode with destructive inflationary force in the years ahead."

"Though wrapped in the tissue of conservative rhetoric," the GOP leaders said, "this allegedly restrained budget will swell our deficit far above its present level, like rice in boiling water."

The Republicans contended that the "real" deficit in the new budget would more likely be closer to $100 billion than the $60.6 billion forecast by Carter.

The Republicans issuing the statement were House Minority Leader John Rhodes (Ariz.); Rep. Barber Conable (N.Y.), ranking minority member of the Ways and Means Committee, and Rep. Delbert Latta (Ohio), ranking Republican on the House Budget Committee.

Rhodes had also appeared in a TV broadcast Jan. 26 as the GOP response to Carter's State of the Union Message.

Rhodes, who offered an alternative to Carter's proposed tax reduction, said that the President's plan "doesn't even really take care of the built-in inflators we have in the tax system." It was a "good start, but no more than that," Rhodes said.

House Republicans, he said, preferred a 30% across-the-board tax cut of 10% a year for three years. This, he said, would aid in capital formation and "give the stimulus that is required to actually make the investments that are necessary to provide the jobs that our economy needs."

Program watered down? Rep. Andrew Maguire (D, N.J.) charged in a statement inserted in the Congressional Record April 24, 1978 that the 1978 tax program Carter had sent to Congress ignored or weakened many of the "ambitious tax reform proposals" recommended to him by the Treasury Department in September 1977. He offered this "summary of major contrasts" between the 1977 and 1978 tax proposals:

I. MARRIAGE TAX PENALTY REDUCTION

Problem: Present law provides a substantial disincentive for marriage, encouraging people to "live together." This is due to higher tax rates for joint income where both partners work, a lower combined zero bracket amount (standard deduction) for couples, and the general tax credit which is half as large for a couple as for two single people. The IRS believes the vast majority of two

BUDGET RECEIPTS

(in billions of dollars)	1977 Actual	1978 Estimate	1979 Without Carter Changes	1979 Carter Proposals
Individual Income Taxes	156.7	178.8	214.0	190.1
Corporation Income Taxes	54.9	58.9	68.8	62.5
Social Insurance Taxes and Contributions	108.7	124.1	142.5	141.9
Excise Taxes	17.6	20.2	18.7	25.5
Other	19.0	18.4	19.8	19.6
Total Receipts	**356.9**	**400.4**	**463.8**	**439.6**

The Federal Budget Dollar

(Proposed by President Carter)

Where it comes from:

Individual income taxes .... 38¢
Social insurance receipts .... 28¢
Corporation income taxes.. 13¢
Borrowing .... 12¢
Excise taxes... 5¢
Other .... 4¢

Where it goes:

Benefit payments to individuals............................. 37¢
Military.. 24¢
Grants to states and localities .... 17¢
Other federal operations.. 14¢
Net interest... 8¢

wage earner couples pay a marriage tax.

September Proposal: In addition to rate cuts and a unified $250 credit which would reduce the penalty somewhat, the Treasury supported a special working spouse deduction equal to 10 per cent of the first $6,000 of earnings by the partner with the lower earnings. Thus, the maximum deduction would be $600.

President's 1978 Tax Program: It contains no relief beyond a $240 credit and rate reductions that will eliminate less than half of the penalty. The September proposal would have eliminated all but 12 percent of the penalty for couples earning $20,000 annually, where the higher earning spouse earns $14,000 of that amount.

II. TREATMENT OF CAPITAL GAINS

Problem: Assets accrued through capital gains, usually by the well off, are accorded exceedingly preferential treatment over assets accrued through earned income. Only half of long-term capital gains (those held more than a year) are fully taxed, and the first $50,000 of such gains may be taxed at a maximum rate of only 12.5 percent. This provision alone is anticipated to cost the Treasury nearly $9 billion from individuals, nearly all in upper income brackets, and $700 million from corporations. Capital gains could be equitably taxed as ordinary income if the purchase price of the asset were adjusted for the effects of inflation.

September Proposal: The September proposal would have fully taxed long-term capital gains, with certain exceptions for rolled-over sales of houses. Capital loss treatment would be changed accordingly. In exchange, the basis value would be indexed to inflation to the extent the asset was held longer than 10 years. A special venture capital rule sustaining present preferential treatment for the initial stock offerings of new corporations would encourage risk capital formation and new enterprise. The changes would have raised $3.5 billion from individuals and closed off the full $700 million loss to corporations.

1978 Tax Program: It only proposes to end the 12.5 percent rate limitation on the first $50,000 of gains, thus raising only $100 million from individuals.

III. DOUBLE TAXATION OF DIVIDEND INCOME

Problem: Profits distributed as dividends are taxed twice, once at the corporate tax rate, and once as individual income to the recipient. Only $100 of dividend income may be excluded by individual taxpayers. Many elderly taxpayers rely upon dividends to supplement fixed incomes. Additionally, the double taxation distorts capital financing in favor of internal earnings, and away from new equity issues.

September Proposal: Pursuant to Mr. Carter's campaign pledges, the Treasury urged partial integration of corporate and individual taxes. Corporate taxes pro-rated to dividends could be claimed as a credit by individual dividend recipients. The $100 exclusion would be ended.

1978 Tax Program: This problem is not addressed.

IV. WITHHOLDING TAX ON INTEREST INCOME

Problem: No tax is withheld on interest income to domestic taxpayers. The Tresaury estimates that up to $8 billion of interest income escapes taxation by not being voluntarily reported to the IRS, an act of illegal tax avoidance.

September Proposal: The Treasury recommended withholding 20 per cent on interest income, except where an exemption certificate was filed stating the expectation that the taxpayer will owe no taxes that year. The Treasury projected this would raise $1.4 billion already legally owed it.

1978 Tax Program: It does not address this problem.

V. GROUP TERM LIFE INSURANCE

Problem: Under current law, taxable employee income excludes premiums paid by employers for the first $50,000 of group term life insurance. There is, however, no reason why such premiums should not be considered constructively received income.

September Proposal: The Treasury recommended the exclusion be reduced to $25,000, chipping away at this loophole which is not available to most lower income workers. Such a change would net the Treasury $165 million.

1978 Tax Program: The Program before Congress does not address this inequity.

VI. PERCENTAGE DEPLETION ON HARD MINERALS

Problem: There is no conceptual reason to permit continued percentage depletion for hard minerals, a tax accounting policy that encourages waste of limited raw resources instead of using recycled resources. Congress has already seen fit to end percentage depletion for major oil companies and the same logic which resulted in that action should apply to the 125 remaining categories of percentage depletion allowed for hard mineral exploitation.

September Proposal: The Treasury urged phasing out percentage depletion over 10 years, a modest proposal designed not to shock the affected industries. Percentage depletion would be replaced with cost depletion that would permit write-off of investments in mineral properties over their useful life as with most other investments. This change would close off $82 million of the loophole in 1979 rapidly increasing to $403 million by 1982, and higher thereafter.

1978 Tax Program: It drops this reform entirely.

AFL-CIO Proposes Economic Stimulus.
The AFL-CIO executive council's prescription for economic stimulus Feb. 20 differed sharply from the Carter Administration's.

The council recommended only about $5 billion more than the $24.5 billion proposed by Carter for economic stimulus.

But the council wanted $13.25 billion more in direct spending programs, such as public service jobs ($4 billion more), public works ($3 billion more) and youth programs ($1 billion more).

The council wanted much less than the Administration in tax reductions. It proposed to eliminate entirely the Administration's proposed $8.4-billion tax reduction for business.

Tax cuts for individuals also should be scaled back, in the council's view, especially for high-income individuals.

The council recommended that the Social Security payroll tax be rolled back to a 5.8% rate. Currently, it was 6.05% and was scheduled to rise to 6.13% in 1979.

The revenue lost because of the rollback, estimated at $5.4 billion, should be replaced by general revenue funds, the council said. All future scheduled hikes in the Social Security tax rates should be funded with general Treasury revenues, the council added.

The council's statement was issued at its midwinter meeting in Bal Harbour, Fla.

Carter & tax-free 'three-martini lunch.'
Touring New England Feb. 17–18, 1978 on a trip split between official and political activities, Carter held a news conference in Cranston, R.I. Feb. 17.

Explaining his tax program, Carter stressed that tax reduction and tax reform "go together."

"As for the famous three-martini lunch," he said, in reference to his proposal to limit tax deductions permitted for business lunches and entertainment, "I don't care how many martinis anyone has with lunch, but I am concerned about who picks up the check.

"I don't think a relatively small minority has some sort of divine right to have expensive meals, free theater tickets, country club dues, sporting events tickets, paid for by heavier taxes on everybody else."

Proposed cut in deduction for business meals—Sen. Edward M. Kennedy (D, Mass.) directed the Library of Congress to make a study of the effect that Carter's proposal to restrict the tax deduction for business meals would have on jobs in the restaurant industry. Kennedy reported to the Senate Feb. 27, 1978:

The study, which was prepared at my request by Jane Gravelle of the Economics Division of the Library of Congress, indicates that any adverse impact of the tax reform would be relatively small, and would be offset by the stimulus for the restaurant industry contained in the general tax reductions in the Carter proposals.

In addition, the study notes that the restaurant industry has been growing significantly faster than other areas of the economy in recent years. The study found this faster growth would continue even under the tax reform proposals, although the rest of the economy would not be lagging as far behind.

Under the Carter proposal, the tax deduction for business meals would be limited to one-half of the expenses incurred. Under present law, such expenses may be deducted in full and have been a long-standing target of tax reformers. Under related aspects of the Carter proposals, tax deductions would be denied entirely for other forms of business entertainment, such as yachts, hunting lodges, country clubs, and sports and theater tickets. Other proposals would restrict tax deductions for foreign con-

Capacity and effort measures for ALL TAXES of State and local governments, by State, 1975

State	Tax Capacity Per Capita	Tax Capacity Index	Potential Tax Yield	Amount Collected	Tax Effort Index	Amount Collected Less Potential Tax Yield
Alabama	$500.95	78	$ 1,810,952	$ 1,425,466	79	$ -385,486
Alaska	917.01	143	334,710	280,664	84	-54,046
Arizona	597.99	93	1,322,756	1,443,212	109	120,456
Arkansas	503.55	78	1,062,484	841,360	79	-221,124
California	709.36	110	15,037,101	17,970,758	120	2,933,657
Colorado	671.32	104	1,705,821	1,564,065	92	-141,756
Connecticut	727.19	113	2,254,305	2,134,842	95	-119,463
Delaware	782.73	122	453,201	389,532	86	-63,669
D.C.	772.71	120	551,637	496,991	90	-54,646
Florida	628.25	98	5,200,037	4,107,125	79	-1,092,912
Georgia	567.15	88	2,796,601	2,441,749	87	-354,852
Hawaii	699.09	109	606,807	726,500	120	119,693
Idaho	556.77	87	452,651	421,477	93	-31,174
Illinois	734.84	114	8,228,027	7,999,697	97	-228,330
Indiana	628.56	98	3,339,527	3,064,328	92	-275,199
Iowa	664.84	103	1,902,097	1,811,807	95	-90,290
Kansas	676.48	105	1,542,375	1,335,591	87	-206,784
Kentucky	575.30	90	1,948,535	1,581,159	81	-367,376
Louisiana	664.99	103	2,530,962	2,085,636	82	-445,326
Maine	476.48	74	504,112	596,499	118	92,387
Maryland	654.28	102	2,696,961	2,808,549	104	111,588
Massachusetts	604.91	94	3,516,967	4,616,687	131	1,099,720
Michigan	648.84	101	5,911,606	6,187,684	105	276,078
Minnesota	632.27	98	2,479,138	2,848,204	115	369,066
Mississippi	448.08	70	1,048,969	1,022,431	97	-26,538

NOTE: *Potential tax yield, amount collected and amount collected less potential tax yield are in thousands of dollars.*

State	Tax Capacity Per Capita	Index	Potential Tax Yield	Amount Collected	Tax Effort Index	Amount Collected Less Potential Tax Yield
Missouri	603.19	94	2,875,387	2,440,224	85	-435,163
Montana	629.95	98	469,946	449,477	96	-20,469
Nebraska	660.10	103	1,019,203	876,035	86	-143,168
Nevada	969.88	151	572,229	398,989	70	-173,240
New Hampshire	626.67	97	508,859	406,173	80	-102,686
New Jersey	715.51	111	5,246,808	5,206,910	99	-39,898
New Mexico	600.16	93	686,581	607,390	88	-79,191
New York	653.99	102	11,821,544	17,913,237	152	6,091,693
North Carolina	538.05	84	2,927,552	2,578,457	88	-349,095
North Dakota	634.77	99	404,351	379,678	94	-24,673
Ohio	656.64	102	7,049,090	5,648,479	80	-1,400,611
Oklahoma	657.53	102	1,785,200	1,261,183	71	-524,017
Oregon	629.73	98	1,438,299	1,419,040	99	-19,259
Pennsylvania	606.34	94	7,191,145	6,918,119	96	-273,026
Rhode Island	552.50	86	514,374	593,201	115	78,827
South Carolina	494.23	77	1,391,745	1,211,446	87	-180,299
South Dakota	582.04	91	396,372	356,999	90	-39,373
Tennessee	530.25	82	2,212,717	1,785,640	81	-427,077
Texas	724.52	113	8,866,741	6,026,158	68	-2,840,583
Utah	549.60	86	661,171	602,666	91	-58,505
Vermont	542.44	84	256,034	310,179	121	54,145
Virginia	598.81	93	2,992,699	2,617,147	88	-365,552
Washington	640.16	100	2,278,325	2,298,072	101	19,747
West Virginia	576.56	90	1,037,228	883,747	85	-153,481
Wisconsin	597.97	93	2,744,075	3,281,113	120	537,038
Wyoming	941.92	147	354,161	258,467	73	-95,694
US Total	$642.76	100	$136,930,239	$136,930,239	100	$0

Source: Tax Wealth in 50 States (National Institute of Education)

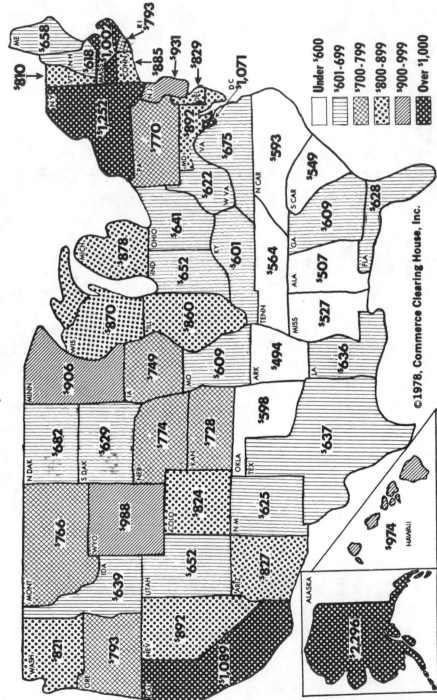

State and Local Per Capita Tax Burden in Fiscal 1976-1977

©1978, Commerce Clearing House, Inc.

Legend:
- Under $600
- $601-699
- $700-799
- $800-899
- $900-999
- Over $1,000

ventions and deny such deductions for first-class air travel. ...

According to the study, tax deductible expenditures for business meals are estimated at $3.2 billion in 1976, or 5.8 percent of total food and business expenditures of $55.3 billion that year. The tax deduction is estimated to save taxpayers who use it $1.2 billion in 1976. Thus, the real cost of the meals for firms and others claiming the deduction in 1976 was only $2 billion, since the Treasury defrayed $1.2 billion of the cost through the tax deduction.

Using standard economic techniques, the study estimated that, if the Carter reform is enacted, expenditures for meals would decline by only 1 percent, or about $550 million.

At the same time, the general economic stimulus in the Carter program of tax cuts for individuals and corporations would produce increased spending on restaurant meals of 1 percent. Thus, the effect of the tax cut would tend to wash out the effect of the loss of the tax deduction on the restaurant industry as a whole. Although not all restaurants would be affected equally, the study found that the overall effect on jobs in the industry would be zero. ...

The study concludes that if President Carter's tax proposals had been in effect in 1976, jobs in the economy as a whole would have grown at a rate of 4 percent that year, or somewhat higher than before, because of the tax reduction measures in the Carter program. At most, therefore, the effect of the tax reform in the area of business meals would have been to narrow by about 1 percent the gap in growth rates between the fast-growing restaurant industry and the slower-growing economy as a whole.

Among comments made in the study:

Two types of problems with the current deduction for entertainment expenses can be identified. The first is simply that such expenditures contain a substantial element of personal consumption regardless of the degree to which they serve a legitimate business purpose. This consumption element accrues both to the individual employee and to the customer being entertained. This element is difficult to measure but clearly exists in some amount. The value of that consumption, because it is deductible to the firm and

not includable in income to the employee, is never subject to taxation.

Consider an employee who entertains a client at lunch. The employee is actually receiving two types of remuneration—the salary the firm pays him for entertaining and selling to customers and the value of the lunch. Similarly, the client being entertained receives two types of remuneration—his salary and the value of the lunch (which in the long run his firm tends to pay for in higher prices for products).

The entertainment element of the remuneration is never subject to tax. Of course, the value to the individuals receiving it may not be equal to its market value, which would make measurement more difficult. An employee who takes a client who likes baseball to such a game who himself dislikes baseball may get no utility from the entertainment; if he likes baseball it may be worth the full value of the ticket. Meals, of course, would be assumed to have some element of benefit.

This problem of a business expense containing consumption items is present in many types of business expenses. Some kinds of firms, selling very expensive products to a small group of clients, may use the entertainment approach such as baseball tickets as a method of sales promotion. A firm which sells, for example, razor blades, may use as a method of sales promotion sponsoring the showing of baseball games on television. This also provides some element of consumption which is not taxed to the viewers of the televised games. However, perhaps the feature that distinguishes these two types of untaxed consumption is that the taxpayers who are ultimately paying for the tax subsidy in the case of mass advertising tend to be the same group as the recipients of the benefits. However, for expense accounts, only a small portion of the taxpayers benefit from these, while the cost of the taxes foregone is borne by all taxpayers.

A second problem is the potential for abuse of the provision by certain taxpayers, particularly closely held corporations, partnerships and self-employed individuals. A large company is more likely to scrutinize expense account entertaining to insure that it has a business purpose. A self-employed individual, where the dividing line between personal consumption and business income tends to be vague in any case, can easily convert much of his personal entertainment and living expenses into deductible items. A similar problem may exist with top executives of firms and closely held corporations. Examples of this type of abuse have been widely documented.

For example, Philip Stern, in his book *The Great Treasury Raid*, described a New York executive who boasted that he had not paid for his lunch in thirty-one years. This feat was accomplished because he belonged to a group of business luncheon companions who took turns charging the lunch to their firms. The Treasury in its papers cited a case

State Government Tax Revenue (fiscal 1977)
(Thousands of dollars)

State	Total	Sales and gross receipts	Individual income	Corporation net income
Number of States using tax	50	50	44	46
All States	101,026,105	52,351,058	25,452,742	9,187,038
Alabama	1,403,674	908,556	261,895	75,874
Alaska	773,787	66,124	210,309	35,759
Arizona	1,160,068	710,534	190,591	51,788
Arkansas	802,913	490,681	163,781	67,210
California	12,589,124	6,004,651	3,620,933	1,641,595
Colorado	1,077,285	550,147	338,920	80,575
Connecticut	1,457,139	1,052,935	59,333	201,742
Delaware	390,882	68,974	168,000	29,036
Florida	3,274,802	2,415,293	(X)	194,199
Georgia	1,903,506	1,134,968	495,639	170,885
Hawaii	685,703	444,892	203,018	27,605
Idaho	367,823	175,932	112,470	31,034
Illinois	5,319,547	3,014,857	1,413,368	384,410
Indiana	2,162,899	1,432,495	479,259	86,198
Iowa	1,292,507	572,115	447,409	91,894
Kansas	969,005	520,649	209,171	122,712
Kentucky	1,560,385	838,101	338,160	131,254
Louisiana	1,714,616	851,520	133,614	95,248
Maine	468,462	295,922	75,157	35,200
Maryland	2,127,712	989,212	806,740	115,297
Massachusetts	2,934,261	1,175,179	1,191,531	397,237
Michigan	4,790,719	2,147,300	1,425,728	802,621
Minnesota	2,485,565	983,370	956,933	258,095
Mississippi	969,251	701,035	131,598	45,873
Missouri	1,598,094	929,413	389,594	105,772
Montana	312,399	82,977	111,862	24,957
Nebraska	610,235	343,083	170,595	41,946
Nevada	329,069	257,327	(X)	(X)
New Hampshire	200,231	113,986	7,066	32,563
New Jersey	3,103,725	1,576,619	709,653	332,775
New Mexico	597,604	376,073	26,639	29,486
New York	10,743,249	3,963,222	4,526,975	1,295,001
North Carolina	2,384,780	1,128,763	782,092	204,291
North Dakota	296,330	164,945	55,037	21,800
Ohio	3,570,771	2,132,628	614,879	315,481
Oklahoma	1,139,000	493,385	216,833	70,635
Oregon	973,145	159,329	561,895	91,104
Pennsylvania	5,590,840	2,804,955	1,178,071	665,993
Rhode Island	438,841	254,778	103,784	40,842
South Carolina	1,187,589	710,710	290,393	106,601
South Dakota	200,115	173,929	(X)	2,504
Tennessee	1,529,531	1,129,592	22,385	156,042
Texas	4,748,947	3,181,034	(X)	(X)
Utah	531,276	307,448	158,268	24,866
Vermont	229,803	112,865	70,334	16,900
Virginia	2,054,831	978,755	714,086	159,152
Washington	2,100,035	1,589,541	(X)	(X)
West Virginia	904,400	654,357	164,671	23,329
Wisconsin	2,733,294	1,053,340	1,144,073	251,657
Wyoming	233,336	132,562	(X)	(X)

(X) Not applicable.

Source: U.S. Commerce Department

State Tax Collections Grew 13.2%. State tax collections in the 50 states totaled $101 billion in fiscal 1977, the Census Bureau reported Jan. 9, 1978.

The total was an increase of 13.2% over the $89.3 billion collected in the previous year. Almost all of the states had fiscal years ending June 30.

A majority share—$52.4 billion, or 51.8%—of all state tax revenue came from sales and gross receipts taxes.

Individual income taxes, the second largest source of state tax revenue, produced $25.5 billion, up almost 19% from fiscal 1976.

Corporate net income taxes rose 26% to the $9.2-billion level.

State motor fuel tax revenue of $9.1 billion represented a 5% increase over the previous year.

More than half of the state tax revenue was collected in eight states: California, $12.6 billion; New York, $10.7 billion; Pennsylvania, $5.6 billion; Illinois, $5.3 billion; Michigan, $4.8 billion; Texas, $4.7 billion; Ohio, $3.6 billion, and Florida, $3.3 billion.

(The above table shows the total tax collections by each state and the amounts from some of the major types of taxes. Not all of the state tax revenue sources are included.)

where a taxpayer deducted every meal for two years with the exception of one day.

There is no way to determine how typical such occurrences are. However, they do illustrate the problem of abuse of this provision. To the extent that this abuse occurs, individuals are avoiding taxes on significant portions of their income. (In the latter case cited the taxpayer took deductions of $31,000 in one year and $32,000 in the next.) This result is inequitable to the majority of taxpayers who cannot take advantage of expense accounts.

The existence of business deductions for what are in part, and in some cases in large part, personal consumption expenses, tends to encourage more expenditures of these types, either as a form of compensation to employees or as a means of competing with other businesses. For those cases where the entertainment expenses deduction is clearly a conversion of personal to business expenses, it makes the consumption entertainment expenses cheaper and thereby encourages such consumption.

Disallowance, or partial disallowance of these expenditures would eliminate or reduce these effects. One question which has been raised about the effect of the proposed changes is what effect will the change have on the competitive position of firms? This question, one would argue, should be easily dismissed. Entertainment may be customary in a business, and more so because it is tax deductible. However, the tax provision will not prevent firms from making these expenditures, but rather will raise the price of them and thereby lead to some curtailment in the expenditures. This increased price, however, will apply to all firms; therefore, there cannot be a competitive problem.

One author notes that the growth of expense accounts began with the high excess profits taxes of the post war period. These expenses continued to grow and achieved a certain amount of notoriety in the 1950's, when few rules or limitations on the deductions existed.

A major proposal for revision in this area was made by the Kennedy Administration in the 1961 tax recommendations. However, the subject was not new to Congress. A series of studies on broadening the tax base published in 1959 by the Committee on Ways and Means contained several articles on travel and entertainment.

In 1961, the Administration tax proposals included a proposal for a significant change in the entertainment expense deduction. Under this proposal:

(1) Deductions for nightclubs, theatres, prize fights, hunting and fishing trips and similar entertainments would be disallowed;

(2) Expenditures on entertainment facilities (yachts, hunting lodges, resort properties, etc.) would be disallowed;

(3) Club dues would be disallowed;

(4) Food and beverages furnished which bear a direct relationship to business would be allowed but only up to dollar limits (proposed at $4 to $7 at that time).

These proposals are very similar to the current proposals, with the substitution of a fifty percent limit rather than a dollar limit on meals.

The Congress stopped far short of these proposals. It made a number of changes which tighten the deductions somewhat, but continued to allow them in general. These changes included adoption of the "directly related" and "associated with" tests (the latter added by the Senate), the partitioning of facility deductions into business and personal use and strict record-keeping requirements. However, the rules continued to allow most of the entertainment expense deduction which had previously occurred.

Carter for 'greater equity.' Carter said at a press conference March 9 that his tax-reduction program would provide "greater equity," in general. He had been asked specifically if he had any plans to have a limit of 50% on all taxable income.

There would be "an alleviation of the tax burden on almost every American" under his tax proposal, he said, although "most of the reductions are not at the $200,000 or $250,000 or higher level. Most of the reductions are in the lower- and middle-income family tax payments."

Other Developments

Property taxes soar. Time magazine reported in its Sept. 12, 1977 issue that rising property taxes were a major cause of the increasing prices of housing.

Property taxes had increased an average 76% since 1970 and 136% since 1967. Time attributed the sharp increase in part to an "expansion of local public services, but more . . . [to] the enormous inflation-sparked increases in the wages and benefits of teachers, police and firemen." Since property taxes were the chief source of revenue for most local communities, reform of an inequitable property-tax structure was difficult.

Capacity and effort measures for INDIVIDUAL INCOME TAXES, by State, 1975

State	Tax Base	Tax Capacity Per Capita	Index	Potential Tax Yield	Amount Collected	Tax Effort Index	Amount Collected Less Potential Tax Yield
Alabama	$ 1,545,769	$ 71.81	71	$ 259,609	$ 207,118	80	$ -52,491
Alaska	475,070	218.59	217	79,787	87,658	110	7,871
Arizona	1,116,108	84.74	84	187,448	157,537	84	-29,911
Arkansas	792,876	63.11	63	133,162	126,192	95	-6,970
California	13,634,564	108.02	107	2,289,900	2,456,573	107	166,673
Colorado	1,620,008	107.07	106	272,077	280,498	103	8,421
Connecticut	2,453,737	132.94	132	412,101	13,578	3	-398,523
Delaware	410,512	119.08	118	68,945	146,103	212	77,158
D.C.	556,819	130.99	130	93,517	171,241	183	77,724
Florida	4,780,662	97.00	96	802,904	0	0	-802,904
Georgia	2,267,581	77.23	77	380,836	373,916	98	-6,920
Hawaii	561,869	108.72	108	94,365	168,670	179	74,305
Idaho	391,087	80.79	80	65,682	91,244	139	25,562
Illinois	8,405,470	126.08	125	1,411,683	1,136,918	81	-274,765
Indiana	3,142,902	99.35	99	527,845	421,091	80	-106,754
Iowa	1,725,842	101.31	101	289,852	358,899	124	69,047
Kansas	1,431,004	105.41	105	240,335	170,044	71	-70,291
Kentucky	1,583,163	78.50	78	265,889	329,888	124	63,999
Louisiana	1,830,662	80.78	80	307,456	108,870	35	-198,586
Maine	457,793	72.67	72	76,886	44,603	58	-32,283
Maryland	3,053,227	124.40	124	512,784	984,825	192	472,041
Massachusetts	3,543,049	102.35	102	595,049	985,616	166	390,567
Michigan	5,663,703	104.40	104	951,209	993,261	104	42,052
Minnesota	2,211,191	94.71	94	371,366	807,108	217	435,742
Mississippi	776,530	55.71	55	130,417	92,687	71	-37,730

NOTE: Tax base, potential tax yield, amount collected and amount collected less potential tax yield are in thousands of dollars.

State	Tax Base	Tax Capacity Per Capita	Index	Potential Tax Yield	Amount Collected	Tax Effort Index	Amount Collected Less Potential Tax Yield
Missouri	2,634,928	92.83	92	442,531	385,605	87	−56,926
Montana	383,827	86.41	86	64,463	88,599	137	24,136
Nebraska	925,566	100.68	100	155,447	78,436	50	−77,011
Nevada	432,201	123.03	122	72,587	0	0	−72,587
New Hampshire	448,364	92.74	92	75,302	8,562	11	−66,740
New Jersey	5,483,916	125.60	125	921,014	45,942	5	−875,072
New Mexico	499,698	73.36	73	83,923	56,575	67	−27,348
New York	11,785,394	109.50	109	1,979,335	4,479,646	226	2,500,311
North Carolina	2,371,474	73.20	73	398,285	549,927	138	151,642
North Dakota	373,934	98.59	98	62,802	64,580	103	1,778
Ohio	6,656,959	104.15	103	1,118,024	953,622	85	−164,402
Oklahoma	1,363,556	84.35	84	229,007	162,741	71	−66,266
Oregon	1,319,595	97.03	96	221,624	427,002	193	205,378
Pennsylvania	7,140,206	101.11	100	1,199,184	1,425,922	119	226,738
Rhode Island	515,361	92.97	92	86,554	79,682	92	−6,872
South Carolina	1,133,769	67.62	67	190,414	210,895	111	20,481
South Dakota	307,962	75.95	75	51,722	0	0	−51,722
Tennessee	2,007,322	80.79	80	337,126	18,436	5	−318,690
Texas	7,581,452	104.04	103	1,273,291	0	0	−1,273,291
Utah	538,251	75.14	75	90,398	104,919	116	14,521
Vermont	212,234	75.52	75	35,644	55,140	155	19,496
Virginia	3,057,695	103.10	102	513,534	547,125	107	33,591
Washington	2,478,530	116.96	116	416,265	0	0	−416,265
West Virginia	908,434	84.81	84	152,570	119,237	78	−33,333
Wisconsin	2,462,388	90.12	90	413,554	873,723	211	460,169
Wyoming	266,383	118.99	118	44,739	0	0	−44,739
US Total	$127,720,597	$100.69	100	$21,450,454	$21,450,454	100	$ 0

N.Y. property tax invalid—New York State Supreme Court Justice L. Kingsley Smith ruled June 23, 1978 that the state's method of funding public schools through the property tax was illegal.

Smith said the funding through use of the property tax discriminated against students from poor districts and thus violated the state constitution's provision for equal protection for all.

The ruling allowed retention of the existing system until the legislature took appropriate action to develop a suitable remedy.

The case was initiated by the Levittown school district, which was joined in the suit by school officials from 31 other districts.

Three States Hiked Sales Taxes in '77. Maryland, Missouri and Nebraska were the only states to increase their general sales tax rates in 1977, Commerce Clearing House reported Jan. 5, 1978.

In Nebraska, the increase in 1977 to 3.5% from 3% reverted to 3% on New Year's Day, 1978.

The increase in Missouri was one-eighth of one per cent, to 3.125% from 3%, effective July 1, 1977. Maryland raised its rate to 5% from 4% on June 1, 1977.

Three states—Rhode Island, Tennessee and Washington—continued sales tax rates that had been due to decrease in 1977.

Twelve states had maintained a steady rate of sales tax during the past decade.

The only states without a general state sales tax were Alaska, Delaware, Montana, New Hampshire and Oregon.

The following table shows state sales and use tax rates, exclusive of all local sales taxes:

Sales Taxes in 1977

State	Current Rate	Rate on July 1, 1967
Ala.	4%	4%
Ariz.	4%	3%
Ark.	3%	3%
Calif.	4.75%	3%
Colo.	3%	3%
Conn.	7%	3.5%
Fla.	4%	3%
Ga.	3%	3%
Hawaii	4%	4%
Ida.	3%	3%
Ill.	4%	4.75%
Ind.	4%	2%
Ia.	3%	2%
Kan.	3%	3%
Ky.	5%	3%
La.	3%	2%
Me.	5%	4%
Md.	5%	3%
Mass.	5%	3%
Mich.	4%	4%
Minn.	4%	3%
Miss.	5%	3.5%
Mo.	3.125%	3%
Neb.	3%	2.5%
Nev.	3%	2%
N.J.	5%	3%
N.M.	4%	3%
N.Y.	4%	2%
N.C.	3%	3%
N.D.	3%	3%
Ohio	4%	3%
Okla.	2%	2%
Pa.	6%	5%
R.I.	6%	5%
S.C.	4%	3%
S.D.	4%	3%
Tenn.	4.5%	3%
Tex.	4%	2%
Utah	4%	3.5%
Vt.	3%	No tax
Va.	3%	2%
Wash.	4.6%	4.5%
W. Va.	3%	3%
Wis.	4%	3%
Wyo.	3%	3%

¹3%, effective July 1, 1978.

IRS Revokes Oil Tax Credits. The Internal Revenue Service Jan. 16, 1978 revoked, effective June 30, two rulings that had enabled oil companies to substantially reduce their U.S. tax obligations by counting as taxes certain payments made to Saudi Arabia and Libya.

Oil companies made payments to Saudi Arabia and Libya based on the "posted price" for oil. The posted price, according to the Treasury Department, was an arbitrary figure that exceeded the market price for oil. The rulings revoked Jan. 16 had allowed the oil companies to count the payments made on the posted price as foreign tax payments. The companies thereby were able to reduce their U.S. tax payments by an amount equal to that paid as a tax to the foreign government.

The rulings had been criticized by some as a giveaway to the oil companies. Critics said the foreign payments should be considered royalties, not foreign taxes. The companies would not be entitled to a dollar-for-dollar abatement of their U.S.

taxes, only a tax deduction as a business expense, if the payments were classified as royalties.

If the two rulings had not been in effect in 1976, Treasury officials said, the companies would have paid the U.S. $600 million in additional taxes.

However, federal tax officials said the new rulings might not result in additional U.S. taxes for the oil companies. The oil companies might be able to restructure their arrangements with Saudi Arabia and Libya to avoid additional U.S. tax burdens, the officials said. Also, Saudi Arabia had indicated it might abandon the use of posted prices, thus rendering the new rulings inapplicable. (The IRS had revoked the old rulings on the basis of rather narrow considerations concerning posted prices and the actual income of the oil companies, thereby avoiding the issue of whether the payments made by the oil companies were in essence royalties or taxes.)

A spokesman for Rep. Benjamin Rosenthal (D, N.Y.), a critic of the tax credit, said the representative was "happy to see the ruling coming out, but he's outraged over what he feels is a $2-billion giveaway to the oil companies" because the ruling was not made retroactive to the spring of 1976. The Treasury Department said in a statement, however, that it had decided against making the ruling retroactive "because taxpayers are entitled to rely on an Internal Revenue Service ruling until the IRS concludes that the ruling is no longer valid."

17 Big Firms Paid No '76 Income Taxes. Seventeen major U.S. firms paid no federal income taxes for 1976 on earnings of $2.6 billion, according to Rep. Charles Vanik Jan. 27, 1978. Another 41 large companies (out of 168 surveyed) paid

taxes amounting to less than 10% of their total worldwide earnings in 1976, Vanik said.

Vanik noted that the companies' actions were entirely legal. They were able to take advantage of provisions in the tax code, such as the foreign tax credit, which allowed them to reduce their U.S. taxes by the amount of taxes they paid abroad. These and other tax breaks enabled the companies to reduce their tax liabilities far below the 48% rate prescribed by law.

Vanik had been compiling these figures for six years. The firms he surveyed in 1972 had paid an effective tax rate of more than 28%. That was more than double the 13.04% rate on 1976 taxes and proof, Vanik said, that many large companies were paying a smaller percentage of their income in taxes.

Vanik said the proportion of total federal revenues derived from corporate taxes had shrunk to 16% from 23% in 1967. Tax payments by individuals, who were paying a larger proportion of their income than before, made up the difference, Vanik said.

The 17 companies that had paid no 1976 taxes were: U.S. Steel Corp., Bethlehem Steel Corp., Armco Steel Corp., Republic Steel Corp., National Steel Corp., LTV Corp., Chase Manhattan Corp., General Dynamics Corp., Phelps Dodge Corp., Singer Co., Texas Gulf Corp., Eastern Air Lines Inc., American Airlines Inc., Pan American World Airways, Southern Co., Pacific Gas and Electric Co. and Philadelphia Electric Co.

Some of the companies that paid an effective tax rate of less than 10% were (rate and earnings in parentheses): Exxon Corp. (8% on $7.4 billion), American Electric Power Co. Inc. (.1% on $337.4 million), American Telephone & Telegraph Co. (9.5% on $6.4 billion), Mobil Corp. (4.5% on $3.8 billion), Gulf Oil Corp. (7% on $2.2 billion) and Esmark Inc. (1% on $114.8 million).

Proposition 13, Kemp-Roth & the Continuing Tax Revolt: 1978-79

Proposition 13 'Shows the Way'

Two tax proposals were said to have made 1978 the "year of the tax revolt."

In California, Proposition 13 was accepted by voters as a way to "send a message" to Sacramento, the state capital, that taxpayers had reached the end of their endurance. Many supporters of tax-cutting proposals hailed Proposition 13 as showing the way to the rest of the nation. Other observers suggested that the measure—which limited real estate taxation to 1% of a property's value—was too restricted in scope for the role some of its more enthusiastic supporters assigned to it.

In Congress, the Kemp-Roth bill—described as the darling of the tax-cutters—was rejected by the House of Representatives. Kemp-Roth would have reduced income-tax rates by about one-third over a three-year period.

Proposition 13 Wins 65% of Vote. California voters approved by an overwhelming margin June 6, 1978 a primary ballot initiative to cut property taxes 57%.

The emotional tax issue completely dominated the California primary and riveted national attention to it as well. Its passage, by a 65% to 35% margin, was seen as a resounding notice of a taxpayers' revolt—against high taxes and wanton government spending—that could spread across the country.

There were similar notices elsewhere in the primary voting June 6. In Ohio, nearly 60% of 198 school levy and bond issues on the ballot were defeated, including those for Cleveland and Columbus.

In New Jersey's Republican senatorial primary, Jeffrey Bell, 33, after a one-issue campaign for a 30% cut in federal income tax rates, won a stunning upset victory over a respected four-term incumbent, Sen. Clifford Case (R).

Actually, various curbs on government spending had been enacted recently by four other states—New Jersey, Colorado, Tennessee and Michigan. Similar action was pending in 17 more states.

A proposed constitutional amendment to bar federal deficit spending also had been endorsed by 23 state legislatures.

Furthermore, tax relief of some kind had been enacted in 1978 by numerous states. According to Commerce Clearing House in Chicago May 25: "Personal income tax rates have been lowered in Maine, Minnesota, New Mexico and New York (beginning in 1979). In Vermont, the 9% income tax surtax has been repealed. Mississippi (beginning in 1979) and New York have increased their standard deductions. Personal exemptions have been increased in Colorado and New York (be-

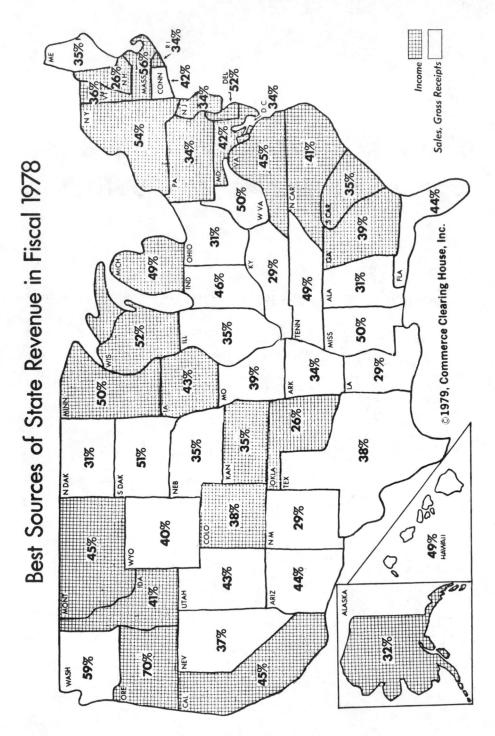

Best Sources of State Revenue in Fiscal 1978

©1979, Commerce Clearing House, Inc.

Income

Sales, Gross Receipts

Text of Property Tax Initiative

Section 1: a. The maximum amount of any ad valorem tax on real property shall not exceed 1% of the full cash value of such property. The 1% tax is to be collected by the county and apportioned according to law to the districts within the counties.

b. The limitation shall not apply to ad valorem taxes or special assessments to pay the interest and redemption charges on any indebtedness approved by the voters prior to the time this section becomes effective.

Section 2: a. The full cash value means the county assessor's evaluation of real property as shown on the 1975 76 tax bill under "full cash value," or thereafter, the appraised value of real property when purchased, newly constructed or a change in ownership has occurred after the 1975 assessment. All real property not already assessed up to the 1975 76 tax levels may be reassessed to reflect that valuation.

b. The fair market value base may reflect from year to year the inflationary rate not to exceed 2% for any given year or reduction as shown in the Consumer Price Index or comparable data for the area under taxing jurisdiction.

Section 3: a. From and after the effective date of this article, any changes in state taxes enacted for the purpose of increasing revenues collected pursuant thereto whether by increased rates or changes in methods of computation must be imposed by an act passed by not less than two-thirds of all members elected to each of the two houses of the Legislature, except that no new ad valorem taxes on real property, or sales or transaction taxes on the sales of real property, may be imposed.

Section 4. Cities, counties and special districts, by a two-thirds vote of the qualified electors of such district, may impose special taxes on such district, except ad valorem taxes on real property or a transaction tax or sales tax on the sale of real property within such city, county or special district.

Section 5: This article shall take effect for the tax year beginning on July 1 following the passage of this amendment, except Section 3, which shall become effective upon the passage of this article.

Section 6: If any section, part, clause or phrase hereof is for any reason held to be invalid or unconstitutional, the remaining sections shall not be affected but will remain in full force and effect.

ginning in 1979). In Colorado, an inflation factor was built into the computation of the state's tax."

The California initiative, a state constitutional amendment to reduce property taxes, was on the ballot as Proposition 13. It was also known as the Jarvis-Gann Amendment after its sponsors, Howard A. Jarvis and Paul Gann.

Jarvis, 74, a long-time crusader for less taxes, was executive director of the Apartment Association of Los Angeles County and the United Organization of Taxpayers. His theory was that "the only way to cut the cost of government is not to give them money in the first place."

Gann, 65, a retired real estate salesman, was president of People's Advocate, another taxpayers' organization, with 30,000 members. In his view, "The government has tried to become uncle, mother and father, and we simply cannot afford it any more."

Needing some 500,000 signatures to put their tax-cut proposal on the ballot, they obtained 1.3 million.

Housing assessments, on which the property tax was based, reportedly had escalated in recent years more rapidly in California than anywhere else in the nation. A boom in Southern California housing had carried market values for single-family homes upward by 1% to 2% a month. Tax rates kept pace with the inflated market because of the state's "good government" practice of doing tax assessments on a three-year cycle.

Ironically, most of the Jarvis-Gann tax cut would not go to the homeowner but to big property owners, such as businesses and farmers. The homeowner portion was estimated to be only about one-third of the total $7-billion reduction expected.

The Jarvis-Gann Amendment – Proposition 13—limited the tax on real property to 1% of the full cash value of the property, according to the assessed value in 1975-76.

It limited increases in assessed values to 2% per year, unless the property changed hands, in which case the property would be assessed at current market value.

It required a two-thirds vote of all state legislators for any increase in state taxes (a majority vote prevailed currently). No new taxes based on the value or sale of real property could be adopted.

A two-thirds vote of all registered voters was also required for local governments to levy any new taxes.

The new tax restrictions went into effect July 1.

Measure's Effect—California property taxes ran to about 3% of market value, not the 1% set in Proposition 13.

Property taxes, expected to produce $12 billion in the year starting July 1, under Proposition 13 were reduced to $5 billion. The $6.6-billion allotment of property-tax revenues for public educa

Capacity and effort measures for all PROPERTY TAXES, by State, 1975

State	Tax Capacity Per Capita	Tax Capacity Index	Potential Tax Yield	Amount Collected	Tax Effort Index	Amount Collected Less Potential Tax Yield
Alabama	$176.75	73	$ 638,940	$ 191,392	30	$ −447,548
Alaska	302.51	125	110,415	75,867	69	−34,548
Arizona	208.88	86	462,036	518,858	112	56,822
Arkansas	180.95	75	381,806	189,626	50	−192,180
California	286.60	119	6,075,459	7,908,946	130	1,833,487
Colorado	238.66	99	606,441	542,198	89	−64,243
Connecticut	297.22	123	921,369	1,088,300	118	166,931
Delaware	299.81	124	173,592	74,006	43	−99,586
D.C.	295.25	122	210,780	140,899	67	−69,881
Florida	215.38	89	1,782,688	1,358,791	76	−423,897
Georgia	215.08	89	1,060,551	799,722	75	−260,829
Hawaii	295.04	122	256,099	130,101	51	−125,998
Idaho	197.82	82	160,826	131,326	82	−29,500
Illinois	287.42	119	3,218,197	3,131,444	97	−86,753
Indiana	236.12	98	1,254,512	1,229,384	98	−25,128
Iowa	249.17	103	712,867	754,415	106	41,548
Kansas	239.24	99	545,477	573,595	105	28,118
Kentucky	199.21	82	674,718	322,264	48	−352,454
Louisiana	228.03	94	867,875	322,826	37	−545,049
Maine	149.51	62	158,181	244,550	155	86,369
Maryland	244.55	101	1,008,030	871,417	86	−136,613
Massachusetts	229.07	95	1,331,802	2,508,894	188	1,177,092
Michigan	256.97	106	2,341,277	2,670,960	114	329,683
Minnesota	244.85	101	960,049	907,582	95	−52,467
Mississippi	159.26	66	372,836	228,076	61	−144,760

NOTE: *Potential tax yield, amount collected and amount collected less potential tax yield are in thousands of dollars.*

State	Tax Capacity Per Capita	Tax Capacity Index	Potential Tax Yield	Amount Collected	Tax Effort Index	Amount Collected Less Potential Tax Yield
Missouri	212.50	88	1,013,009	875,751	86	-137,258
Montana	239.91	99	178,976	227,203	127	48,227
Nebraska	229.50	95	354,354	434,043	122	79,689
Nevada	285.93	118	168,699	149,987	89	-18,712
New Hampshire	191.74	79	155,693	257,725	166	102,032
New Jersey	296.40	123	2,173,468	3,018,580	139	845,112
New Mexico	185.89	77	212,662	109,494	51	-103,168
New York	252.20	104	4,558,817	6,681,183	147	2,122,366
North Carolina	200.84	83	1,092,753	641,621	59	-451,132
North Dakota	215.76	89	137,440	121,768	89	-15,672
Ohio	258.37	107	2,773,616	2,175,534	78	-598,082
Oklahoma	235.62	97	639,715	317,300	50	-322,415
Oregon	221.62	92	506,174	633,857	125	127,683
Pennsylvnaia	226.47	94	2,685,954	1,931,081	72	-754,873
Rhode Island	188.83	78	175,802	250,240	142	74,438
South Carolina	184.45	76	519,419	283,557	55	-235,862
South Dakota	195.08	81	132,852	182,099	137	49,247
Tennessee	187.12	77	780,834	489,101	63	-291,733
Texas	254.77	105	3,117,919	2,343,100	75	-774,819
Utah	194.98	81	234,560	183,058	78	-51,502
Vermont	165.38	68	78,061	140,992	181	62,931
Virginia	230.15	95	1,146,396	782,142	68	-364,254
Washington	248.01	103	882,685	814,741	92	-67,944
West Virginia	191.95	79	345,324	181,552	53	-163,772
Wisconsin	224.12	93	1,028,465	1,248,886	121	220,421
Wyoming	306.97	127	115,419	105,889	92	-9,530
US Total	$241.72	100	$51,495,923	$51,495,923	100	$ 0

Source: Tax Wealth in 50 States (National Institute of Education)

tion in the coming fiscal year would drop to about $2.7 billion.

Total revenues for public elementary and high schools and local governments—the counties and municipalities that levied the property taxes—were reduced by about 22% on July 1. In the current fiscal year, local governments were receiving total income of about $31.4 billion, of which $12.4 billion came from property taxes.

As for the schools, about half their income, on a statewide basis, came from the property tax.

Immediate Effects—The day after the election, California Gov. Edmund G. Brown Jr. put an immediate freeze on the hiring of state employees.

Local officials had warned during the emotional primary campaign of impending cutbacks in services that Proposition 13 would force. In some areas, layoff notices were sent out. Similar warnings from the schools were sent home with pupils.

After the vote, the warnings became official.

Los Angeles County officials announced June 7 that 37,000 of the county's 73,000 employees would be laid off, including sheriff's deputies, firemen and hospital workers.

Los Angeles Mayor Tom Bradley said that 8,300 of the city's 29,000 employees would be laid off, including 1,080 police.

San Diego County officials planned to eliminate 1,500 jobs, Contra Costa County officials 25% of their workers.

Los Angeles school officials announced June 7 they would have to cancel summer classes and drop 20,000 of the district's 30,000 teachers. Beverly Hills school officials planned a 60% cutback in programs.

Local Autonomy—There was a source of reprieve for the suddenly deprived local governments and schools. The state had reaped a budget surplus estimated at about $5 billion from its progressive income tax.

But observers noted that if the funds were used to help keep schools open or police on duty, the cherished principle of local control of those matters would be that much diminished.

Brown on the Spot—Gov. Brown, his presidential prospects hinging on his handling of the volatile issue, spoke June 7 of the "great opportunity" presented by adoption of Proposition 13.

"I began my governorship with a pledge of no new state taxes," he said. "I've carried out that promise. I began the effort at government frugality, and what I hear out of this vote is that people want more of it."

Brown, who was nominated for a second term over nominal opposition in the primary June 6, had started out in opposition to Proposition 13.

He had advocated Proposition 8 on the primary ballot, which, in conjunction with recently enacted state legislation, would have provided a 30% cut in property taxes and limited increases in the tax to the rate of inflation. It earmarked the existing state surplus to property tax relief and pegged the rate of growth of state tax revenues to the rate of growth of state personal income.

But, adoption of Proposition 8 was conditional upon the defeat of Proposition 13, which was to prevail if both were adopted. So Proposition 8 lost when 13 won.

Brown fought against Proposition 13 until a week before the primary, when he canceled public appearances to stay in Sacramento to prepare his administration to handle Proposition 13, which, he conceded, appeared unstoppable.

Brown appeared June 8 before a quickly convened joint session of the Legislature. He told it the state should use all its $5-billion budget surplus to help local governments, schools and state agencies cope with the Jarvis-Gann strictures. He also urged a $300-million cut in state spending in the next fiscal year.

A Constitutional Challenge—A suit challenging the constitutionality of Proposition 13 was filed in state Supreme Court June 7 by the California Teachers Association.

It contended that equal protection under the law would be denied people who purchased new homes once the proposition went into effect. Because a new assessment at current market values was permitted only when a home changed hands, a new owner would be paying more tax than a person with a comparable home who did not sell it.

Why Taxpayers Revolt

Dr. Lyle C. Firth, president of the Institute of Public Administration, testified July 25, 1978 before the Joint Economic Committee of Congress on the phenomenon of taxpayer revolt. The following is excerpted from his testimony:

In brief, what has happened in the last 20 years is that the unit cost of goods and services purchased by local governments, in order to provide public services, has increased by some 189 percent, compared with an increase in the cost of consumer goods and services of something like 104 percent. There has been a dramatic inflation in the cost of the inputs going into the State and local government process, compared with the cost of consumer goods.

Second, the amount of resources used by State and local governments per capita increased by 100 percent in the last two decades. In other words, State and local governments are now using twice the amount of resources for each man, woman, and child that they did two decades ago.

Now, I doubt if many taxpayers feel that they are getting double the services. On the contrary, they see many evidences of declining public sector effectiveness, such as increases in school dropouts, more traffic congestion, dirtier streets, more potholes, worsening public transportation, rising delinquency, and the rest.

Proposition 13 Impact Studied. California's Proposition 13 would have an "insignificant" impact on national economic growth but a measurable impact on inflation, according to a Congressional Budget Office report July 6.

It could produce a .2 percentage point reduction in the consumer price index in 1978 and a .4 percentage point reduction in 1980, the study estimated.

This would come about because a cut in property taxes would lower the cost of housing, which was a major component of the consumer price index, the government's measure of inflation.

The impact of California on the index was substantial because of the state's 10% share of the nation's population.

As for economic growth, the report estimated that Proposition 13 would cause a .1 percentage point reduction in the nation's output of goods and services in the first quarter of 1979.

Reduced spending by government units in California, induced by the drop in tax revenue, would slow the economy more than the tax cut would stimulate it, the study concluded, based on the reasoning that individuals would save some of their tax reductions.

Largely because of the layoffs and other cutbacks in the ranks of public employees necessitated by Proposition 13, the study estimated that national employment figures would be cut by 60,000 in 1978. This would represent "a negligible effect on the unemployment rate," the study pointed out.

The picture would turn around somewhat after 1978, in the view of the congressional economists. The stimulative effects of the tax reduction were expected to show up by the second quarter of 1980 and increase the national economic growth by a little less than .1 percentage point. At that point, the study estimated that employment would be 30,000 less than it would have been without the tax cut.

As for the impact on federal revenue,

Capacity and effort measures for all taxes of State and local governments, by State, 1975

STATE	Tax Capacity per Capita	Index	Potential Tax Yield	Taxes Collected Amount	Taxes Collected per Capita	Tax Effort Index	Amount Collected Less Potential Tax Yield
Alabama	$500.95	78	$1,810,952	$1,425,466	$394.32	79	$-385,486
Alaska	917.01	143	334,710	280,664	768.94	84	-54,046
Arizona	597.99	93	1,322,756	1,443,212	652.45	109	120,456
Arkansas	503.55	78	1,062,484	841,360	398.75	79	-221,124
California	709.36	110	15,037,101	17,970,758	847.76	120	2,933,657
Colorado	671.32	104	1,705,821	1,564,065	615.53	92	-141,756
Connecticut	727.19	113	2,254,305	2,134,842	688.66	95	-119,463
Delaware	782.73	122	453,201	389,532	672.77	86	-63,669
D.C.	772.71	120	551,637	496,991	696.16	90	-54,646
Florida	628.25	98	5,200,037	4,107,125	496.21	79	-1,092,912
Georgia	567.15	88	2,796,601	2,441,749	495.18	87	-354,852
Hawaii	699.09	109	606,807	726,500	836.98	120	119,693
Idaho	556.77	87	452,651	421,477	518.42	93	-31,174
Illinois	734.84	114	8,228,027	7,999,697	714.45	97	-228,330
Indiana	628.56	98	3,339,527	3,064,328	576.76	92	-275,199
Iowa	664.84	103	1,902,097	1,811,807	633.28	95	-90,290
Kansas	676.48	105	1,542,375	1,335,591	585.79	87	-206,784
Kentucky	575.30	90	1,948,535	1,581,159	466.83	81	-367,376
Louisiana	664.99	103	2,530,962	2,085,636	547.99	82	-445,326
Maine	476.48	74	504,112	596,499	563.80	118	92,387
Maryland	654.28	102	2,696,961	2,808,549	681.36	104	111,588
Massachusetts	604.91	94	3,516,967	4,616,687	794.06	131	1,099,720
Michigan	648.84	101	5,911,066	6,187,684	679.14	105	276,078
Minnesota	632.27	98	2,479,138	2,848,204	726.40	115	369,066
Mississippi	448.08	70	1,048,969	1,022,431	436.75	97	-26,538

NOTE: Potential tax yield, Amount collected and Amount collected less potential tax yield are in thousands of dollars. Per capita is in dollars.

STATE	Tax Capacity per Capita	Index	Potential Tax Yield	Taxes Collected Amount	Taxes Collected per Capita	Tax Effort Index	Amount Collected Less Potential Tax Yield
Missouri	603.19	94	2,875,387	2,440,224	511.90	85	-435,163
Montana	629.95	98	469,946	449,477	602.52	96	-20,469
Nebraska	660.10	103	1,019,203	876,035	567.38	86	-143,168
Nevada	969.88	151	572,229	398,989	676.25	70	-173,240
New Hampshire	626.67	97	508,859	406,173	500.21	80	-102,686
New Jersey	715.51	111	5,246,808	5,206,910	710.07	99	-39,898
New Mexico	600.16	93	686,581	607,390	530.94	88	-79,191
New York	653.99	102	11,821,544	17,913,237	991.00	152	6,091,693
North Carolina	538.05	84	2,927,552	2,578,457	473.89	88	-349,095
North Dakota	634.77	99	404,351	379,678	596.04	94	-24,673
Ohio	656.64	102	7,049,090	5,648,479	526.17	80	-1,400,611
Oklahoma	657.53	102	1,785,200	1,261,183	464.52	71	-524,017
Oregon	629.73	98	1,438,299	1,419,040	621.30	99	-19,259
Pennsylvania	606.34	94	7,191,145	6,918,119	583.32	96	-273,026
Rhode Island	552.50	86	514,374	593,201	637.17	115	78,827
South Carolina	494.23	77	1,391,745	1,211,446	430.20	87	-180,299
South Dakota	582.04	91	396,372	356,999	524.23	90	-39,373
Tennessee	530.25	82	2,212,717	1,785,640	427.90	81	-427,077
Texas	724.52	113	8,866,741	6,026,158	492.41	68	-2,840,583
Utah	549.60	86	661,171	602,666	500.97	91	-58,505
Vermont	542.44	84	256,034	310,179	657.16	121	54,145
Virginia	598.81	93	2,982,699	2,617,147	525.43	88	-365,552
Washington	640.16	100	2,278,325	2,298,072	645.71	101	19,747
West Virginia	576.56	90	1,037,228	883,747	491.24	85	-153,481
Wisconsin	597.97	93	2,744,075	3,281,113	715.00	120	537,038
Wyoming	941.92	147	354,161	258,467	687.41	73	-95,694
US Total	$642.76	100	$136,930,239	$136,930,239	$642.76	100	0

Source: Tax Wealth in 50 States (National Institute of Education)

the study expected a boost from Proposition 13 of about $600 million in fiscal 1979 and $900 million in fiscal 1980. The increases would come from the smaller property tax deductions that would be claimed on federal income taxes.

Calif. Allocates Budget Surplus—In California, Gov. Edmund G. Brown Jr. signed legislation June 24 allocating $5 billion of the state's $5.8-billion budget surplus to cities, counties and schools facing drastic cutbacks because of the tax revenue loss from Proposition 13.

The measure, put together in two weeks by six legislative leaders, applied $2.27 billion of the total as a grant to schools. The counties' share of $1.48 billion included $1 billion from a transfer to the state of welfare and health costs normally paid at the county level.

Cities were allotted $250 million and special districts $125 million.

A $900-million loan fund was established for local agencies to draw on if they had immediate cash flow problems.

Local government spending was expected to drop by a net 9.7% average in the coming fiscal year because of the new tax and budget actions.

Speaking to a statewide audience via television June 24, Brown said, "I want to reassure the people of this state that the provisions of Proposition 13 that have been enacted by 65% of the people will indeed be put into effect."

Brown also proposed putting in the state constitution a limit on local and state spending. The limit would be based on the growth of personal income in California. "If personal income goes up, so may government spending," he said.

In signing a $14.73-billion state budget July 6, Brown noted it was "the first time in 17 years that the budget has gone down instead of up." The budget was $10.6 million less than the previous year.

Other Reaction—Proposition 13, as a possible harbinger of a national tax revolt, was a major issue at conventions across the country as delegates from unions and other organizations assembled in regular annual meetings.

In Dallas, many delegates to the National Education Association convention sported buttons showing dice and the tagline, "13 You Lose."

There were those "who treat the politics of California as an aberration," President John Ryor told the delegates July 5. "I'm here to tell you that the fears, anxieties and aspirations of Californians are not significantly different from those of citizens of New Hampshire, South Carolina, Michigan or Texas."

Proposition 13 was mentioned "a million times" during a convention in Denver of the National Conference of State Legislatures, according to the organization's president, Fred Anderson, who was president of the Colorado Senate.

The consensus at the July 6 meeting, as Minnesota House Speaker Martin O. Sabo put it, was that the Proposition 13 posed "a very serious threat to the fabric of government."

Convention delegates of Americans for Democratic Action, meeting in Washington June 17, were told that politicians across the country were "chasing and fanning the popular whirlwind" and "seeking a mandate to govern by running against government itself."

The characterization came from outgoing president, Sen. George McGovern (D, S.D.).

McGovern said support for Proposition 13 had "undertones of racism" because it reflected a desire to reduce social services for minorities.

Economist John Kenneth Galbraith made a similar point June 28 in addressing a convention of the AFL-CIO American Federation of State, County and Municipal Employees in Las Vegas.

Proposition 13 was "a disguised attack on the poor," he said, because "an attack on public services singles out the poorest of our citizens for the greatest deprivation."

Union President Jerry Wurf had told the delegates June 26 that the movement in California was not a tax rebellion but "a public outcry for fair play" that could be answered only by tax reform.

Commerce Secretary Juanita Kreps, in a speech to the U.S. Conference of Mayors in Atlanta June 21, cautioned that "tax rebellions" such as the Proposition 13 vote could create "potentially the most vicious of cycles" that would contribute to urban decay.

A cutback of urban services, because of cutbacks in tax revenues, could "produce panic out-migrations of firms and residents, further diminishing the tax base and further reducing the ability of affected cities to meet minimum needs," she said.

Her advice was that the states, in the short run, should assume a greater share of the cost of urban services and, in the long run, should "lessen the dependence of cities on real property as the primary revenue base."

Campaign Vs. Property Tax. The campaign against property taxes produced legislation for property tax relief in 23 states during 1977, reported Rep. Joseph R. Biden Jr. (D. Del.) Aug. 14, 1978 as he introduced a bill to set up a program of federal grants to states and local government units that provide such relief. Biden said in a statement accompanying his legislative proposal:

In recent years, States, and to an even greater degree, local governments and school districts, have been forced to rely more heavily on the real property tax. Local governments, faced by soaring costs as a result of inflation, but in many cases, with property tax bases still eroded from the recession, have been forced to increase their property taxes in an ever upward spiral.

"Tax revolts" are an integral part of American history. There is a new tax revolt with us today, in modern form. It is the increasing dissatisfaction with the property tax. People feel not only that it is too high, but also that it is inequitable. In a recent survey taken in Delaware, when people were asked whether—if necessary to continue essential State services—they favored an increase in income taxes, a sales tax, or a statewide property tax, only 16 percent opted for the property tax. Yet on the local level particularly, the property tax is the only major revenue source for providing essential local services.

One usually thinks of the homeowner as bearing the burden of property taxation. The fact is that many of the people who can least afford it pay property taxes through their rent, as the owner passes along tax increases in the rent he charges. Thus no one is immune from the burden which this tax imposes and which together with inflation eats away at the money needed for subsistence.

Last year, property tax relief was enacted in one form or another in 23 States. But such relief is essentially hit or miss and that does not begin to take care of the problem. Based on 1974 figures, average relief from circuit-breaker programs nationally provided tax relief benefits of only $143 per participant. While this has undoubtedly risen some, so have property taxes as the following figures show.

In the decade from 1966 to 1976, State and local property taxes have climbed at an amazing rate of 131 percent. Total revenues from property taxes in 1976 were $57 billion, a staggering sum that is about half of all Federal collections from the individual income tax. The per capita real property tax burden grew from $135 per capita to $266 in the decade.

The two groups often hit the hardest are the elderly who live on fixed incomes in these inflationary times and families of modest incomes seeking to raise and educate a family. In particular, the elderly find that the property tax can threaten a secure future in their own home, no matter how carefully that future was planned. For modest income families it is a barrier to a reasonable standard of living and to our national goal of a decent home for every family.

This reliance on the property tax places a strain on local governments which are the backbone of our Federal structure of our Government. In some ways, the Federal Government, by virtually monopolizing the income tax, has forced this reliance on property taxes. The Federal Government has an obligation to help ease the burden on those unable to bear it and, in fact is in a unique position to do so. However, its help must leave the flexibility to local governments to plan their finances to meet local needs.

The bill I am introducing today is broad in scope and nature. It seeks to give maximum flexibility to State and local governments in designing a program of real property tax relief to homeowners and renters to meet the specific problems or needs of their locality. The bill provides for a Federal grant equal to half of the tax relief granted under the tax relief program, but with maximum amounts per property to assure that reasonable levels of relief are observed.

The Local Property Tax

John Sherman, assistant director of the Advisory Commission on Intergovernmental Relations, testifying July 25, 1978 before the Joint Economic Committee of Congress, was asked whether it still made "political and economic sense to retain the property tax as a major source of local revenue in an inflation ridden economy." He replied:

Despite obvious defects and a very poor public image, the property tax has significant political and fiscal virtues. First, it is the one major revenue source directly available to local government and, therefore, serves as a traditional defense against fiscal centralization.

Second, it is the only major tax that can capture for the community the property values created by the community.

Third, it has a high visibility, and it can work in the direction of greater public accountability.

But beyond these three considerations, there is an inescapable element of fiscal realism. The Nation's local governments will not quickly come up with an acceptable substitute for this powerful $65 billion revenue producer. That figure alone is more than the gross national product of most of the members of the United Nations. We are talking about a revenue instrument that produces more than the individual income tax and the sales tax at the State levels combined.

In view of the conservative mood of the country, it is also not likely that many State legislative bodies will be willing to solve the local property tax problem by granting broad discretion to local governments to levy income and sales taxes or by quickly relieving the local property tax of all responsibility for the financing of schools.

State legislators are much more likely to use their surplus funds to grant tax relief to property owners, rather than work out fiscal relief strategies for local governments. The State-financed plans of aid to property owners will take a variety of forms, and we are seeing it now: expanded circuit breakers, State reimbursement for partial homesteading exemptions, more tax rebates for part of the school taxes, part—not all—of the school taxes borne by homeowners.

. . .

Because State takeover of local school costs is an extremely expensive venture, we are not likely to see many dramatic breakthroughs on this front immediately. It is happening over time, but is going to be slow-going.

Well, for all of these reasons, prudent public policy would dictate the adoption of measures at the State level, designed to conserve the local property tax by reducing as much as possible the high irritant content of this levy.

The program can cover property tax relief to homeowners, or renters, or both. Tax relief must be related to income to qualify, but the specific relationships are left to each locality to determine based on local conditions. Finally, to assure fiscal soundness, there is a limit on the total Federal funds to be given to any State based on a per capita amount.

Governors Urge Budget Restraint. Restraint in government spending was a major topic at a meeting of the National Governors' Association in Boston Aug. 28–29, 1978.

Two prominent speakers at the meeting Aug. 28—Sen. Edward M. Kennedy (D, Mass.) and Gov. Edmund G. Brown Jr. (D, Calif.)—tied their messages to Proposition 13.

Brown said the taxpayer revolt signified by passage of Proposition 13 "could well unravel the Democratic coalition" unless the federal government responded to "the rising wrath of the middle class" without forsaking the party's "historic commitment to the poor and the dispossessed."

As a course of action for the governors, Brown advocated a stand that the federal government reimburse states and localities for the cost of implementing programs mandated by Congress or Administration officials.

If the federal government required, for example, that new buildings paid for with federal funds must have ramps, then the federal government should pay for the ramps.

In California, the state was required to help local governments pay for state-mandated programs.

"What I'm suggesting is real truth in spending," Brown said. His goal was to slow down federal spending and help state officials like himself who had been "born again to the spirit of austerity and tax cut."

Kennedy, appearing at a session on national health policy Aug. 28, said Proposition 13 was "in the minds of governors and of people all over the country."

"If there's one example of government out of control, it is in the health area," he said. "If there is one example of inflated cost with less services, it is in the health area."

A long-time supporter of national health insurance, Kennedy urged the governors to support such a program as a way to fight inflation and promote competition in the health-care field.

He contended that a national program would hinder cost increases since it would force states to budget health-care programs many years in advance.

The speaker at the conference's concluding session Aug. 29 was Robert S. Strauss, President Carter's special aide on inflation.

He said the President was prepared to "veto any budget-busting bills."

In a resolution adopted Aug. 29, the governors expressed "great concern" about federal spending as an ever-increasing share of the gross national product.

The resolution called for a balanced federal budget by fiscal 1981.

Gov. James B. Hunt Jr. (D, N.C.), who proposed the resolution, said he thought "the problem is in Congress." "They're voting every day to spend more money," he said.

The association refused to approve Aug. 29 a proposal by Gov. Meldrim Thomson Jr. (R, N.H.) that favored a constitutional limit on state and federal spending.

The governors also approved Aug. 29 the resolution endorsed by Gov. Brown to have the federal government reimburse states and localities for the costs of federally mandated programs.

Tax Votes. During the nationwide elections Nov. 7, 1978, voters in Arizona approved a constitutional amendment that would limit state spending to 7% of personal income. The ballot initiative, an outgrowth of the tax protest raised by California's Proposition 13, was adopted by a three-to-one margin.

Hawaii voters, approved, two to one, an amendment linking and limiting increases in government spending to economic growth.

An initiative modeled after Proposition 13 was adopted in Idaho by a 56% margin. The proposal required a cut in realty taxes to 1% of market value.

Michigan voters backed, by a narrow

THE GREAT AMERICAN TAX REVOLT

margin, a provision to limit spending by the state to a fixed percentage of the state's personal income. An amendment to drastically cut property taxes and a measure to institute a voucher plan to finance public education were defeated.

In a Nevada initiative, a proposal limiting property taxes to 1% of market value was approved by a three-to-one margin. Before it could become law, however, the proposal would have to be approved again in 1980.

The tax issue was involved in Oregon's gubernatorial contest. Incumbent Democrat Robert Straub lost to his Republican challenger, state Senate Minority Leader Victor Atiyeh.

Both candidates had responded to the swelling tax protest that had originated in neighboring California, but they favored rival ballot proposals to implement tax cuts.

Atiyeh supported a plan called Measure 6, which was nearly identical to California's Proposition 13. The Oregon plan would limit property taxes to 1.5% of assessed value.

Straub was opposed to Measure 6, saying it offered little tax relief to renters and homeowners. He convened a special session of the legislature in September to draft an alternative, Measure 11. Straub's proposal called for the state to pay half of each homeowner's property tax, up to $1,500, and would limit increases in state and local spending.

Both measures were defeated because supporters of the rival plans canceled each other out.

Texas voters approved an initiative to link state spending to the growth of the state's economy.

Tax-Cutting & Kemp-Roth

The campaign to cut taxes grew almost explosively in 1978. In an article entitled "Revolution of 1978," published in the Oct. 27, 1978 issue of National Review, Bruce Bartlett recalled that when Rep. Jack F. Kemp (R, N.Y.) and Sen. William V. Roth Jr. (R, Del.) had announced July

14, 1977 that they were co-sponsoring a bill to cut income taxes by about a third, "only three reporters showed up for the press conference." A year later, however, after the Kemp-Roth Tax Reduction Act had acquired 179 Congressional co-sponsors and wide support, the Senate Finance Committee July 14, 1978 opened hearings on the measure "in a packed hearing room filled with reporters and television cameras." The bill, brought to the House floor as an amendment to an Administration bill, was rejected Aug. 10 by 240-177 vote. Five days later a much altered tax-cutting bill was passed by both houses.

Kemp-Roth under attack. Rep. Charles A. Vanik (D, Ohio) warned in a statement in the Congressional Record Aug. 2, 1978 that "adoption of a tax cut in the dimension contemplated in the [Kemp-Roth] bill is extremely risky business." "[T]he deficit caused by such a tax cut would almost double the current deficit" and increase inflation, he said. He submitted for the Record a study prepared at his request by Donald W. Kiefer, Library of Congress specialist in taxation and fiscal policy. According to the study of the Kemp-Roth bill:

In summary, it might be observed that the overall shape of the Kemp/Roth tax cut is rather conventional. The largest portion of the tax cut would go to individual taxpayers (over 90 percent, which is a larger portion than for most recent tax cuts), and lower-income taxpayers would receive proportionately larger tax cuts. The revised distributions of the individual income tax burden across income classes and the nature of the corporate income tax cuts in the Kemp/Roth bill and the Carter Administration's tax cut proposal announced early in 1978 are very similar. Thus, the primary distinguishing characteristic of the Kemp/Roth proposal versus other measures, including the Administration's, is its magnitude.

While the proponents of the Kemp/Roth bill have advanced a number of arguments on its behalf, two contentions have received the principal emphasis and gained the most attention. The first involves reference to the 1964 tax cut as an appropriate historical precedent for the Kemp/Roth bill, and the second is the assertion that a general tax cut can be self-financing....

. . .

With regard to the 1964 tax cut the Kemp/Roth advocates have advanced essentially four propositions: (1) that there is a strong analogy between the economic conditions in 1964 and at the present, (2) that the 1964 tax cut was a successful fiscal policy worthy of emulation, (3) that the economic "feedback effects" of the 1964 tax cut were completely unanticipated, and (4) that the increase in tax revenue which was generated by the more rapid economic activity resulting from the 1964 tax cut more than offset the original revenue loss attributable to the tax cut.

The 1964 tax cut was the first major countercyclical tax reduction adopted in the United States. The tax cut had been proposed the previous year by President Kennedy as a remedy for high unemployment and slow economic recovery. Individual income tax liabilities were cut an average of 20 percent in two stages covering 1964 and 1965. The cut was accomplished by a revision of the tax rate schedule; rates were cut from a range of 20 percent in the lowest bracket to 91 percent in the highest bracket before the tax cut to a range of 14 percent to 70 percent after the tax cut. Corporate income taxes were cut approximately 10 percent; the top corporate tax rate was reduced from 52 percent to 48 percent. When the tax cuts had become fully effective in 1965, individual income taxes were reduced approximately $11 billion and corporate taxes about $3 billion.

While there are important similarities between present economic conditions and those which existed in 1964, there are also crucial dissimilarities. In 1978 we are approximately three years into an economic recovery from a recession, as we were in 1964. The 1975 recession was the most severe postwar recession, and so the recovery is taking considerable time. Presently, as was the case in 1964, the consensus forecasts imply that, in the absence of stimulative policy, economic recovery will subside shortly, perhaps to a level which will no longer make progress in reducing unemployment.

In mid-1978, as in 1964, we have an unemployment rate which is lower than during the depth of the recession, but nonetheless allows some room for further improvement. The present unemployment rate is 5.7 percent, down from 9.1 percent during May of 1975. The definition of full employment is presently the subject of considerable debate, but it is most likely in the range of 4.5 to 5.5 percent. Thus, while full employment has not yet been attained, the economy is nonetheless in the range where further progress in reducing unemployment must be accomplished gradually to avoid contributing to inflationary pressures. In 1964 the unemployment rate (on an annual basis) was 5.2 percent, down from 6.7 percent in 1961. At that time full employment was regarded to be in the neighborhood of 4 percent so, then as now, further improvement was possible.

The two eras are also similar in terms of industrial capacity utilization, indicating room for expansion of output. In 1964 the capacity utilization rate for total manufac-

turing, using the Federal Reserve Board measure, was 85.7 percent, up from 77.3 percent in 1961 but still substantially below full capacity. In May, 1978, the rate was 83.6 percent, up from the 70.9 percent rate experienced in the first quarter of 1975, but below the 1964 level and substantially below full capacity.

The concept of the GNP gap, which is an estimate of the difference between actual gross national product (GNP) and potential GNP, is a way of combining the diverse economic indicators into a single measure of the degree of slack in economic performance. Some caution is necessary in using this concept because different analysts have different estimates of potential GNP, depending on their views of the level of full employment, capacity utilization, etc. The 1978 annual report of the Council of Economic Advisors provides their estimates of actual and potential GNP from 1952 through 1977.[10] Using this measure, the 1975 recession was considerably more severe than the 1961 recession, and in 1978 there remains considerably more slack in the economy than existed in 1964. These data indicate that, in 1972 dollars, 1961 actual GNP was $755.3 billion and potential GNP that year was $798.6 billion, indicating a GNP gap of $43.3 billion of 5.4 percent. By 1964 potential GNP had reached $890.3 billion, actual GNP was $874 billion, leaving a gap of $15.9 billion or 1.8 percent. In 1975 actual GNP was $1,202.1 billion compared to potential GNP of $1,316.9 billion, leaving a gap of $114.8 billion or 8.7 percent. The 1977 data indicate a potential GNP of $1,412.0, an actual GNP of $1,397.6 billion, and a resulting GNP gap of $74.4 billion or 5.3 percent. Thus, the output shortfall in 1977 was substantial and considerably larger than existed in 1964. ...

. . .

In addition to the above similarities between present economic conditions and those in 1964, there are also several important differences. First, and perhaps foremost, the inflation rate is much higher in 1978 than it was in 1964. The consumer price index (CPI) increased only 1.3 percent in 1964 and had advanced an average of 1.24 percent per year for the first 5 years of the 1960's. In mid-1978, however, the CPI is advancing at an average annual rate of over 10 percent, and the average for the past 5 years is an annual rate of 7.7 percent. ...

Kemp defends proposal—Kemp announced Aug. 8 that he intended to introduce the Kemp-Roth bill as an amendment to the House tax-cut bill. He said:

··· The Kemp amendment is the only measure being discussed in the entire tax debate in Congress and the Nation which assures that the increases in all kinds of Federal taxes which are going to otherwise occur will be offset....

Federal taxes are increasing—and at an astonishing rate. I have placed into the RECORD on several occasions the table prepared by the Joint Committee on Taxation staff, detailing the higher social security taxes, the higher personal income taxes—as a result of inflation pushing the taxpayers into tax brackets where the percentages they pay in taxes on additional dollars of income are increasingly higher, the higher energy taxes if the energy bill becomes law.

The joint committee's table shows $22.9 billion more in inflation-pushed and social security taxes in fiscal year 1979; $35.1 billion more in those taxes in fiscal year 1980. If you add prospective new energy taxes, resulting from the House-passed bill, we will be facing $25.8 billion more in fiscal year 1979, $47.4 billion more in fiscal year 1980.

But these are not all of the higher taxes the American taxpayer will be paying in fiscal year 1979 and beyond. He and she will be paying $5.3 billion more in excise taxes, and another $1.2 billion in customs, estate, gift, and other taxes. This means from over $29 billion to over $32 billion more in Federal taxes in fiscal year 1979.

To the fiscal year 1980 figures in the joint committee's table, we also have to add $5.6 billion more in excise taxes and $1.3 billion more in customs, estate, gift, and other taxes. That would mean from $42 billion more to over $54 billion more in fiscal year 1980.

But billions are difficult to comprehend. What the individual taxpaying family is more interested in is the effect of these higher taxes upon them. Let us take a look, then, at what these higher taxes will mean to the average family:

Additional tax dollars which will be paid by the average family of 4

Tax	Fiscal year 1979	Fiscal year 1980
Personal income	$224	$374
Social security	158	212
Energy	48	205
Excise	88	93
Customs, estate, gift and others	20	22
Total taxes increase	538	906

That is a staggering total Federal tax increase to ask, to expect, the American people to shoulder. And it is wrong to think that these tax increases will be offset either by inflation-pegged wage

gains or by real income growth. Because for each 1-percent inflation-pegged or real income growth wage increase, the Federal total tax burden goes up an average of 1.2 percent. It goes up 1.5 percent for personal income taxes, 1 percent for social security, and 0.5 percent for other taxes. Thus, with these levels of taxes, the harder the wage earner works to get ahead, the less they really do.

This is a critical point: Inflation is pushing people into higher and higher marginal tax rate brackets. It is true whether the person is in a lower, middle, or higher income category. . . .

The Kemp amendment is the only bill or amendment which will be before the House that comes close to offsetting these high taxes, to offsetting the effect of inflation in pushing taxpayers into higher and higher marginal tax rate brackets.

The only way to deal with this, and this is the reason the Kemp amendment is structured the way it is, is to reduce the marginal rates. Increases in thresholds, increases in personal exemptions, and so forth, only offset a small portion of these increases, and they do not effect incentive and reward, therefore they do not assure increased individual or total economic activity. . . .

Hatch backs Roth-Kemp—In Senate debate on the tax measure Oct. 5, Sen. Orrin G. Hatch (R, Utah) was one of several senators supporting the Roth-Kemp proposal. Hatch said:

. . . What about Roth-Kemp and its inflationary effects? Will not Roth-Kemp create a sudden and huge surge in consumer spending, creating the inflationary situation of too many dollars chasing too few goods? Even if investment spending increases at this time as capital stock is put in place, will not this too be inflationary, particularly in the short run?

There are two effects of a tax rate reduction along the lines of Roth-Kemp. One, which this question addresses, is the increase in after-tax incomes of workers and investors.

In the first year of Roth-Kemp, this increase "in consumer pockets" would amount to $20 billion in a gross economy 100 times as large. But while $20 billion goes, in effect, into consumer pockets,

$18 billion comes right out as a result of increased social security taxes and inflation-related tax increases. This $2 billion net is only one-thousandth the size of the economy itself—hardly enough to overwhelm capacity with great surges in consumer demand as the gloomy inflation scenarios predict.

In addition, to the degree the economy sees that this $2 billion must be paid back to finance the bonds that make it available, the economy will save, not spend, the $2 billion. Particularly in the lowest income classes, where credit is often necessary for survival, the net result of Roth-Kemp would tend to pay down debt, thus going into savings, not consumption.

The second, more important effect of Roth-Kemp is to remove unnecessarily high barriers to production. That is, a lower tax rate not only affects the current paycheck—or interest payment, or dividend check. It holds out greater incentive to work, save or invest in the future. The increased willingness of workers to produce plus the increased willingness of capital to assemble workers in new or added enterprise—there now being a greater reward for such effort—lifts the entire economy to a higher level of efficiency. Even if the physical effort expended, in aggregate, remains the same, production of goods and services increases by increased efficiency—produtivity.

As to the effects of increased investment spending, a tax rate reduction cannot focus on either labor or capital to the exclusion of the other. If tax rates on labor were zero and tax rates on capital 100 percent, there would be no employment, thus no enterprise, and no revenues. Roth-Kemp, of course, applies across-the-board on the incomes of workers, savers and investors.

There would also be no short-run inflationary effect from Roth-Kemp. The economy simply does not await actual passage of a tax cut to begin expanding work, saving and investment. ...

Another question: How did Roth-Kemp arrive at the 30 percent tax cut figure—10 percent each year for 3 years?

If inflation is the major fear of Roth-Kemp, why not expand the tax cut time frame to 5 years, beginning the first year at a relatively low tax cut rate, increasing it year by year at an increasing rate?

Roth-Kemp is designed as an ex poste adjustment of tax rates to offset the debilitating inflation rates of the 1970's. If the progressive income tax rates had been indexed since 1970 to annually adjust for the rate of inflation, thereby preventing real increases in tax rates from occurring, the income thresholds would have been adjusted upward by more than 60 percent in that period—except that if the rates had been indexed, the deficits, contraction and inflation would not have been as severe as we have experienced.

In light of this, Roth-Kemp's 30 percent tax cut over 3 years is a relatively modest attempt to return to a sense of reasonableness in Federal income taxation.

As to the second question, Representative KEMP originally planned a 1-year adjustment, conceding to requests for a cautious phase-in. To extend the phase-in over 5 years would not adjust for the inflation the Carter administration forecasts for the future, let alone the last 8 years of inflation. ...

If the goal of Roth-Kemp is to generate economic expansion on the supply side of the economy, why is the proposal so stingy with cuts in the corporate income tax? Should not the corporate income tax cuts be at least equal in magnitude to the personal income tax cuts to accomplish your called-for rate of economic expansion?

It is a mistake to think of corporate taxes as taxes on capital and personal taxes as taxes on consumption. Both are taxes on production, with the former applied selectively to corporate income, the latter applied to all forms of productive income.

In the final analysis, all income flows through to individuals, which is why Roth-Kemp emphasizes cuts in personal income taxes. An across-the-board reduction in individual income tax rates treats all forms of primary income sources without bias. In other words, individuals receive taxable income from wages and salaries, interest, dividends, royalties and capital gains, and all of these must encounter the personal income tax schedules.

There is a second reason why personal income tax cuts are so important. Any tax plan that cuts business taxes but neglects personal income taxes will do nothing to raise the rate of return on work effort. Nor will it increase the after-tax rate of return on savings. And increased savings is an important by-product of any tax cut plan.

Compromise tax cut passed. Congress Oct. 15, 1978 passed a compromise bill revising the tax code and providing a tax cut of $18.7 billion for 1979. President Carter signed the bill Nov. 6.

President Carter had threatened to veto an earlier version of the bill, passed by the Senate, that mandated a cut of $29.3 billion for 1979. But White House adviser Stuart Eizenstat, appearing Oct. 15 on the CBS-TV program *Face the Nation,* said the final version of the bill put together by the House-Senate conference committee was "much closer to the type of bill which we requested."

Treasury Secretary Michael Blumenthal called the bill "much improved" over the earlier House and Senate versions, the Wall Street Journal reported Oct. 16.

Carter had objected that the Senate version would cost the government too much revenue, and he had criticized the House version as allocating too much of the tax relief to upper-income individuals. Among the steps taken by the House and Senate conferees to make the bill more acceptable to Carter:

■ A House provision to "index" capital gains against inflation (so that the part of the appreciation in value that was due to inflation would not be subject to tax) was eliminated.

■ A college tuition tax credit was eliminated.

■ A tax break for homeowners selling their houses was trimmed somewhat.

■ A Senate provision mandating automatic tax reductions in future years provided the government held down spending and achieved a balanced budget by 1982 was diluted into just a statement of intention. The Senate's version of the bill had been projected as providing tax cuts of $130 billion in 1983, and this provision would have accounted for almost half of those cuts. The provision, opposed by Carter, was described by the Washington Post Oct. 11 as a Democratic version of the GOP Roth-Kemp tax cut proposal.

■ The amount of tax reduction slated by the Senate for capital gains was cut by about one-third.

The conference committee finished its work in the early morning hours of Oct. 15. Later the same day the Senate approved the final version, 72 to 3, and the House cleared it, 337–38.

Even after the conference committee changes, the final version of the bill departed considerably from Carter's original proposals. According to the Oct. 16 Washington Post, 79% of the tax cuts for individuals would go to those with annual incomes of $15,000 or more, while only 21% would go to those making less than $15,000. Also, the tax breaks for capital gains were still greater than Carter had wanted.

The bill's $18.7 billion in cuts for 1979 broke down as follows: $12.7 billion in cuts for individuals, $3.7 billion in business tax cuts, and $2.2 billion in reductions in capital gains taxation.

Republicans, who had favored a 33% cut spread over three years, criticized the $18.7-billion reduction as too little. Republicans argued that even with the $18.7-billion cut, many taxpayers would pay higher taxes next year because of scheduled increases in Social Security taxes and because inflation tended to lift taxpayers into higher tax brackets.

The bill was also attacked by some liberals. Robert Brandon, director of Ralph Nader's Tax Reform Research Group, said the bill "reverses over 10 years of tax reform efforts," the Wall Street Journal reported Oct. 16.

Brandon continued, "The long effort to eliminate the special treatment of capital gains—the biggest loophole in the tax system for the wealthy—would be dealt a knockout blow, unless the President rejects the bill."

Details of the major provisions:

Individual Taxes—The existing $750 personal exemption for each taxpayer and dependent would be raised to $1,000. The higher exemption would be provided in place of the existing personal tax credit, which equaled $35 per exemption or 2% of the first $9,000 of taxable income.

The zero bracket amount, formerly known as the standard deduction, would go up to $2,300 from $2,200 for single persons and to $3,400 from $3,200 for married couples filing joint returns.

Existing law provided 25 tax brackets, with income in each bracket taxed at different rates, ranging from 14% (for single persons with taxable income between $2,200 and $2,700, or married coupled filing jointly with income between $3,200 and $4,200) up to 70% (for income over $102,200 for a single taxpayer, or for income over $203,200 for a couple filing jointly). The bill would replace this system with a smaller number of wider brackets. Single taxpayers would have 16 brackets; couples would have 15 brackets.

Fewer brackets would tend to reduce the impact of inflation, since higher earnings would not move taxpayers so quickly into higher brackets. The bill also set some rate cuts in middle-income brackets.

Business Taxes—The top tax rate on corporate income would be cut to 46% from 48%.

The rate on the first $25,000 of corporate income would be pared to 17% from 20%, and the rate on the next $25,000 would be cut to 20% from 22%. The bill set a tax rate of 30% for the third $25,000 of income and 40% for the fourth 25,000; currently that money was taxed at the top rate. The top rate, under the bill, would apply to income over $100,000.

The existing general jobs tax credit would be replaced with a new credit aimed at encouraging businesses to hire individuals from certain underemployed groups. The credit would be worth up to $3,000 for the first year of employment and up to $1,500 the second year. There would be eight targeted groups, including certain welfare recipients, Vietnam veterans, convicted felons and handicapped persons. The credit, in effect for 1979-1981, would apply to employees hired after Sept. 26, 1978.

Capital Gains—Various changes would be made in the rules affecting taxation of capital gains—the profits from the sale of real estate, stocks or other assets—with the effect of reducing the maximum tax rate for individuals on capital gains to 28%

from 49%. The minimum rate would go down to 5.6% from 7%, and intermediate rates would also be cut.

Changes made in the treatment of capital gains for businesses would have the effect of lowering the maximum tax rate to 29.67% from 31.125%.

The effective date of a rule from the 1976 Tax Reform Act dealing with tax on capital gains from inherited property would be pushed back. Prior to the 1976 law, only the appreciation in value that occurred between the death of the benefactor and the sale of the property was subject to the capital gains tax. The 1976 law established a new "carry-over" policy: all appreciation in value, from the time the benefactor originally acquired the property, would be subject to the tax. However, the 1976 law cushioned the impact of the new rule by applying it only to the future: a "basis" date of Dec. 31, 1976, was set, and appreciation in value that occurred prior to that date would not be subject to the capital gains tax. The new bill would delay, through 1979, imposition of the "carry-over" policy.

Home Sales—A one-time tax break would be made available for the sale of homes by persons 55 years and older. They would not be taxed on the first $100,000 in profits on the sale of their homes, provided they had owned and occupied the residence for three of the previous five years. The effective date of the provision would be retroactive to July 26, 1978.

Other Provisions—Other provisions of the bill would:

■ Liberalize the tax credit businesses received for investing in machinery and equipment. (Money spent after Nov. 1 to rehabilitate industrial and commercial buildings that had been in use for at least 20 years would qualify for the credit.)

■ Expand, in certain cases, the tax credit for installing pollution control facilities to 10% from 5%.

■ Enlarge the category of industrial bonds and bonds to construct water facilities that would pay tax-exempt interest.

132 THE GREAT AMERICAN TAX REVOLT

■ Increase the maximum tax credit for political contributions to $50 from $25, for an individual, and to $100 from $50, for a couple filing jointly.

■ Exempt from taxation the tuition paid by an employer for courses being taken by an employee, unless the courses dealt with sports, games or hobbies. (Under current law, employees had to pay taxes on company-paid tuition unless the course related directly to their current jobs.)

■ Liberalize rules governing individual retirement accounts, pension plans and other financial arrangements for retirement.

■ Allow working parents to take a tax credit for child-care payments made to a grandparent.

■ Allow businesses to carry back losses arising from product liability claims seven years (instead of the three years for operating losses provided by existing law). Businesses would still be able to carry the losses forward the seven years provided by existing law.

■ Revise sections of federal tax law dealing with oil and gas drilling, railroads, housing, mutual funds, cooperatives, farms, student loans and a variety of other subjects.

Carter 'Reforms'—Many of Carter's proposals to raise revenue and eliminate "loopholes" were rejected by Congress.

Congress did agree to eliminate the deduction for state and local taxes on gasoline and other motor fuels not used for business purposes. And the bill would end the existing business deductions for yachts, hunting lodges, fishing camps and similar entertainment facilities. But country club dues, first-class air fares and "three martini" lunches would still be deductible. Also, Congress eliminated the Administration's proposed cuts in deductions for medical expenses.

Unemployment pay would be subject to tax if received by a single person with an income over $20,000, or by a couple filing jointly with an income over $25,000. Existing law treated unemployment compensation as tax-exempt.

Kemp scores bill—Rep. Kemp charged in a statement in the Congressional Record Jan. 18, 1979 that instead of taxes being cut, they would actually rise under the 1978 tax-cutting bill. He said:

Congress allowed most of the meaningful tax relief which it had approved to be eliminated from its final tax bill under the threat of a Presidential veto. A House-Senate conference committee deleted the Nunn amendment to enact significant reductions in personal income tax rates over 5 years. In fact, the administration and majority leadership announced their backing for enormous tax increases, by rejecting measures to index capital gains and income taxes against inflation-caused automatic tax increases. Also rejected was a delay in imposing massive scheduled increases in the social security payroll tax, which took effect January 1, 1979.

By the time the conference committee was finished, it had produced a bill it called a $12.7 billion tax cut for individuals—which was really a $13.7 billion increase for 1979 alone, because of $26.4 billion in tax increases due to inflation and social security. . . .

. . .

All of these amounted to massive increases in disincentives which block economic growth, and the financial world correctly recognized them as such. Beginning the day the conference committee began to demolish the tax bill, the stock market began a sickening decline. The value of the Nation's capital stock, as measured by the New York Stock Exchange, lost $110 billion in the space of 2 weeks.

The stock market acts on the oldest of economic principles: when you tax something, you get less of that thing. When you tax production, capital, work, savings, entrepreneurial activity and excellence, you get less of all of those. Such taxation can be increased explicitly, through legislation like the rise in social security payroll taxes. Or, with our steeply progressive system of tax rates, it can be increased through production, or inflation, or both.

Consider the baker, who, by way of example, is taxed 20 percent on the first loaf of bread he and his employee bake, 40 percent on the second loaf, 60 percent on the third, 80 percent on the fourth, and 100 percent on the fifth, and who, given the level of technology in his economy, is capable of producing only one loaf of bread per day. His objective is clearly to increase his output of bread loaves to increase his income. Under the tax system just described, however, his rewards from pushing forward on the frontiers of baking technology are reduced again and again for each additional loaf that he bakes. When he is at the level of four loaves, or at the margin, the 100-percent tax rate, all incentive to increase his baking productivity is ended. It is ended without any inflation because if the baker were to produce a fifth loaf of bread, it would be taxed entirely away.

Productivity combined with a progressive tax system means higher taxes, and so does inflation combined with a progressive tax system. Inflation, though, acts more swiftly than increased productivity in pushing people into higher tax brackets. Inflation speeds the process of crushing out incentive when the government levies its tax on the nominal value of the bread. If the baker sells one loaf for one paper dollar, and the Government taxes 20 percent of a dollar's income, then the incentive to increase efficiency is removed more quickly than as the Government reduces the value of a dollar.

The combined effect of inflation and progressive taxation has reduced productivity in the last decade, from 3.2 percent a year on the years 1947–67, to 1.6 percent since. ...

Taxes to Rise for Most—A congressional study had predicted in 1978 that under tax-cut legislation then pending, most taxpayers would pay more taxes in 1979 than in 1978.

The study, prepared by economists for the Joint Committee on Taxation, concluded that higher Social Security taxes and inflation would outweigh the effects of the tax cut for all but a few taxpayers. Inflation raised tax bills by pushing taxpayers into higher tax brackets.

According to the study, only those earning about $15,000 per year would have a lower tax obligation in 1979—and their bills would be down by only $2 or $3.

A single person earning $10,000 would have a tax bill about $40 higher in 1979 than in 1978, the study said. A married person with two children earning the same amount would have to pay about $29 more in taxes.

For persons earning $20,000 to $30,000, taxes would go up by $66 to $241 in 1979 for single persons, and by $22 to $105 for married persons with two children, the study said.

Taxes, the Budget & the Economy

Democrats on Carter's Programs. President Carter's budget plans and anti-inflation program were supported by resolution of the Democrats in a midterm conference Dec. 10, 1978.

But strong discontent with Carter's priorities was evident throughout the conference, which was held in Memphis Dec. 8–10.

The climax of the conference was an 822-521 vote Dec. 10 to reject a resolution strongly critical of the Administration's budget priorities.

The almost 40% vote of dissent was cast despite heavy Administration pressure to support the President's position. The conference was controlled by Carter supporters and the President showed up at the conference with a large contingent of aides.

The emotional climax of the conference came when Sen. Edward M. Kennedy (D, Mass.) aroused the delegates with a ringing attack on the Administration's budgetary conservatism.

"I support the fight against inflation," Kennedy shouted at a workshop on national health insurance Dec. 9. "But no fight against inflation can be effective or successful unless the fight is fair."

"The party that tore itself apart over Vietnam in the 1960s cannot afford to tear itself apart today over budget cuts in basic social programs.

"There could be few more divisive issues for America and for our party than a Democratic policy of drastic slashes in the federal budget at the expense of the elderly, the poor, the black, the sick, the cities and the unemployed.

"We cannot accept a policy that cuts spending to the bone in areas like jobs and health but allows billions of dollars in wasteful spending for tax subsidies to continue and adds even greater fat and waste through inflationary spending for defense."

Kennedy's speech was wildly cheered.

The Administration's position at the session was presented by Joseph A. Califano Jr., secretary of health, education and welfare, and Stuart E. Eizenstat, the President's chief domestic adviser. Their argument was that while national health insurance was the goal, how to phase it in was the problem, especially in view of the country's economic problems. They favored a slower course and smaller package than that advocated by Kennedy.

President Carter received only polite applause for a half-hour speech to the convention Dec. 8.

Reviewing a broad range of programs to be undertaken, the President stressed that the most crucial test of the party's success would be the battle against inflation.

"It is an illusion to believe we can preserve a commitment to compassionate, progressive government if we fail to bring inflation under control," he told the delegates.

Carter appeared at several issue workshops Dec. 9. Challenged repeatedly to justify cutting back domestic spending programs while boosting military spending, Carter replied, "I do not have any apology to make at all for maintaining a strong defense."

Discontent with the President's budget proposals was heard again and again from blacks and from labor and urban leaders at numerous other workshops at the conference Dec. 9.

The dissident budget proposal defeated Dec. 10 requested that "human needs" be budgeted at no less than in the current services budget. It was sponsored by Douglas A. Fraser, president of the United Auto Workers. A current services budget was the level of funds needed to maintain all existing services, despite rising prices.

Before the vote rejecting the Fraser proposal, Vice President Walter Mondale warned the delegates that if the Democrats "don't end the ever-rising cost of living, we will be driven out of office as we were by the Vietnam war."

"If we don't end inflation," he said, "it will stop all our efforts for social progress. . . . Inflation will make a progressive nation a nasty, uncaring, illiberal society. . . . It has happened to other societies and it can happen to us."

As for the President's budget, Mondale assured the conference that "it will not be just the domestic programs that will be analyzed, so will the defense budget."

Budget dispute continues—President Carter Dec. 14 defended his budget plans in the face of growing criticism and protests from special interest groups against reported spending cutbacks in their areas.

Much of the criticism focused on the President's intention to increase defense spending while cutting most other programs.

Carter told television interviewer Barbara Walters of ABC-TV that "I do not intend to go back on my commitment" to maintain "a strong defense."

Carter reaffirmed his commitment to a 3% "real" increase in defense spending. The commitment had been made in May by the U.S. and other North Atlantic Treaty Organization members.

Some key congressional leaders had objected to the President's plan to spare only defense from budget cutting.

Sen. Edmund Muskie (D, Me.), chairman of the Senate Budget Committee, said Dec. 14 he saw "no reason" why defense spending could not be cut along with civilian programs.

Muskie indicated that this could be done even without breaking the commitment to increase NATO spending.

House Budget Committee Chairman Robert Giaimo (D, Conn.) expressed a similar view Dec. 14. "Defense, like everything else, is going to have to tighten its belt," he said.

"We've got lots of crises, including one in defense," Giaimo said, "but the major, immediate, pressing crisis is the economy."

Muskie spoke critically of the budget's deficit and tax assumptions.

"That $30-billion figure may be over-sold," he said of Carter's plan to try to hold the deficit to that amount.

The $30-billion deficit could be reached in the budget year, he said, if the economy had the same "real" growth as in the current year. The estimate for calendar 1978 was for a 3.75% "real" growth, or growth beyond the inflation factor.

But, Muskie said, the "economic signs" were pointing to slower growth in calendar 1979, many in the range of 2.5% to 3%.

The Congressional Budget Office's estimate for 1979 growth was tentatively set at 2.4%, Muskie noted.

The Administration's own estimate, reaffirmed by Treasury Secretary Michael Blumenthal in testimony Dec. 14 to Congress's Joint Economic Committee, was for the growth in 1979 to be in the range of 2% to 3%.

Muskie pointed out that an economic slowdown would lead to less tax revenues and more federal spending on unemployment insurance and, hence, a larger-than-expected budget deficit.

Inflation put the projected budget deficit in jeopardy as well, Muskie said, because a tax cut was very probable if inflation kept pushing people into higher tax brackets.

"Congress has got to hold the effective tax rate stable," he said.

Muskie also observed that Congress could be pushed into tax cuts by an aroused public. There could be considerable reaction, he said, "if people see their taxes rising" because of inflation.

White House Press Secretary Jody Powell had conceded Nov. 28 that inflation could alter the President's specific economic goals.

A goal of a 3% growth in defense spending might be unattainable, Powell said, if inflation persisted.

"Certainly you've got to assume that, with the problem with inflation, you aren't going to be able to do as much there [defense spending] as you otherwise would be," he said.

Powell also indicated that the 3% goal for defense increases might not survive the budgetary thrust to keep the federal deficit at or below $30 billion.

Continuing his budget orientation hearings with various groups, Carter had sepa-rate meetings Dec. 20 with eight big-city Democratic mayors and with seven governors from both political parties.

The mayors expressed concern about a cutback in urban aid, which they said could total as much as $15 billion. "We of the cities are the walking wounded," Syracuse, N.Y. Mayor Lee Alexander protested.

A cutback of that magnitude would "result in the disintegration" of the Administration's urban program, Alexander said.

Boston Mayor Kevin White warned that such reductions were "deep and dangerous to the Democratic Party" because they threatened key constituencies, the party's "building blocks" in the 1980s.

The governors were more sympathetic to Administration plans. They said they could live with the necessary budget cutbacks. But they urged the Administration to be flexible, as well, by relaxing red tape, especially on the programs that were required of states and cities but not funded by the federal government.

"Somebody has got to suffer," Gov. Julian Carroll (D, Ky.) commented, and mayors "might as well get ready" as well.

Tax Total Budgeted at Over $500 Billion. President Carter Jan. 22, 1979 submitted a budget that anticipated more than $500 billion in federal taxes in fiscal 1980. The budget was designed primarily to restrain inflation by gently slowing the economy.

One hazard to avoid, Carter Administration officials felt, was the recession that was being forecast by many nongovernment economists for late 1979 or 1980.

The new budget called for outlays of $531.6 billion in fiscal 1980, which would begin Oct. 1. The total was a 7.7% increase over the estimate for the current 1979 fiscal year's spending level.

Revenues were projected at $502.6 billion for fiscal 1980, which would bring the budget deficit in at the $29 billion promised previously by the President.

The spending level would "disappoint those who seek expanded federal efforts across the board," Carter said.

"This policy of restraint is not a casual one," he said. "It is an imperative if we are to overcome the threat of accelerating inflation. If that threat is realized, it would severely disrupt our economy and the well-being of our society. Americans with low and fixed incomes would suffer the most. Restraint would eventually become an inescapable necessity. But the longer we wait, the more severe and costly the inevitable restraint will be."

Carter referred to the spending level projected for fiscal 1980 as "well below that suggested by the recent momentum of federal spending."

The 7.7% increase from the current year compared with a 12.1% average annual increase in federal spending from 1973 to 1978.

The President, however, predicted that the course of restraint would bring the federal budget into "approximate balance" by fiscal 1981. The projected fiscal 1980 deficit of $29 billion compared with the $37.4 billion deficit estimated for the current 1979 fiscal year.

On the other hand, if Carter's "wage-insurance" proposal did not survive, a widely predicted eventuality, the government would save the $2.5 billion put in the fiscal 1980 budget to cover its cost.

The proposal was part of the President's wage-price guideline plan. It would provide tax cuts for workers abiding by the guidelines if inflation exceeded 7%.

A number of changes in tax collection were proposed in the budget to tighten or accelerate payment of withheld and estimated taxes. Most of the proposals would require congressional action.

The Administration looked upon deferral of tax liabilities as a matter of "interest-free loans from the government." While loopholes in this area were to be closed, however, the Administration also proposed to reduce the number of taxpayers required to make quarterly payments of their estimated taxes.

One of the proposed changes would speed up deposits of state and local Social Security taxes. Other proposed revisions applied to taxes on inherited property, railroad retirement, aviation, independent contractors, fringe benefits and tips.

Even with the outlays expected under Carter's "real wage insurance" proposal, the tax revisions would increase revenues $2.2 billion in fiscal 1980, $5 billion in

The Federal Budget Dollar

(Proposed by President Carter)

Where it comes from:

Individual income taxes	43¢
Social insurance receipts	30¢
Corporate income taxes	13¢
Borrowing	5¢
Excise taxes	4¢
Other	5¢

Where it goes:

Benefit payments to individuals	39¢
Military	24¢
Grants to states and localities	16¢
Other federal operations	12¢
Net interest	9¢

1981 and $5.3 billion in 1982.

The real wage insurance plan, part of the Administration's anti-inflation program, would extend a tax credit to workers whose pay increases were held to 7% or less. The credit would be limited to the first $20,000 of wages and three percentage points of inflation above 7%.

In other areas, the Administration planned to:

■ Speed up collection of customs duties and tobacco excise taxes (in 1981 and 1982);

■ Establish an oil-cleanup fund from a fee of three cents a barrel on oil received at refineries or terminals;

■ Restrict the use of tax-exempt state and local mortgage bonds to low- and moderate-income families.

Budget Balancing Issue. The question of a constitutional amendment requiring a balanced federal budget should be approached "very gingerly," President Carter said at his press conference Jan. 17, 1979.

Such an amendment had been endorsed by Gov. Edmund G. Brown Jr. (D. Calif.), as well as by others.

It would be difficult to devise such an amendment, Carter said, "without adding provisos that would let us deal with unanticipated military or security needs and unanticipated needs when we have a depression, for keeping our people at work and providing for large numbers of those who might be poor, or hungry or needing services."

Carter especially opposed a constitutional convention as the method of getting an amendment prohibiting deficit spending. Such a procedure would be "extremely dangerous," he said, because a convention could be "completely uncontrollable." The Constitution "could be amended en masse," he said.

The President stressed his commitment to a balanced budget.

A call for a constitutional convention to mandate a balanced federal budget had been approved by at least 26 state legislatures, according to the National Taxpayers' Union, which had been pushing the proposal since 1975.

By the start of 1979, the group claimed backing of 22 states.

But the exact count of states in the drive was disputed. Sen. Alan Cranston (Calif.), Democratic whip, counted only 14 states Feb. 6 as having filed proper petitions with Congress.

Sen. Birch Bayh (D, Ind.), chairman of the Judiciary Subcommittee on the Constitution, counted 16 Feb. 6. The Bayh count, for example, excluded several states where the measure approved differed in the two houses of the legislature.

Specific language for a proposed amendment had been approved by several states, which was thought to be another possibly improper procedure.

Amending the Constitution by the convention process had never been attempted. All amendments had come by way of the congressional route—approval by two-thirds of each house, then submission to the states and ratification by three-fourths of them.

The Constitution authorized Congress to call a "convention for proposing amendments" when requested by two-thirds of the states.

Opponents of such a procedure for the budget-balancing amendment, who included President Carter, contended such a convention could get out of hand and lead to wholesale revision of the Constitution.

Opponents of the budget-balancing proposal also argued that such a requirement would be a straitjacket allowing no adjustment for crises. They also said it would be ineffective in controlling federal spending.

That method, controlling spending, was being promoted by the National Tax Limitation Committee as a "reasonable alternative" to the balanced-budget approach.

Economist Milton Friedman, in presenting the committee's proposal Jan. 30, said, "If you have a simple budget-balancing amendment, even with emergency escape valves, it turns out to be impossible to implement.

His group, whose home base was in California, was proposing a constitutional amendment putting specific limits on government spending.

In general, it would limit the percentage increase in each year's federal spending to the percentage rise in the gross national product, or total output of goods and services.

The spending limit would be cut back further whenever the inflation rate exceeded 3%. Any surpluses would be used to reduce the national debt. And Congress would be allowed to authorize emergency spending by a two-thirds vote.

The plan would "let the budget balance itself" over a period of years, according to Friedman.

Lewis Uhler, president of the committee, said, "We're putting this on the table to contribute to the national dialogue on this issue."

The subject was taken up also by a large group of Republican Party officials—the Tidewater Conference—at an informal meeting in Easton, Md. The meeting was open to all Republicans in Congress and in statewide elective office. On Feb. 4, the conference rejected, after a two-hour debate, endorsement of a proposal for a constitutional amendment to require a balanced federal budget.

Instead, the conference called on Congress to balance the budget for the fiscal year 1981 and to consider immediately a constitutional amendment to "limit federal spending."

The issue divided the Republicans at Easton. Some desired endorsement before the issue became associated primarily with "born-again Democratic fiscal conservatives."

But GOP National Chairman Bill Brock, House Minority Leader John J. Rhodes (Ariz.) and Rep. Barber B. Conable Jr. (N.Y.), ranking minority member of the Ways and Means Committee, led a successful drive against the amendment.

"I just don't like gimmickry," Rhodes said. Conable said he did not feel the Constitution should be "the repository of all kinds of nitpicking amendments."

"We're talking too much about the budget as if it was a panacea," Brock told reporters later. "Inflation isn't caused just by deficits."

The resolution the conference did adopt Feb. 4 blamed the Democrats for "mounting deficits" of the federal budget.

In other action taken at the conference, the Republicans called for "indexing the tax system" to insure that taxpayers did not pay a higher proportion of taxes if their income did not keep pace with inflation.

Sen. Roger R. Jepsen (R, Iowa) told the Senate March 21 that because of inflation's effect on tax rates, "it would not have been necessary for any [spending] cuts to have been made in any existing programs since 1975 ... for us to have achieved a balanced budget by fiscal 1978." He said:

The reason why this is possible is that inflation causes tax revenues to increase at a faster rate, approximately 1.6 percent for every 1 percent inflation. Thus the Congressional Budget Office estimates that inflation and real income growth will increase income taxes on the American people by $8 billion in 1980, $18 billion in 1981, $34 billion in 1982, $51 billion in 1983 and $71 billion in 1984.

This inflation-tax increase lies at the heart of President Carter's budget strategy for the next 2 years. The figures in his fiscal 1980 budget prove that his promise to balance the budget in 1981 will be accomplished on the backs of the taxpayers. They show that in 1980 personal income tax revenues are expected to rise 1.9 percent faster than personal income, in 1981 they will increase 8.3 faster, and in 1982 taxes will increase 6.2 percent faster than personal income.

Therefore, I believe that we must do several things in order to balance the budget in a responsible manner. First, we must slow the growth of Government spending, preferably to less than the rate of inflation. Since this will mean a real reduction in Government spending across the board we must also begin to cut away at programs which no longer

serve a useful purpose and eliminate fraud and waste in all other programs. This will insure that adequate funds are available for critical needs.

Rep. John H. Rousselot (R, Calif.) had told the House March 20:

Despite all the myths around, we must face the cold facts as to what budget deficits are, and are not. Budget deficits represent an obligation that the Government has to those citizens from whom it has borrowed. It is an obligation to levy taxes on the general citizenry upon the maturity of the debt. In some instances the budget deficit is financed via the Federal Reserve bank's printing presses, and this can be inflationary. Historically, however, the Fed's role in financing the debt has not been as great as many people have been led to believe. The blame for our current inflation is only partially attributable to our large deficits. The real problem with running budget deficits is that in most cases they are simply an expedient way of transferring wealth from one segment of society to another segment by forcing future generations to pay for the tab.

Unfortunately, today's generation of taxpayers is already paying part of the tab. With deficits growing, the Federal Government's obligation to increase tax rates has also been growing. As a consequence our Nation's financial managers have been systematically turning down high risk projects with paybacks too far off in the future. The bottom line has been that investment has been dropping off over a period of years, and along with it productivity. The only reason investment is perking up now is because of the tax cuts we enacted last session. With after-tax incomes for business and individuals, higher after the tax cut, the economy is surging along quite nicely. In short, all the things we said last summer about the positive effect tax cuts can have on incentives in the marketplace have come true.

Obviously in light of the positive effects tax cuts can have on the economy, we must not undermine the tax cutting movement by forcing the Congress to raise taxes to balance the budget. Across-the-board tax cuts will naturally lead to "paper" deficits because the Treasury is simply not able to calculate the supply-side effects that cutting tax rates have on the economy. Therefore, balanced budget proposals which make tax cutting impossible and tax increases inevitable must be avoided.

Mr. Speaker, there can be no doubt of the need to balance the budget. Large deficits associated with increased Federal spending serve only to stifle investment because of the expectation of higher taxes in future years. Nor can there be any doubt that the Founding Fathers ever intended to provide the Congress with a free ride to spend to their heart's content by virtue of inflation and the progressive tax code. They adopted provisions to limit the Federal Government but adoption of the 16th amendment has lead to the emergence of powerful special interest groups in society who are competing for larger and larger shares of a growing Federal spending pie. Mr. Speaker, I will introduce an amendment to the U.S. Constitution which requires that there be a balanced budget; and requires that Congress offset the effect inflation has on the collection of tax revenues; provides that the Congress will only be able to spend more than the amount it collects upon favorable action by a three-fifths majority of both Houses of Congress; and tax increases will require three-fifths majority.

In the amendment I propose, it will be easier for the Congress to enact tax cuts than spending increases and tax increases. Spurring economic growth, and in the process expanding the tax base is a far better way to increase tax revenues, than by raising taxes from a shrinking tax base.

It is true that this course of action which I am proposing is somewhat unconventional, but I hope that my Colleagues in this House will agree that it is a wise one—long overdue. This amendment will make it more difficult to increase spending and taxes. More importantly, it will enable us to decrease taxes, without violating the balanced budget rule.

By limiting spending and balancing the budget, this plan enables all Members of Congress to feel more comfortable in voting in favor of cutting the heavy burden of taxes which is destroying economic incentive and productivity in our society. It also gets to the heart of the fears that many of my colleagues and constituents are expressing over rising

deficits. These fears are justified. Congress has been known to legislate spending programs that are wasteful, tax increases which are economically counterproductive, and tax rebates that do not improve incentives in the marketplace. It is for this reason that we need a plan to guard against legislative proposals which, although well intended, can lead to deficits which are inflationary—if financed by the Federal Reserve Bank—or to deficits which result in a redistribution of income with the bill being paid by future generations.

'Tax Spending' Problem. A little known aspect of the "tax revolt" is the campaign to reduce "tax spending." Tax spending is a term used to designate the tax benefits and "loopholes" that result in decreased tax revenue. They are considered spending because the benefits cost the government money. It is pointed out that this cost must be made up by taxpayers who do not share the benefits.

Sen. Edward M. Kennedy (D, Mass.) told the Senate Jan. 15, 1979 that the "missing ingredient" in the Carter Administration's budget-cutting "is any effort to reduce the massive amount of federal tax spending." He said:

This approach to the budget is seriously defective. It means that programs involving large amounts of Federal spending have been arbitrarily exempted from budget review and from the threat of budget cuts.

At a time of austerity in Federal spending, it is unfair to concentrate on cuts in direct spending alone, while providing to blank check for all the spending programs contained in the Internal Revenue Code—the tax expenditure programs.

Nothing turns on whether a Federal dollar is spent as a tax subsidy or another form of subsidy. It is a familiar fact that any Federal spending program can be structured either as a direct spending program or as a tax spending program, as demonstrated by the vigorous congressional debate last year between tuition tax credits and direct educational grants as a means of providing increased Federal aid for education.

Federal law now contains almost 100

Proposition 13 & Government Budgets

From the Economic Report of the President, transmitted to Congress January 1979:

As a result of the increased growth in purchases and the pressure for tax reduction, the aggregate budget surplus in the State and local sector declined sharply in 1978. The surplus on current and capital account (but excluding social insurance trust accounts) fell from a peak of $12.8 billion (annual rate) in the third quarter of 1977 to $1.8 billion a year later. Of the $7.5-billion decline that occurred between the second and the third quarters, roughly $5¾ billion is attributable to California's Proposition 13, which mandated a reduction of about 50 percent in local property taxes, or about one-fourth in total local revenues. This local tax cut was followed by a substantial redistribution of funds from the State government, which had been incurring a surplus, to the local governments.

Proposition 13 and similar measures in other States suggest the likelihood of significantly slower growth in State and local spending in the near future and an approximate balance or a deficit in the aggregate current and capital account of this sector. In the fall elections, 11 States had proposals on their ballots that would immediately limit State and local taxes or expenditures or both. Such measures passed in eight of these States. Referenda mandated substantial reductions of property taxes in Idaho and personal income taxes in North Dakota. The measures in other States differ in their form and the degree to which they will constrain taxes and expenditures, but their enactment—by large margins in some cases—clearly indicates public sentiment for budgetary restraint. This is likely to put downward pressure on both spending and the current and capital account surplus.

separate tax expenditure programs, which are listed annually in the tax expenditure budget. Tax expenditures are found in all of the budget categories into which direct spending programs are divided—in some cases, the dollar amount of tax expenditures is equal to, or exceeds, the amount for direct spending programs in the same budget function.

For fiscal year 1980. Federal revenues spent through the tax laws will total approximately $150 billion, while direct expenditures will total approximately $550 billion under the so-called current serv-

ices budget. Total Federal spending in 1980, therefore—counting both tax spending and direct spending—will reach $700 billion, with tax spending representing over 20 percent of the total.

As a matter of budget policy, therefore, it would be appropriate for any necessary budget cuts to be allocated in a 4-to-1 ratio between direct spending programs and tax spending programs. For example, to reach the administration's target of a deficit of $30 billion for 1980, it is likely that total spending will have to be reduced by approximately $15 to $20 billion. If the cuts are allocated properly, then $12 to $16 billion of the cuts should come from direct spending programs, and $3 to $4 billion of the cuts should come from tax spending programs. Clearly, direct spending programs should not be required to bear the full brunt of any spending cuts that may be necessary.

Tax expenditures have always had a preferred—but undeserved—position in the budget, because they have an automatic first priority in the allocation of Federal revenues. Direct spending programs compete for the revenues left after all the tax expenditures have been funded. Thus, responsible development of the Federal budget must include an evaluation not only of relative priorities among direct spending programs, but also of the priorities involved in tax expenditure programs.

Unfortunately, there is no evidence that the $150 billion tax expenditure budget is even being given consideration as a source of possible spending cuts by the administration in the preparation of the 1980 budget. Yet, the President's $30 billion deficit figure can be reached as easily by cutting tax expenditures programs as by cutting direct expenditure programs. There is no reason why this large component of the Federal budget should be exempted from examination and from bearing its fair share of the fourthcoming austerity that is likely to be imposed.

The Treasury should be required to justify each dollar spent through the tax expenditure budget with the same degree of precision required of all other agencies in justifying their proposals for direct spending programs. In addition, each item in the tax expenditures budget should be reviewed to determine its priority compared to the direct spending programs in the same budget category that are candidates for budget cuts.

Careful review of the tax expenditure budget is also essential because it is the part of the total Federal budget that is rising the most rapidly and that is most clearly out of control. In the current decade, the number of tax expenditure programs has more than doubled, from 40 to nearly 100. Between 1971 and 1978, the total revenues spent through the tax expenditure budget increased from $51 billion to $112 billion, an increase of 141 percent. By contrast, direct spend-

ing climbed from $211 billion to $448 billion in the same period, an increase of "only" 112 percent.

I therefore urge both Congress and the administration, as part of the budget process, to examine the tax expenditure budget with the same care they give to the direct spending portion of the budget. I am confident that such study will reveal spending programs in the tax expenditure list that should be cut before some of the proposed direct spending cuts are made.

To demonstrate this point, I have made a preliminary survey of some of the proposed spending cuts that have received publicity in recent weeks. Then, I have examined tax expenditure programs in the same budget areas. This analysis reveals that often, cuts in tax expenditure items can and should be made before direct spending programs are reduced from present levels. Indeed, reduction or elimination of some of the most wasteful tax expenditures could well free up additional funds for direct spending programs that have higher priority. Clearly, however, cuts contemplated in worthwhile, direct programs could more easily and more equitably be made in tax programs in the same budget category.

First. Nutrition. The administration is reportedly planning to cut $400 to $500 million from the food stamp program, the special milk program for schoolchildren, and the school lunch program.

By comparison, the $1 billion tax spending program that subsidizes lavish meals and martini lunches for corporate executives, doctors, laywers and other high income business persons will apparently remain untouched. Before Congress makes budget cuts in food stamps and school lunch programs for the poor and middle class, or eliminates the milk program, it ought to cut back this lavish tax subsidy which provides food stamps for the rich.

Last year, the President recommended that the deduction for business meals should be limited to 50 percent of the cost of the meal. Congress did not adopt the President's proposal, but the revenue saved would be more than enough to eliminate the need for the currently proposed cuts in the food stamp, school milk and school lunch programs.

It would be unconscionable for Congress and the administration to continue to provide federally subsidized lunches and alcoholic beverages for high income corporate executives, while cutting back on the basic nutritional needs of the poor and the schoolchildren of the Nation. The President should squarely confront Congress with this situation, and insist that the rich must take a place at the rear of the subsidized lunch line, behind the more deserving families of the Nation.

Second. Health care. There has already been extensive discussion and debate over the level of spending for health care in the direct budget. In recent weeks, the administration has restored some of the needed funds. But many important programs are still scheduled for unacceptable cuts, and I am hopeful that the additional funds will be restored as the budget process develops.

By contrast, the tax expenditures that provide health care largely for a privileged few would remain untouched. In fiscal 1980, tax subsidies for health care will exceed $11 billion. Of this amount, $1.5 billion will go to those with the top 1 percent of incomes in the country—those with over $50,000 income annually.

If we are to have an austere budget on health, the question must be faced as to whether these health subsidies for the rich—provided through tax expenditures—have a higher priority than the direct spending programs slated for drastic cutbacks, especially the programs in the areas of biomedical research and aid to medical schools, where cuts are still planned totaling approximately $500 million.

My own view is that we should move forward now to national health insurance, as the best means of controlling costs and providing adequate health care to all our citizens. But until that goal is achieved, we must make the most efficient use of the Federal funds currently available for health care. Paying 50 percent to 70 percent of the medical bills and private health insurance premiums in the highest income families in the country hardly represents a pressing health priority for the Nation. Revenues should therefore be diverted from these tax expenditure programs in order to held fund higher priority direct health care needs.

Third. Housing. Budget cuts are also being considered for federally subsidized low- and middle-income housing, which will reduce housing units by about 20 per-

cent next year. At the same time, tax expenditures for real estate construction will remain untouched, and will total almost $1.3 billion next year. The direct spending programs benefit low- and middle-income people. But over 75 percent öf the tax expenditures for real estate go to the 1 percent of individuals with the highest incomes in the country. It is a distortion of the Nation's housing priorities to reduce Federal spending for low-and middle-income persons, but to continue massive Federal spending in the form of real estate tax subsidies for the over-$50,000 income group.

Even worse, only 6 percent of the tax expenditures for real estate is used to fund low-income housing projects. The remaining 94 percent goes to provide Federal subsidies for luxury apartments, high rise office buildings, motels and similar facilities. Congress would certainly not provide indirect subsidies for these real estate projects, and we should not be subsidizing them through the tax laws. Direct subsidies for low- and middle-income persons should be held at present levels and the necessary budget reductions should come from cuts in real estate tax expenditures.

Fourth. Income security. A number of social security programs are apparently also in jeopardy in order to achieve spending cuts of $500–$600 million. Again, tax expenditure programs in the same budget category would remain untouched.

One of the programs scheduled for elimination is the modest $255 survivor's benefit, which will save $220 million in the 1980 budget. By contrast, a current tax expenditure program will provide almost $10 billion of benefits to survivors of decedents in fiscal 1980. This enormous Federal subsidy is made available through the exemption of tax on the gains in property transferred at death. For the top 1 percent of families, the tax subsidy provides an average survivor's benefit of over $5,000, at a cost of over $6 billion. It makes no budget sense to retain these handsome survivor's benefits for the richest families in the Nation, while slashing the meager $255 direct subsidy that largely goes to low- and middle-income families.

Another direct program to be cut back is the social security benefit for orphaned students. Under present law, students receive benefits until the age of 21. But the administration would phase this down to age 18, for a budget saving of $169 million. There is also a tax expenditure for orphans in the estate tax, which provides a special deduction that benefits orphans through age 21—but only for the wealthiest 2 percent of families in the country, those with the largest estates. The wealthier the parents, the larger is the Federal tax subsidy for their orphaned children. It makes no sense to provide a Federal tax subsidy for children of the country's wealthiest families until they reach 21, but to cut off orphaned students of low- and middle-income parents when they reach age 18. The tax expenditure program should be reduced or eliminated and the direct social security benefit should be retained at present levels.

Other proposed social security cutbacks would reduce minimum benefits for intermittent workers, place a cap on the maximum benefits that a disabled person can receive, and terminate benefits for mothers of dependent children when those children reach 16. These actions are apparently designed to save approximately $250 million in fiscal year 1980. Tax expenditures for private pension plans are, however, to remain unaffected. The tax subsidy for private pension plans will exceed $15 billion in 1980. Over $3 billion of this amount goes to those with incomes above $50,000 a year. Moreover, annual distributions from these plans can be as much as $90,000 per person, many times the social security benefits that are to be cut back. Surely we should be able to agree that a more likely candidate for a budget cut in the pension area is the $3 billion retirement tax subsidy for the rich, instead of direct social security benefits for low and middle income individuals.

Fifth. Education. In addition to the reduction in social security benefits for students discussed above, the administration is reportedly considering a reduction of $200 million in the basic educational opportunity grants program and a larger amount in the Elementary and Secondary Education Act program. Students in middle income families will be the hardest hit by these proposed cuts.

Yet, tax expenditures for education will exceed $1.1 billion in 1980. Of that amount, the 1 percent of families with incomes over $50,000 will receive over $130 million. In short, elimination of tax spending for students from the country's wealthiest families would permit us to come closer to fulfilling the promise of an affordable quality education for students from middle income families. The Nation's priorities are clear, and the budget should reflect them. . . .

According to a Common Cause study in 1978, the federal government was expected to reach $136 billion in tax spending in fiscal 1979. Among items in the summary of the study:

Some tax expenditures are controversial. Calling them loopholes, their opponents raise arguments of costly ineffectiveness and inefficiency. But there are some tax expenditures that are accepted with little or no argument. For example, there are few, if any, opponents to the tax-free status of veterans' pensions or welfare payments.

Common Cause examined the hearing records of the House Ways and Means Committee and the Senate Finance Committee, and the floor debates on tax bills considered during the 92nd, 93rd, and 94th Congresses. Our purpose was not to make judgments on the merits of particular tax expenditures, but rather to determine the thoroughness of Congressional oversight and evaluation of existing tax expenditures and to examine the process by which new tax expenditures are enacted.

Our findings support the wisdom of the theory on which many interest groups have acted for some time: getting a tax benefit is better than getting a grant or loan from the government, because once a tax benefit is enacted, there is a minimal chance of oversight and an even smaller chance that the benefit will be taken away.

Nearly ninety percent of the items in the tax expenditure budget as of January 1, 1978 are permanent and do not have to be reauthorized periodically. As a result, oversight occurs at the whim of the tax committees. If a tax expenditure is by chance chosen for oversight, the bulk of the witnesses who appear to testify on it are those who benefit from it. The tax committees generally do not hear from agencies of government which are operating direct spending programs in analogous policy areas to see if the conditions which prompted the tax expenditure in the first place still exist. Nor do the tax committees make any attempt to determine from either the agencies or the other substantive committees of Congress that write the programs if the tax expenditure complements or conflicts with direct spending programs.

Because these programs are run through the tax system, they are not subject to the institutional checks and balances of Congress that apply to direct spending programs. They do not require the approval of the Appropriations Committees, which means that tax expenditures are not scrutinized twice by Congress in the same way that direct spending programs are.

Given the existing undisciplined process of writing tax laws, it is not surprising that tax expenditures are multiplying in number and getting more expensive each year. The tax expenditure budget has grown even faster that the budget for direct outlays over the past decade. Since 1968, direct spending outlays have increased by 180%; the tax expenditure budget increased by 209%.

In addition to reducing the amount of revenues available to the federal government and either adding to the deficit or freezing out money for other worthy programs, tax expenditures often result in an upside-down welfare program—the richer the taxpayer, the greater the benefit he, she, or it receives.

Since nearly 97% of the dollars spent in the tax expenditure budget can continue to be spent indefinitely and can even increase without any Congressional action, oversight of this budget is especially important. We found that neither the Senate Finance nor House Ways and Means Committee carries out a systematic or responsible evaluation of tax expenditures. Items in the tax expenditure buget continue year after year without either committee determining that the particular tax expenditure is effective, efficient, or wise in light of other government priorities. Specifically, we found that during the six year period from 1971 through 1976—

Over $161 billion was spent in tax expenditures without a single vote of approval or disapproval appearing on the public record by any member in a tax committee, much less any Member on the House or Senate floor; and

38 of 86 tax expenditures were not addressed by a single witness before the Senate Finance Committee while the Ways and Means Committee did not hear testimony on 25 tax expenditures during the same period.

In those cases where hearings on certain tax expenditures were held, other deficiencies were apparent. The bulk of testimony received by the committees came from witnesses with pecuniary interests in the continuation or expansion of the tax expenditures on which they testified. A disproportionate amount of testimony was given by trade associations and businesses. We found that during the six year period from 1971 through 1976—

Private commercial interests comprised 65% of all witnesses before the Senate Finance Committee and 45% of all the witnesses before the Ways and Means Committee;

Citizen groups represented 4% of the witnesses before the Senate Finance Committee, and 12% before the Ways and Means Committee;

Research organizations, academics, and other experts accounted for 10% of the witnesses before the Senate Finance Committee, and 17% of the witnesses before the Ways

and Means Committee; and

Only 14 witnesses before the Senate Finance Committee and 13 witnesses before the Ways and Means Committee represented federal agencies other than the Treasury Department, although these agencies are likely to have valuable information on the activities which tax expenditures affect.

Although scores of existing tax expenditures were not subject to oversight hearings, Congress and its tax committees did not hesitate to create new ones. We found that:

16 new tax expenditures were enacted between 1971 and 1976, and

Only 2 tax expenditures were repealed, while 3 more failed to be reauthorized.

Although 16 new tax expenditures were enacted, many had been proposed. While the Ways and Means Committee proposed 16, the Senate Finance Committee, in addition to approving 10 new tax expenditures previously adopted by Ways and Means, also proposed another 15 new tax expenditures for a total of 25.

We found a sharp contrast between the Ways and Means Committee and Senate Finance Committee in the number of times each has proposed increasing or decreasing specific tax expenditures. Between 1971 and 1976, the Senate Finance Committee proposed increasing specific tax expenditures in 39 instances, while it proposed decreasing them in only 12; the Ways and Means Committee proposed increasing specific tax expenditures in 27 instances, and decreasing them in 27.

In the three major tax bills enacted during 1971–1976—the Revenue Act of 1971, the Tax Reduction Act of 1975, and the Tax Reform Act of 1976—we found that in each case the Senate Finance Committee version would have increased tax expenditures more than the bill as reported by the Ways and Means Committee. This was especially apparent in the Tax Reform Act of 1976, in which revenue losses for fiscal year 1977–1981 due to increases in tax expenditures would have been $39.7 billion in the Senate Finance Committee version compared with $14.4 billion in the Ways and Means Committee version.

The Senate Finance Committee, in fact, turns out to be one of the biggest spenders of government tax dollars. Senate floor amendments tend to follow the "big government spending" lead provided by the Senate Finance Committee. Of 43 amendments offered on the Senate floor in 1971–1976 to increase tax expenditures, 37—or 86%—passed. By contrast, of the 45 amendments offered to decrease tax expenditures, 33—or 73%—failed.

The low public visibility of the tax expenditure budget is a major reason for Congressional negligence in this area. The public would never tolerate such blatant neglect of direct spending programs by Congress.

Furthermore, tax subsidies are thought by many—including, apparently, the Senate Finance Committee—to be "free". While no money is appropriated for them, they are certainly not free. Tax dollars not collected because of tax privileges must be made up by other taxpayers. For example, if a family requires $100 a week to pay its bills, and one member is not required to contribute, the remaining members must contribute larger amounts of money so that the $100 is collected.

Congress and its tax writing committees have done an irresponsible job of monitoring the tax expenditure budget. Mechanisms must be put in place that will assure oversight and accountability. Currently, almost all of the tax expenditure budget is permanent. The tax committees are under less pressure than any other Congressional committees to take their oversight responsibilities seriously.

And because of the unique status of tax legislation, if the tax committees do not conduct oversight, there is no other forum in Congress to fill that void. Tax legislation is not subject to the checks and balances inherent in the two-step authorization and appropriation process. Once a tax expenditure is enacted—or authorized—the spending can begin and can increase without control. No further action by anyone but taxpayers is necessary.

Tax Cut Not Likely in 1980. Despite the political attractiveness of a tax cut in an election year, President Carter said at his press conference May 29, 1979 that he doubted "very seriously that we will have any tax cut in 1980."

"My own major responsibility is to deal with the inflation question," he said. "Part of that, of course, is to be fiscally responsible in reducing the federal deficit.

"If we have the option between substantial reduction in the deficit and controlling inflation on the one hand and having tax reductions for the American people in an election year on the other, I would forgo the tax reduction and insist upon controlling inflation and cutting the deficit."

Nearly a month earlier the chairmen of both of the congressional tax-writing committees had told members of the U.S. Chamber of Commerce April 30 it was unlikely that Congress would enact a major tax reduction before the next election.

In a statement to a group attending the chamber's annual meeting, Rep. Al Ullman (D, Ore.), chairman of the House Ways and Means Committee, said the "absolute necessity" of a balanced budget "eliminates any possibility of a major tax

reduction in fiscal 1981." Fiscal 1981 would begin Oct. 1, 1980, about a month prior to the next election.

Sen. Russell Long (D, La.), chairman of the Senate Finance Committee, said he favored a big tax cut "as soon as we could arrange it." But, he added, "I don't think we ought to do it to the extent of unbalancing the budget."

Other Developments

Value-Added Tax Proposed. The chairman of the Senate Finance Committee, Sen. Russell Long (D, La.), said Nov. 30, 1978 that he would like to repeal the Social Security payroll tax, cut the federal income tax, and make up the lost revenue with a value-added tax (VAT).

Long made his proposal, which he had advanced before, at a seminar on taxes at Tulane University in New Orleans.

The VAT would be a charge at each step of production or distribution of a product. It would be a complex form of "a national sales tax" and would be levied in the states as a product was made.

Long claimed the VAT could be a vehicle for cutting individual and corporate income taxes to a level that he said would not "discourage work or investment."

U.S. News and World Report of Dec. 18 said the major disadvantage of the VAT was that it would be regressive, taking a larger share of lower incomes than of higher ones.

Long also said Nov. 30 that the VAT would reward efficiency. He said firms that held down costs would be taxed less. He also claimed the VAT would encourage exports and curtail imports because the tax would be levied on goods coming in but rebated on those exported.

Finally, the Louisiana senator said the VAT was the "least painful way of collecting money, because it applies across the board," and reached consumers "somewhat like a hidden sales tax."

But Charles Schultze, chairman of the President's Council of Economic Advisers, criticized the idea in an appearance on the ABC broadcast program *Issues and Answers* Dec. 3.

Schultze said "a sales or value-added tax goes right into the consumer price index," thereby fueling inflation. During periods of high inflation, he said, it was a "difficult time to make that sort of a tax adjustment because it does tend immediately to raise costs and prices."

On Dec. 6, Rep. Al Ullman (D, Ore.) said he would support a VAT and pledged to work closely with Long in 1979 to see what could be developed.

Ullman, chairman of the House Ways and Means Committee, said, however, that such a tax would have to be "low-level" and not a "retail federal sales tax." His insistence that the VAT be kept low seemed to rule out any attempt at a major shift in Social Security financing.

Excess Profits Tax Urged for Oil. With the U.S. energy problem "getting worse," President Carter April 5, 1979 ordered the gradual decontrol of domestic oil prices and proposed to tax windfall profits the oil companies might make from decontrol. The revenue, he recommended, should be used for developing alternative energy sources. The proposal was subject to congressional approval.

In a nationally televised address, Carter noted "Our national strength is dangerously dependent on a thin line of oil tankers stretching halfway around the Earth, originating in the Middle East and around the Persian Gulf, one of the most unstable regions in the world." The Iranian revolution and the recent 9% price increase voted by the Organization of Petroleum Exporting Countries, he said, "have sent us stern warnings about energy."

"But our nation has not yet responded to these warnings," Carter continued. Because of the lengthy congressional debate on energy legislation, "we have lost precious time that we could not afford," he said.

"With new legal authority, I am now able to act without delay," Carter declared. "This is a painful step, and I'll give it to you straight. Each of us will have to use less oil and pay more for it."

Carter said the industry would reap additional profits from the decontrol of domestic oil prices. For this reason, he said, "we must have a new windfall profits

tax to recover the unearned billions of dollars" from the oil companies.

An Energy Security Fund would be established with the tax money, Carter said. The fund would be used to help low-income families pay the higher fuel bills, to finance public transportation construction and to promote research and development of alternative energy sources.

In addition to taxing the companies, Carter said, "I will demand that they use their new income to develop energy for America, and not to buy such things as department stores and hotels. . . ."

The President called for the elimination of "foreign tax credit loopholes" that benefited oil companies and for the lifting of tariffs on imported petroleum and petroleum products.

Carter warned oil firms April 10 that he would not hesitate "to put restraints" on them to make sure that their profits from higher prices would be plowed back into energy exploration and development.

Speaking at a news conference, Carter said he would push vigorously for enactment of a tax on the "windfall" profits. He said it was estimated that the oil companies would gain $6 billion in new income from higher oil prices over the next three years even with the windfall profits tax.

He did not specify what "restraints" he would invoke against the companies.

But "the nation has a right to expect," he said, "that all of this new income will be used for exploration for oil and gas and not to buy timberlands and department stores."

"I am making the passage of this tax and the establishment of the Security Fund for Energy one of my highest legislative priorities," he said.

Carter April 23 assailed critics of the proposed oil profits tax.

In a speech in Washington to the National Academy of Sciences, Carter said that "many of those who only a few weeks ago were dedicated to killing outright the windfall-profits tax have now given up on that fight."

But, he continued, "their new strategy seems to be to try to hoodwink the American people by passing a windfall-profits tax that in fact is a charade, a tax designed primarily to provide loopholes to the oil companies so they will get another $4 billion or $5 billion in unearned profits on top of the $6 billion they would get under decontrol with an honest windfall-profits tax.

"They will try to pass this charade off on the American people as a so-called 'plowback' provision. But it isn't a 'plowback'; it's a 'plow under' and a 'kickback,' and what is going to be plowed under is the Energy Security Fund with its aid to research and its aid to the poor, and what is going to be kicked back to the oil companies is the money that would go to finance these absolutely necessary programs."

The prospects for passage of the President's proposal to tax windfall profits had changed drastically since he had introduced it three weeks earlier. Then the consensus was that the outlook was bleak indeed.

By April 23, when the President spoke to the scientists, Senate Republican Leader Howard H. Baker Jr. (Tenn.) was telling reporters the President could get congressional approval of the oil tax "virtually for the asking."

"I'm hard-pressed to find anybody who's opposed to it," Baker said.

Sen. Robert C. Byrd (W.Va.), the Democratic leader, said the same day that rising oil company profits would put additional pressure on Congress to pass the proposal. "If there isn't a demand now, there will be," he said.

Carter sent his oil-profits bill to Congress April 26.

Chairman Al Ullman of the House Ways & Means Committee said April 26, after meeting with the President, that Carter and his committee "are in full agreement about the windfall profits tax."

The windfall profits tax, he said, was "the only thing that stands between the oil companies and a huge bonanza of unearned, . . . and unjustified profits."

Carter warned Congress against caving in to the oil companies and adding to the tax plan "loopholes you could sail an oil tanker through."

Carter had said since first announcing his intention to tax "windfall" profits that the proposed levy would take 50% of the extra profits that were expected to result from the decontrol of oil prices. Adminis-

tration figures indicated, however, that only 21% of the industry's additional revenue would be taxed during the three-year period 1979–1981. But Administration officials added that the federal government's share of the additional profits would jump to 55% as a result of the regular income tax on corporate earnings.

Under the Administration's plan, the first-year revenues from the new tax would be earmarked as follows, for the fiscal 1982 year: $800 million for assistance for the poor, $200 million for mass transit and $2.9 billion for various energy supply and conservation projects.

Increased 1st Quarter Oil Profits—The nation's largest oil companies earned greatly increased profits in the first quarter of 1979, the Wall Street Journal reported April 27.

On an industry-wide basis, the Journal said, the 13 largest petroleum products companies reported a 48.5% surge in earnings—$3.24 billion in the first quarter of 1979, as against $2.18 billion in the first quarter of 1978.

Mobil Corp. led the way among the giant transnational oil companies, posting earnings in the first quarter of 1979 that were 82% ahead of its earnings in the same period of 1978. Texaco Inc. reported an 81% increase and Gulf Oil Corp. a 61% gain.

Many of the companies attributed the increases to higher oil prices, particularly in overseas markets, arising from the cutback in Iranian production and what they claimed was a resultant tightening of world oil supplies.

1979 1st Quarter Oil Profits

Company	Earnings (in millions)	% Rise (from 1978)
Exxon	$955.0	37
Mobil	$437.0	82
Texaco	$307.0	81
Standard Oil (Calif.)	$347.0	43
Gulf Oil	$249.0	61
Standard Oil (Ind.)	$349.1	28
Shell	$224.0	16
Standard Oil (Ohio)	$167.5	303
Continental Oil	$161.8	343
Sun	$120.3	43

Carter-Kennedy dispute—President Carter April 30 bitterly rejected criticism of his oil-pricing policies and proposals. The criticism came from Sen. Edward Kennedy (D, Mass.).

In a speech to the American Society of Newspaper Editors in New York the same day, Kennedy said, "The overbearing power of the oil lobby has exerted its influence in two new and unacceptable ways.

"First, it has intimidated the Administration into throwing in the towel without even entering the ring on the issue of oil price decontrol.

"And second, it has also intimidated the Administration into submitting a token windfall tax that is no more than a transparent fig leaf over the vast new profits the industry will reap."

At a televised news conference that day, Carter was asked to comment on Kennedy's remarks.

"That's just a lot of baloney," Carter began. "I really can't believe that Sen. Kennedy said this unless the phrases were taken out of context."

Carter said that everyone in Congress knew that oil-price decontrol was scheduled by law to be completed by October 1981. "This is not a decision that I made. I am complying with an existing law."

Carter maintained that he was trying "to minimize the impact of decontrol" by phasing it in over a 28-month period instead of effecting it immediately.

He defended his proposal to tax the windfall profits, or profits that would accrue from decontrol, as "eminently fair."

The President said his tax proposal would let the oil companies keep just 29¢ of each dollar they gained from decontrol.

However, if Congress, "including Sen. Kennedy," he said, wanted to "tighten up on that" he would "gladly support" a "more stringent" version.

Carter said he would not support any move in Congress "to make the windfall tax more lenient on the oil companies."

In reference to the 29¢ to be retained by the oil companies on each dollar gained from decontrol, the President earlier in the conference had explained that this "other part of the dollar" would be going for federal taxes, state and local taxes and payment of royalties.

He defended the retention of some of the additional profit by the companies as necessary to ensure increased oil production. The proposed tax cannot be "confiscatory," he said.

Tax Inequity Based on Marital Status. Rep. G. William Whitehurst (R, Va.) May 21, 1979 summarized complaints about tax inequities that "apply to single persons and married couples in which both partners work." Introducing legislation to correct such inequities, Whitehurst said:

The bill I have introduced proposes a substantial tax cut for single persons and married couples, in which both partners are employed. In the latter category alone, there are approximately 44 million individuals who stand to benefit from this legislation.

Much has been made in the past decade of the so-called marriage tax or marriage penalty, which unfairly penalizes the married couple composed of two career-minded individuals. The magnitude of this issue becomes increasingly obvious as more and more women join the labor force. The figures for the past year show that 50 percent of all women are in the labor force and that they now make up 42 percent of all workers in the United States. In the 20-year period from 1956 to 1976, the labor force participation of married women doubled from 11 million to 22 million. In many cases, women are joining the labor force out of necessity in order for their families to continue to maintain their accustomed life styles.

As the emergence of women into the labor force has been clearly defined, our tax laws have not kept pace with this phenomenon. Far from it; our tax laws do nothing to encourage the two-career-minded couple from reaching their potential in professional life or the non-working spouse who decides to work a part-time job to supplement the family's income. These millions of taxpayers are growing increasingly bitter and disillusioned as they observe the growing gap in the degree of work and sacrifice they expend and the amount of tax dollars they must pay. I refuse to believe that it is simply coincidental that the rate of persons of the opposite sex living together outside of marriage has risen by 80 percent since 1970. At present, there are approximately 2 million persons living with an unrelated person of the opposite sex. To that I would add that it is small wonder that the number is not far higher in light of the inequities built into the tax laws of this country.

Indeed, the married couple in which each partner wishes to pursue a career is sometimes even driven to divorce to shelter themselves from the voracious appetite of the Internal Revenue Service. In effect, what the tax laws are saying to the spouse of a married couple who chooses to enter the labor force is that he/she will have to pay extra taxes for the right to work while maintaining a marriage. One reason for this is that since all of the income reported on a joint return is combined for purposes of taxation rather than taxed according to the individual rates which apply to the earner, each dollar earned by secondary workers in the family is taxed at that family's marginal or highest tax rate.

The married couple with two workers is also penalized by the social security system. Since all payments into the system are based on individual earnings, although benefits are predicated on a per family basis, once the one-earner family passes the taxable base it pays nothing further into the system. This is not true with the two-earner family, which can pay to a maximum of double the amount of a one-earner family.

While much has been heard of the "marriage tax," let us not overlook by any means the cries of single taxpayers, on whom we continue to heap a disproportionate share of taxes. Their angry pleas are familiar around the Halls of Congress and will certainly grow in intensity until we take positive steps to alleviate this condition.

What I am proposing before this Congress is to apply the same tax rate schedule to every individual's income, regardless of marital status.

State-Local Tax Collections Up. State and local tax collections increased to $198.3 billion in calendar 1978, a rise of 8.5% from the previous year, Commerce Clearing House reported May 16, 1979.

The biggest individual source of revenue for state and local governments was the property tax, which brought in a total of $64.9 billion in the year ending December 1978. The total, however, was only 1.3% higher than the year earlier, a relatively low rate of increase said to reflect the impact of Proposition 13 in California and similar trends in other states to limit property tax assessments and collections.

Property tax collections for the October–December 1978 quarter were less than those for the same period in 1977, the report noted. It was the first time that property tax collections had decreased from the corresponding prior year's quarter since the data had first been collected in 1962.

There were higher rates of increase in other categories of the state and local tax collections.

Collections from individual income taxes rose 15.1% to a total of $35.5 billion for the year. Corporate net income taxes increased 14.8%, reaching $11.1 billion.

General sales and gross receipts tax revenue was up 14.3%, to a total of $44.3 billion. Motor vehicle and operator's license fees were 7.9% higher at $5.4 billion. Alcoholic beverage taxes rose 6.7%, to $2.5 billion; motor fuel taxes rose 4.4%, to $9.8 billion, and tobacco taxes rose 2.6%, to the $3.8 billion level.

State tax cuts urged—Gov. Hugh L. Carey (D) of New York, opening the state Legislature Jan. 3, 1979, called for a $225-million state tax cut over the next three years.

Gov. Edmund G. Brown Jr. (D) of California, making his second inaugural speech, proposed in Sacramento Jan. 8, 1979 a $1-billion state income tax reduction and a reduction of 5,000 jobs in state government.

Brown pointed to the federal government as a chief culprit in the fight against inflation. "People know that something is wrong when the federal government stimulates inflation," he said, "and inflation raises the face value of prices, income and property so that taxes on each grow higher and higher."

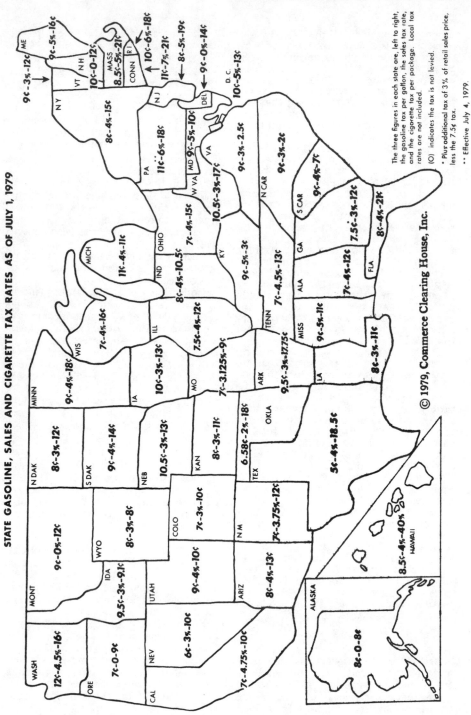

STATE GASOLINE, SALES AND CIGARETTE TAX RATES AS OF JULY 1, 1979

The three figures in each state are, left to right, the gasoline tax per gallon, the sales tax rate, and the cigarette tax per package. Local tax rates are not included.

(O) indicates the tax is not levied.

* Plus additional tax of 3% of retail sales price, less the 7.5¢ tax.

** Effective July 4, 1979.

© 1979, Commerce Clearing House, Inc.

Cleveland Votes Tax Rise. Cleveland voters Feb. 27, 1979 approved a local income tax rise and retention of the city electric light system.

The votes were considered victories for Mayor Dennis J. Kucinich, who had been locked in battle since becoming mayor with the City Council and Cleveland's banking and business interests while the city drifted into default. The default happened in December 1978, when Cleveland could not repay $14 million in notes.

Kucinich stood alone among city leaders in his support for retention of the Municipal Electric Lighting System, known as Muny Light. He had made Muny Light a symbol of his stand against the power and influence of big business in the city's life.

The tax increase, approved by a 74,402–34,586 vote, would raise the income levy to 1½% from 1%. Four other attempts to raise the tax had failed since 1968.

The increase was seen as a first step in the city's climb from default. It would bring in an estimated $25 million in extra revenue. But this was not expected to cover the city's total financial problem.

Index